MYP Biology

A concept-based approach

Years 4&5

Andrew Allott
David Mindorff

OXFORD
UNIVERSITY PRESS

OXFORD
UNIVERSITY PRESS

Great Clarendon Street, Oxford, OX2 6DP, United Kingdom

Oxford University Press is a department of the University of Oxford. It furthers the University's objective of excellence in research, scholarship, and education by publishing worldwide. Oxford is a registered trade mark of Oxford University Press in the UK and in certain other countries

© Oxford University Press, 2017

The moral rights of the authors have been asserted

First published in 2017

British Library Cataloguing in Publication Data
Data available

978-0-19-836995-0

10 9 8 7 6 5 4 3

Paper used in the production of this book is a natural, recyclable product made from wood grown in sustainable forests. The manufacturing process conforms to the environmental regulations of the country of origin.

Printed in India by Manipal Technologies Limited

Acknowledgements

We are grateful to the authors and publishers for use of extracts from their titles and in particular for the following:

Steve Connor: 'Smallest known genome to support a living cell created by scientists' The Independent, 24 March 2016, http://www.independent.co.uk. Reproduced by permission.

Eva Garde et al: Extract from 'Age-specific growth and remarkable longevity in narwhals (Monodon monoceros) from West Greenland as estimated by aspartic acid racemization' the Journal of Mammology, 27 February 2007. Reproduced by permission.

Theo Jansen: quote from http://www.strandbeest.com/contact.php. Reproduced by permission.

Denis J Murphy: 'Palm oil: scourge of the earth or wonder crop?' from http://theconversation.com. Reproduced by permission.

Trudy Netherwood et al: 'Assessing the survival of transgenic plant DNA in the human gastrointestinal tract' from Nature Biotechnology, 1 February 2004. Reprinted by permission from Macmillan Publishers Ltd.

F P Perera: Extracts from 'Molecular Epidemiology: On the Path to Prevention?' in the Journal of the National Cancer Institute (2000) 92, pp 602–612. Reproduced by permission.

Extract from https://www.cbd.int/island/intro.shtml. Reproduced by permission.

'In what ways do zoos model the habitat of animals?' from National Geographic, http://www.nationalgeographic.org. Reproduced by permission of National Geographic Creative.

Pine trees growth (Data-based question from IB Biology Higher Level exam paper, Paper 2, Monday, 21 May 2001. Reproduced by permission.

From Science Netlinks, Genes and Geography (http://sciencenetlinks.com/science-news/science-updates/genes-andgeography/). Readers may view, browse, and/or download material for temporary copying purposes only, provided these uses are for non-commercial personal purposes. Except as provided by law, this material may not be further reproduced, distributed, transmitted, modified, adapted, performed, displayed, published, or sold in whole or in part, without prior written permission from the publisher. Reprinted with permission from AAAS.

The publishers would like to thank the following for permissions to use their photographs:

Cover: Paul Souders/Getty Images; p2t: Intrepix/Shutterstock; p3r: Danielle Dufault; p2b: Pixtal/Stocktrek/Getty Images; p9b: OUP and Six Red Marbles; p3l: strandbeest.com; p4: Ashley Cooper/Corbis Documentary/Getty Images; p5r: Wiktor Bubniak/Shutterstock; p5l: Kostyantyn Ivanyshen/Alamy Stock Photo; p5m: DR Juerg Alean/Science Photo Library; p6: Nigel Cattlin/Science Photo Library; p6: Cordelia Molloy/Science Photo Library; p8: Brian Gadsby/Science Photo Library; p7t: Anyaivanova/Shutterstock; p9t: Photodisc/Getty Images; p10t: Sputnik/Science Photo Library; p10m: Smereka/Shutterstock; p10b: Jason Lindsey/Alamy Stock Photo; p12: Design Pics/Getty Images; p13: Michael Ready/Visuals Unlimited, Inc./Science Photo Library; p14t: Adrian Muttitt/Alamy Stock Photo; p14b: T Service/Science Photo Library; p15l: Amana Images Inc./Getty Images; p15m: Image Source/Getty Images; p15r: Photodisc/Getty Images; p16tl: Digital Vision/Getty Images; p16tr: National Geographic; p16tml: Claffra/Shutterstock; p16tmr: Amar and Isabelle Guillen - Guillen Photo LLC / Alamy Stock Photo; p16bml: Ingram/Alamy Stock Photo; p16bmr: David Cappaert/Agstockusa/Science Photo Library; p16bl: Steve Gschmeissner/Science Photo Library; p16br: Photodisc/Getty Images; p17t: Mike Pellinni/Shutterstock; p18: Willyam Bradberry/Shutterstock; p19tl: DR P. Marazzi/Science Photo Library; p19tr: Corbis; p19bl: Claire Ting/Science Photo Library; p19bml: Sinclair Stammers/Science Photo Library; p19bmr: Digital Vision/Getty Images; p19br: Frans Lanting, Mint Images/Science Photo Library; p20: Photodisc/Getty Images; p26t: Nick Upton/Alamy Stock Photo; p26b: Andrew F. Kazmierski/Shutterstock; p27t: Everything possible/Shutterstock; p27b: Excitations/Alamy Stock Photo; p28: By Mogens Engelund (Own work) [CC BY-SA 3.0 (http://creativecommons.org/licenses/by-sa/3.0)], via Wikimedia Commons; p26t: Alfie Photography/Shutterstock; p26b: Liu Fuyu/123RF; p35: Lagutkin Alexey/Shutterstock; p36: Madlen/Shutterstock; p38: By Li, H. et al, (2009), Refined Geographic Distribution of the Oriental ALDH2*504Lys (nee 487Lys) Variant. Annals of Human Genetics, 73: 335–345. doi:10.1111/j.1469-1809.2009.00517.x; p43 all:Research Collaboratory for Structural Bioinformatics PDB; p46: Jps/Shutterstock; p50: National Human Genome Institute/SCIENCE PHOTO LIBRARY; p53: Ollyy/Shutterstock; p56: By Perry, GH, et al. Diet and evolution of human amylase gene copy number variation, Nature Genetics 39:1256-1260 (2007); p57: By Perry, GH, et al. Diet and evolution of human amylase gene copy number variation, Nature Genetics 39:1256-1260 (2007); p58: Science Museum, London/Wellcome Images; p60l: Brian Lasenby/Shutterstock; p60r: Kurt G/Shutterstock; p61tr: SCUBAZOO/SCIENCE PHOTO LIBRARY; p61tl: Lightboxx/Shutterstock; p61br: Dirk Ercken/Shutterstock; p61bl: aquapix/Shutterstock; p62: Rawpixel.com/Shutterstock; p64l: Nikoncharly/istockphoto; p65: By Henrik L/istockphoto; p65: By Jerzy Strzelecki - Own work, CC BY-SA 3.0, https://commons.wikimedia.org/w/index.php?curid=3356426; p66l: Yuriy Kulik/Shutterstock; p67tl: Anna Kucherova/Shutterstock; p67tm: Kristian Bell/Shutterstock; p67bl: Nature's Images, INC.'/Science Photo Library; p67br: Georgette Douwma/Science Photo Library; p67r: Corbis; p68l: J. Bicking/Shutterstock; p69: (c) Thomas Christensen, www.rightreading.com; p70tl: Prisma Bildagentur AG/Alamy Stock Photo; p70tr: Jameslee999/Vetta/Getty Images; p70bl: Johner Images; p70br: robertharding/Alamy Stock Photo; p71tl: Javier Trueba/MSF/Science Photo Library; p71tr: Tony Camacho/Science Photo Library; p71mr: The Jane Goodall Institute/ By Fernando Turmo; p71br: Ingram/Alamy Stock Photo; p72l: Reinhard Dirscherl, Visuals Unlimited/Science Photo Library; p72r: Shalamov/istockphoto; p73tl: Corel; p73tr: Johan Swanepoel/Shutterstock; p73br: Jeremy Woodhouse/Photodisc/Getty Images; p74: Ian Scott/Shutterstock; p76tl: Gail Jankus/Science Photo Library; p76tr: Maria Mosolova/Science Photo Library; p76bl: Royal Botanic Garden Edinburgh/Science Photo Library; p76br: Bob Gibbons/Science Photo Library; p77tl: Ian Gowland/Science Photo Library; p77tr: JIL Photo/Shutterstock; p78t: Sanamyan/Alamy Stock Photo; p78b: F. Peyregne/CNRI/Science Photo Library; p79l: John Durham/Science Photo Library; p79r: By gwenole camus from Cournon d'auvergne, France (P1030792) [CC BY-SA 2.0 (http://creativecommons.org/licenses/by-sa/2.0)], via Wikimedia Commons; p80tl: M.I. Walker/Science Photo Library; p80bl: By Anatoly Mikhaltsov (Own work) [CC BY-SA 4.0 (http://creativecommons.org/licenses/by-sa/4.0)], via Wikimedia Commons; p80r: Steve Gschmeissner/Science Photo Library; p81l: Ted Kinsman/Science Photo Library; p81m: Science Photo Library; p81r: Jan Hinsch/Science Photo Library; p82t: Photodisc/Getty Images; p82b: Brand X Pictures/Getty Images; p83: By Hand_zur_Abmessung.jpg:2D4Dderivative work: Thetesting2d4dratio (talk) - Hand_zur_Abmessung.jpg, Public Domain, https://commons.wikimedia.org/w/index.php?curid=14515285; p85l: Sheila Terry/Science Photo Library; p85r: Natural History Museum, London/Science Photo Library; p86: Dorling Kindersley/UIG/Science Photo Library; p87t: Matthias Wolf/123RF; p87b: Ted Kinsman/Science Photo Library; p88: Corel; p89t: Claffra/Shutterstock; p89b: WEellcome Dept. Of Cognitive Neurology/Science Photo Library; p95: David S. Goodsell (The Scripps Research Institute and the RCSB PDB); p90: DR. Donald Fawcett, Visuals Unlimited/Science Photo Library; p11b: David S. Goodsell (The Scripps Research Institute and the RCSB PDB); p91: Monkey Business Images/Shutterstock; p93tl: Thomas Deerinck, NCMIR/Science Photo Library; p93tr: Steve Gschmeissner/Science Photo Library; p93ml: Steve Gschmeissner/Science Photo Library; Continued on last page

Contents

Introduction

The MYP biology course is inquiry based. MYP structures inquiry in sciences by developing conceptual understanding. Key concepts represent big ideas that are relevant across disciplines. Related concepts are grounded in specific disciplines and are useful for exploring key concepts in greater detail. Each chapter of this book is focused on a single related concept and one or two key concepts.

Every chapter opens with ways in which the related concept is explored in other disciplines. This structure will help to develop an interdisciplinary understanding of the concepts. After the interdisciplinary opening pages, the concepts are introduced more deeply in relation to the content of the chapter.

The objectives of MYP Science are categorized into four criteria, which contain descriptions of specific targets that are accomplished by studying this programme:

A Knowing and understanding

B Inquiring and designing

C Processing and evaluating

D Reflecting on the impacts of science

Within each chapter, we have included activities designed to promote achievement of these objectives, such as experiments and data-based questions. We also included factual, conceptual and debatable questions, and activities designed to promote development of approaches to learning skills. The summative assessment found at the end of each chapter is framed by a statement of inquiry relating the concepts addressed to one of the six global contexts, as in the MYP eAssessment.

For those students taking the eAssessment at the end of the MYP programme, the International Baccalaureate Organization provides a subject-specific topic list. Great care has been taken to ensure all topics from the list are covered within this book.

Overall, this book is meant to guide a student's exploration of biology and aid the development of specific skills that are essential for academic success and getting the most out of this educational experience. In particular, the content of this book will provide a sound foundation for the study of DP Biology, both at Standard and Higher Level.

How to use this book

To help you get the most of your book, here's an overview of its features.

Concepts, global context and statement of inquiry

The key and related concepts, the global context and the statement of inquiry used in each chapter are clearly listed on the introduction page.

Activities

A range of activities that encourage you to think further about the topics you studied, research these topic and build connections between biology and other disciplines.

Experiment

Practical activities that help you prepare for assessment criteria B & C.

ATL Skills

These Approaches to Learning sections introduce new skills or give you the opportunity to reflect on skills you might already have. They are mapped to the MYP skills clusters and are aimed at supporting you become an independent learner.

Data-based question

These questions allow you to test your factual understanding of biology, as well as study and analyse data. Data-based questions help you prepare for assessment criteria A, B & C.

1 A grey circle appears before a conceptual question.

2 A red circle appears before a debatable question.

Summative assessment

There is a summative assessment at the end of each chapter; this is structured in the same way as the eAssessment and covers all four MYP assessment criteria.

 These icons indicate which criterion is assessed in that section.

Glossary

The glossary contains definitions for all the subject-specific terms emboldened in the index.

Topics overview

The MYP eAssessment subject list for Biology consists of nine broad topics:

Cells

Organisms

Processes

Metabolism

Evolution

Interactions with environment

Interactions between organisms

Human interactions with environments

Biotechnology

These topics are further broken down into sub-topics and the mapping grid below gives you an overview of where these are covered within this book. It also shows you which key concept, global context and statement of inquiry guide the learning in each chapter.

Chapter	Topics covered	Key concept	Global context	Statement of inquiry	ATL skills
1 Energy	Movement Energy transfer Cell respiration, aerobic and anaerobic respiration Food chains/webs	Change Systems	Globalization and sustainability	Humans need to find sources of energy that do not cause harmful and irreversible changes to ecosystems and the environment.	Critical thinking skills: Revise understanding based on new information and evidence Thinking in context: How can we make human energy use more sustainable?
2 Transformation	Biochemistry and enzymes Word and chemical equations Photosynthesis	Change	Scientific and technical innovations	Science is applied to mitigate the transformations associated with aging but sometimes anti-aging science is misrepresented.	Creative thinking skills: Generate metaphors and analogies Communication skills: Use a variety of organizers for writing tasks
3 Form	Cell structure Tissues Organs Systems Classification	Relationships	Identities and relationships	Relationships between organisms are revealed by similarities and differences between the myriad of forms.	Communication skills: Use and interpret a range of discipline-specific terms Information literacy skills: Understand and use technology systems Information literacy skills: Preview and skim videos to build understanding
4 Function	Cell functions Nutrition Digestion Receptors Senses	Systems	Orientation in space and time	Each component in a system must perform its specific function at the right time and place for the system as a whole to be successful.	Critical thinking skills: Making reasonable predictions Affective skills: Practicing resilience
5 Movement	Diffusion Osmosis Tropisms Transpiration and translocation Gas exchange Transport and circulation	Change	Fairness and development	The changes in the weather patterns caused by current economic activity may not be fair to future generations.	

Chapter	Topics covered	Key concept	Global context	Statement of inquiry	ATL skills
6 Interaction	Nervous system Competition Pathogens/parasites Predator/prey Interdependancy	Relationships	Identities and relationships	When two or more individuals interact, they form relationships that, over time, impact and contribute to their identity.	**Creative thinking skills:** Generating analogies **Thinking in context:** What is the relationship between video games and identity? **Organization skills:** Preparing for eAssessment
7 Balance	Homeostasis Hormones Ecosystem Cycles including nutrient, carbon, nitrogen	Systems	Fairness and development	Development is only sustainable if systems remain in balance.	**Information literacy skills:** Present information in a variety of formats and platforms **Critical thinking skills:** Addressing counterclaims
8 Environment	Habitat **Habitat change or destruction** **Pollution/ conservation**	Change	Personal and cultural expression	Environments provide aesthetic benefits and influence human cultural expression, but human induced changes undermine these benefits.	**Thinking in context** **Communication skills:** Collaborate with peers and experts using a variety of digital environments and media
9 Patterns	Unity and diversity in life forms DNA **Genome mapping and application** Cell division Mitosis Meiosis Reproduction Life cycles	Relationships	Orientation in time and space	Observing patterns allows scientists to propose new theories that explain how the living world works.	**Creative and innovative thinking skills:** Generate a testable hypothesis **Critical thinking skills:** Evaluating evidence and arguments
10 Consequences	Inheritance and variation Natural selection **Speciation and extinction** Genetic modification Cloning Ethical implications	Change	Scientific and technical innovation	Scientific and technical innovations can change the impacts that we have on the world.	**Critical thinking skills:** Draw supported conclusions **Reflection skills:** Consider ethical, cultural and environmental implications
11 Evidence	Factors affecting human health Vaccination	Relationships	Scientific and technical innovation	Healthy lifestyles can be based on evidence of relationships between types of behaviour and risks of disease.	**Information literacy skills:** Finding, interpreting, judging and creating information
12 Models	**Overexploitation** **Mitigation of adverse effects** 3D tissue and organ printing **Human influences**	Systems	Globalization and sustainability	Methods of achieving sustainability can be developed using models that explore differences between systems.	**Critical thinking skills:** Is modelling an essential part of all research in biology? **Communication skills:** Take effective notes in class and make effective summary notes

1 Energy

Energy is invisible, but its effects are easily observed.

◀ More energy is available to living organisms in some regions on Earth than in others. For example, the poles are the regions where there is least available energy. What is the reason for this?

▼ A huge amount of energy is needed to get a space shuttle into orbit. To generate this energy, hydrogen and oxygen are used as fuel. The plumes trailing behind the shuttle are water. Hydrogen is obtained using fossil fuels formed millions of years ago out of the remains of living organisms. What is the source of the oxygen?

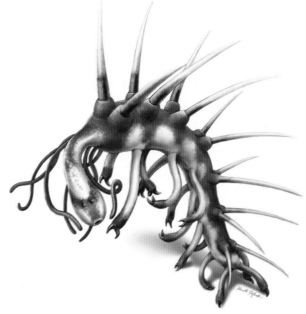

▲ All aspects of life rely on energy. Based on this idea, Dutch physicist and artist Theo Jensen refers to his gigantic Strandbeests as "animals" that "live" on the beach. The organisms made of plastic tubes and sheets have stomachs, muscles, wings and legs, and use wind energy to move. They can also store energy, which allows them to continue moving even when the wind is not blowing. While moving, their legs throw sand in the air, leading to the formation of dunes which protect the coasts from rising sea levels. What other impacts could these animals have on their environment? Is this a strategy that could be used in other countries too?

▲ *Hallucigenia* lived on Earth 500 million years ago. It had muscles for movement, like animals alive today. It used energy from chemicals rather than wind. How did *Hallucigenia* obtain chemical energy? How can animals still obtain the chemical energy that they need for movement despite using it for more than half a billion years?

"

Over time, these skeletons have become increasingly better at surviving the elements such as storm and water and eventually I want to put these animals out in herds on the beaches, so they will live their own lives.

Theo Jensen

"

Introduction

Energy is what makes things happen. In physics this is stated more formally: energy is the capacity to do work. Energy cannot be created or destroyed, but it can be converted from one form to another or transferred between objects. Energy is therefore closely related to the key concept of change.

Energy for body functions comes from food. Energy for industry, transport and for homes comes from a variety of sources including oil and gas. There are major issues about where energy will come from in the future, so the global context of this chapter is globalization and sustainability.

Key concepts: Change, Systems

Related concept: Energy

Global context: Globalization and sustainability

▽ Rapeseed (*Brassica napus*) is a very versatile crop, producing vegetable oils for human consumption and for the production of biodiesel, as well as a protein-rich animal food. Could growing such crops solve the problems of energy supply in the future?

Statement of inquiry:

Humans need to find sources of energy that do not cause harmful and irreversible changes to ecosystems and the environment.

All aspects of life rely on energy:

- Movement is possible because of kinetic energy. A falcon diving through the air to catch its prey and pollen grains blown by the wind have kinetic energy. Blood flowing through arteries also has kinetic energy. The concept of movement is the theme of Chapter 5.

- Atoms interacting to form molecules (chemical energy), neurons sending and receiving messages (electrochemical energy) and tissues changing shape (elastic energy) are all possible because of potential energy. Potential energy is energy that is stored and which exists because of a change in position, shape or state.

- Plant growth is possible because of a form of radiant energy: light. Other forms of radiant energy are gamma rays, microwaves and radio waves.

All the cells in living organisms, as well as the air around them, are made up of particles that may vibrate, rotate and move in random directions. This movement of particles is a source of thermal energy: the more rapid the movement, the greater the thermal energy and the higher the temperature. Heat is thermal energy that is being transferred, generally from a material with a higher temperature to materials with a lower temperature, for example, from the human body to the environment. In nature, energy is lost from all ecosystems in the form of heat.

What kind of energy is needed to split firewood? What is the source of this energy? Firewood is a source of energy itself—what kind and how is it released?

Changes to the form of energy

The table gives examples of two energy transformations in biology. Draw up an expanded version of the table to include more forms of energy.

Light to chemical	**Chemical to light**
Production of foods by photosynthesis	Bioluminescence in fireflies

How do plants obtain energy?

Plants grow towards the light and do not grow well if they are deprived of light. When you walk under trees, the shade shows that leaves block some of the sunlight. These observations suggest that plants absorb light and use it as an energy source. Light energy must be changed into chemical energy inside the plant. Although this seems obvious, scientists look for evidence, usually from experiments. You can obtain evidence for the conversion of light energy into chemical energy inside plants by doing a simple experiment, using a pondweed such as *Elodea* or *Cabomba*.

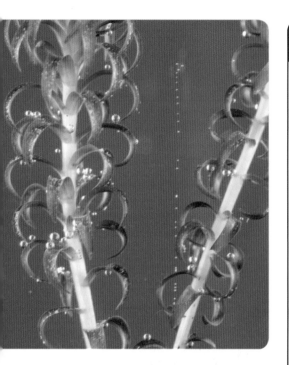

▲ *Elodea* releasing bubbles of oxygen

Ⓐ Ⓑ Ⓒ Ⓓ Experiment

Hypothesis

When plants convert light energy to chemical energy they produce oxygen.

Materials

A stem of *Elodea* or *Cabomba*; a clean, transparent container; tap water

Method

Fill a clean, transparent container with water. Choose a stem of *Elodea* or *Cabomba* that has plenty of leaves. Place it upside down in water and cut the end of the stem.

Observations

Bubbles of gas should emerge from the cut end of the stem and rise to the water surface.

Suggestions for further stages in your experiment:

1. Collect and test the bubbles to confirm that they are oxygen.

2. Carry out a simple test to show that light energy is needed for the production of oxygen.

3. Obtain further evidence of the need for light energy by measuring the bubbling rate at different light intensities.

Extension to your experiment

Devise a method for measuring the bubbling rate of a pondweed stem when it is placed in three different samples of water: a) tap water, b) water that has been boiled and then cooled to remove dissolved gases and c) sparkling water. Before you perform the experiment you should write a hypothesis. When you have obtained your results, you can analyse them to see whether they support your hypothesis. Do the results of this experiment change your understanding of photosynthesis?

Revise understanding based on new information and evidence

Sometimes the results of experiments support our hypothesis and reinforce our understanding, but in science it is not unusual to get surprising results. These may be due to an error in procedures, which should be found and corrected. On other occasions, the results are not in error and they show that we need to revise our understanding. The results of the extension experiment may cause you to revise your understanding of photosynthesis.

Another example of revising our understanding comes from isotope experiments. Consider the summary equation for photosynthesis:

$$6H_2O + 6CO_2 \rightarrow C_6H_{12}O_6 + 6O_2$$

This equation indicates that some of the oxygen released must come from the carbon dioxide that is used. Experiments with isotopes show that this is incorrect. The normal isotope of oxygen is ^{16}O. When plants are given water containing ^{18}O rather than ^{16}O, all the oxygen that they release is also ^{18}O rather than ^{16}O. This shows that all the oxygen produced in photosynthesis comes from the splitting of water into oxygen and hydrogen. Twelve molecules of water must be split per glucose, but six new water molecules are subsequently produced, giving the net use of six molecules shown in the equation. Clearly, photosynthesis must be a more complicated process than the summary equation suggests.

Discuss in your class the meaning of the following terms in relation to this text:

dogmatic   steadfast   open-minded.

How similar are leaves and solar panels?

Leaves have evolved over millions of years; solar panels have been developed by electrical engineers over recent decades. Consider how similar leaves and solar panels are by making a list of similarities and a list of differences. You could include size, shape, energy source, energy conversion and efficiency.

▶ Solar panels are being installed on satellites, roof tops and increasingly in large arrays on former farmland

---

How do plants build up stores of energy?

PLANTS

A pigment is a chemical substance that absorbs light. Chlorophyll is the main pigment in plants and it plays an important role in absorbing energy. Chlorophyll absorbs red and blue light, but reflects green light. This is why chlorophyll, and leaves, look green.

When photons of red or blue light reach the chlorophyll, they cause particular electrons in the molecule to jump to a higher energy level. This is how light is converted into chemical energy. The high-energy electrons are very unstable, however, and they cannot store energy for more than a fraction of a second. In order for the chemical energy to be stored, the high-energy electrons must be used quickly in the production of chemical compounds such as glucose. Plant cells can only store small amounts of glucose, so when there is rapid photosynthesis they convert it to starch. This leads us to a testable hypothesis: starch is only produced by photosynthesis if there is chlorophyll in a leaf cell.

▲ Variegated plants have chloroplasts containing the green pigment chlorophyll in some parts of the leaf but not others. Where the cells lack chloroplasts, the leaf appears yellow or white. Normal and variegated varieties of privet are shown here

▲ The leaves of this *Coleus blumei* plant have green, white and purple areas

ⒶⒷⒸⒹ Experiment

Hypothesis

Starch is only produced by photosynthesis if there is chlorophyll in a leaf cell.

Method

1. Put a variegated *Pelargonium* plant in darkness for a few days.

2. Test a leaf from the plant for starch to confirm that none is present.

3. Cover part of a healthy leaf with a black card to exclude light.

4. Put the plant in bright light for a few hours.

5. Remove the leaf and test it for starch.

    a) Dip the leaf into boiling water for 20 seconds to destroy all the cell membranes.

    b) Put the leaf in a test tube of boiling ethanol for about two minutes to dissolve out the chlorophyll from the leaf and allow test results to be seen more clearly.

    c) Rinse the leaf in water to remove the ethanol.

    d) Spread the leaf on a white tile so that all of it is visible.

    e) Put iodine solution over the whole of the leaf and wait for a few minutes to allow the iodine to diffuse into the cells where starch could be located.

    f) Any parts of the leaf that turn black contain starch. Any parts that remain brown do not contain starch.

Analyse your results by considering the reasons for starch being present or absent from each of these regions of the leaf: green illuminated, green in darkness, white illuminated and white in darkness.

Extension to your experiment

Some leaves are either totally purple or have purple areas. Suggest a hypothesis for whether starch can be produced by photosynthesis in purple leaf cells and test your hypothesis using plants such as *Coleus blumei*. You may have to revise your understanding when you get your results, but remember that as there are many different patterns of purple leaf colour, you cannot accept or reject your hypothesis by testing just one type.

How much chemical energy is there in a seed?

Plants store energy in seeds so that when the seed germinates there is enough energy available for the early stages of growth. All seeds contain chemical energy but sunflower seeds, cashews and almonds are suitable choices for this experiment.

A simple method for measuring the chemical energy content of a seed is to burn the seed and use the heat released to increase the temperature of water. Energy is measured in joules (J). To raise one millilitre (ml) of water one degree Celsius requires 4.2 J of heat energy, so energy content of seed (J per gram of seed) = temperature rise (°C) × water volume (ml) × 4.2 J / mass of food (grams).

▲ Seeds contain stores of chemical energy

ⒶⒷⒸⒹ Experiment

Method

1. Clamp a tube at an angle of about 45° with the clamp at the top of the tube.

2. Put 20 ml of water in the tube.

3. Put a thermometer into the tube and measure the temperature before burning the seed.

4. Measure the mass of a seed using an electronic balance.

5. Fix the seed onto a mounted needle and set it alight by holding it in a Bunsen burner flame.

6. When it is burning, hold the seed under the tube of water so that the flame touches the tube (see diagram).

7. When the seed has finished burning, stir the water with the thermometer and measure its temperature again.

Results

Draw up a results table to record the type of seed, its mass, the water temperature before and after burning the seed, the temperature rise and the energy content per gram of the seed.

Evaluation

Dietary information on food packaging gives these values for energy content:

- sunflower seeds: 24,800 J per gram

- cashew nuts: 24,700 J per gram

- almonds: 24,500 J per gram.

Discuss the reasons for the differences between your results and the results given on food packets.

Suggest improvements to the method that you used.

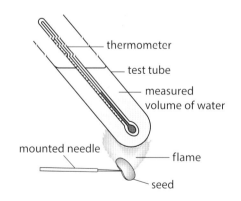

thermometer
test tube
measured volume of water
mounted needle
flame
seed

Biodiesel

The seeds used in the previous experiment have relatively large amounts of chemical energy because of the oil they contain. Oil extracted from seeds is used as an alternative to diesel fuel in some parts of the world. Find out whether "biodiesel" is produced or used in your part of the world. What are the advantages and disadvantages of using biodiesel instead of fossil fuels?

▲ Biodiesel fuel pump in Spain

METABOLISM

How is energy released in cells?

Molecules such as glucose or fat contain a relatively large amount of chemical energy—more than needed for most tasks in a cell. Energy released from these food molecules is therefore used to make a large number of molecules that contain a smaller amount of energy. It is a remarkable fact that all organisms use the same molecule for storing and then supplying small packets of energy in the cell. This molecule is adenosine triphosphate (ATP). It is made by linking a phosphate group onto adenosine diphosphate (ADP). This is achieved using energy from glucose, fat or other foods. The reactions that release energy from glucose and other foods and produce ATP are called cell respiration.

If oxygen is used, the process is aerobic respiration. This is a long sequence of reactions, but these can be summarized in one equation:

glucose + oxygen ⟶ carbon dioxide + water

ADP   ATP

▲ Corn has starchy seeds. The starch can be digested into sugars. Yeast can then be used to produce ethanol from the sugar by anaerobic respiration

If oxygen is not available, some cells can perform anaerobic respiration, which is a shorter sequence of reactions that produces much less ATP. In some organisms, such as humans or mealworms, the summary equation for anaerobic respiration is:

glucose ⟶ lactic acid

ADP   ATP

▽ E85 is a fuel consisting of 15% gasoline and 85% ethanol

In fungi, such as yeast, and in plants the summary equation for anaerobic respiration is:

glucose ⟶ ethanol + carbon dioxide

ADP → ATP

Both these versions of anaerobic respiration produce less ATP per glucose molecule than aerobic respiration because the glucose has not been fully broken down. Ethanol and lactic acid contain chemical energy that has not been released and used to make ATP. Ethanol produced by anaerobic respiration in yeasts is used as a fuel for cars, where the remaining energy is released by combustion.

Refer to the diagram in the margin and research ATP to find out these things:

1. In the diagram of ATP, what do the letters C, H, N, O and P represent?

2. What do the single and double lines represent?

3. What are the names of each of the differently colored parts of the molecule?

4. What is removed from ATP to make **a)** ADP, **b)** AMP and **c)** adenosine?

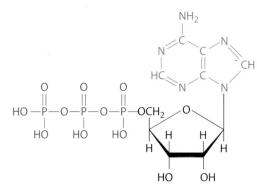

▲ Adenosine triphosphate (ATP)

How can we measure the rate of energy release in cells?

METABOLISM

Rate means how much of something happens in a certain time. Energy is released in cells by respiration, so to find the rate of energy release, you measure the amount of respiration occurring in a period of time. The diagrams in the experiments below show methods for doing this.

Experiment

Method A

Set up the apparatus shown in the diagram and leave it running for several days. An electronic balance is needed that gives a mass reading to a hundredth of a gram

1. Explain what type of respiration the yeast cells must be carrying out.

2. The mass of the apparatus is expected to decrease steadily. What causes this loss of mass?

3. Explain these possible trends in mass loss:

    a) a gradual increase in the rate of mass loss.

    b) higher mass loss in daytime than at night.

    c) no further mass loss after a few days.

4 Suggest one advantage of recording the results with a data logger.

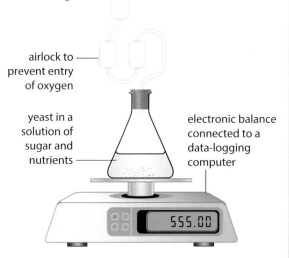

airlock to prevent entry of oxygen

yeast in a solution of sugar and nutrients

electronic balance connected to a data-logging computer

555.00

Experiment

Method B

Set up the three tubes shown in the diagram and place them in a hot block heater or a water bath at 30°C. When they have heated up, inject a small drop of colored fluid into the capillary tubes, near the top. If the fluid starts to move down the tube, measure how far it moves in millimetres every minute.

colored fluid

air

glass beads

mesh basket

dry peas

germinating peas

cotton soaked in potassium hydroxide solution

1. What is the purpose of the potassium hydroxide solution?

2. The fluid is expected to move downwards in the tube containing germinating peas. What causes this movement?

3. What are the correct units for measuring the rate of movement of the fluid?

4. What is the purpose of:

   a) the tube with glass beads instead of germinating peas?

   b) the tube containing the dry peas?

5. Explain how the method could be modified and improved so that the rate of energy release could be compared accurately in different types of seed.

METABOLISM

What is energy needed for in cells?

Many different tasks are performed in cells using energy from ATP:

- Energy is used to transform small molecules into larger molecules such as proteins and DNA. These transformations are called anabolic reactions and are explored more fully in Chapter 2.

- ATP also provides energy for pumping ions and other particles across cell membranes from a lower to a higher concentration. This process is called active transport. Energy is changed from chemical to electrochemical during active transport.

- Energy is also required for movement. Chemical energy is changed into kinetic energy. ATP supplies energy for moving components from one part of a cell to another and also for moving the whole cell. Muscle cells in particular use considerable amounts of ATP when they are contracting. Movement is explored in Chapter 5.

- In a few species, ATP supplies energy for chemical reactions that make part of the body flash or glow, so chemical energy is changed into light.

▲ Cells on the surface of roots transfer ions such as potassium from the soil into the plant. The concentration of these ions is already much higher inside the cells than in the soil, so energy from ATP has to be used to pump the ions into the cells by active transport

Data-based question: Energy requirements of humans

The table shows the energy requirements of different groups of humans.

| Age range (years) | Energy requirement (MJ per day) | | | | | |
| | Females | | | Males | | |
	Low activity level	Moderately active	Very active	Low activity level	Moderately active	Very active
1–2		3.6			4.0	
7–8	5.5	6.5	7.5	6.0	7.1	8.2
14–15	8.7	10.2	11.8	10.6	12.5	14.4
15–16	8.9	10.4	12.0	11.3	13.3	15.3
17–18	8.9	10.5	12.0	12.1	14.3	16.4

1. State two processes in human cells which require energy.

2. Suggest a reason for increasing energy requirements as boys grow older.

3. **a)** Calculate the percentage increase in energy requirement for a 14–15-year-old boy that stops playing computer games and starts training with a football team.

   b) Explain how the extra energy is used in the boy's body.

4. Explain what will happen in a boy's or girl's body if:

   a) they eat food each day containing more energy than their requirement

   b) they eat food each day containing less energy than their requirement.

5. **a)** State the trends in energy requirement as boys and girls grow from 15–16 to 17–18 years old.

   b) Suggest a reason for the different trends in boys and girls.

6. Draw a bar chart to display the energy requirements for moderately active boys and girls, for all boys or for all girls.

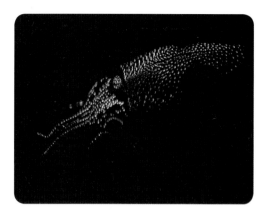

▲ The firefly squid (*Watasenia scintillans*) lives in the Western Pacific at depths where little light penetrates. It emits flashes of light from groups of light-emitting cells, using energy from ATP and an enzyme (luciferase). The flashes of light are used to attract the small fish on which it feeds.

How is thermal energy generated and lost in living organisms?

METABOLISM

Whenever energy changes from one form to another inside cells, some of it is changed into thermal energy. The energy change causes any particles involved to vibrate or move around more rapidly, so their temperature rises. Thermal energy is also generated during most chemical reactions—the products of the reaction are at a

▼ Despite cold winter weather and light clothing, these hockey players are warm, but the umpire standing behind needs more insulation

higher temperature than the reactants, because some chemical energy changes into thermal energy. For example, we experience a temperature increase when we run. Chemical energy in glucose is used to generate the kinetic energy of our moving body, but at the same time some of the chemical energy of the glucose changes to heat in our muscles.

All normal cellular activities therefore generate thermal energy. This is true for all organisms and can be demonstrated with a simple experiment using vacuum flasks and peas.

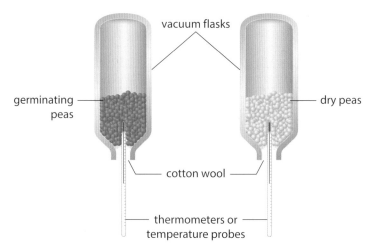

Generation of thermal energy in living organisms often makes them hotter than their surroundings. Heat passes from a hotter to a colder system, so living organisms usually lose heat to their surroundings. There are of course exceptions to this—you may be able to think of some. They are only ever temporary—all organisms generate thermal energy and eventually lose it to the environment in the form of heat.

Data-based question: Infrared photography

Some cameras can take photographs using infrared radiation instead of visible light. The images that they produce show the temperature of the subjects. This image shows a tarantula spider in a person's hands. The temperature of the dark blue areas was coolest (22.8°C or less) with increasing temperatures showing as green, yellow, orange and red (35.9°C or more).

1. How was the camera able to measure the temperature of the spider and the hands?

2. Which was losing more heat to the surroundings, the spider or the hands? Give reasons for your answer.

3. Explain the temperature difference between the palms of the hands and the fingers.

4. Was the spider losing heat to the environment or gaining heat from it? Explain your answer.

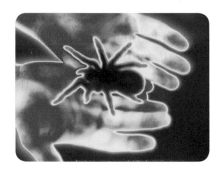

How can we make human energy use more sustainable?

You can explore this issue by debating the answers to these questions:

1 The total energy requirements of humans on Earth are huge. What are the reasons for this?

2 Energy in food is released by respiration to fuel activities in our cells. Are there any humans living on Earth today that do not use any other energy source apart from food?

3 Is food production for humans sustainable?

4 What are the sources of energy other than food that humans use?

5 The photographs show one person exercising on a rowing machine and another commuting to work in a car. What is the source of energy in each case and what energy conversions are happening in their daily lives?

6 What can we do in our everyday lives to make human energy use more sustainable?

▲ Spraying pesticide on a food crop

▲ Exercising on a rowing machine

▲ Commuting to work

How do animals obtain energy?

ECOLOGY

Animals obtain their energy by consuming other organisms. Each cell in an animal's body is supplied with substances produced by digesting the consumed organism. These substances contain chemical energy. Fats and carbohydrates are particularly useful as sources of energy.

We can divide animals into categories according to what they consume. These are called trophic groups.

● Animals that consume plants are called primary consumers.

● Animals that consume primary consumers are called secondary consumers.

● Animals that consume secondary consumers are called tertiary consumers.

● Animals that consume dead organic matter and micro-organisms are detritivores.

● Plants are not consumers because they make their own food instead of obtaining it from other organisms. They are in a trophic group called producers.

Trophic levels

Study the photographs in the table and deduce the trophic level of each organism.

▲ Tiger

▲ Monarch butterfly caterpillar

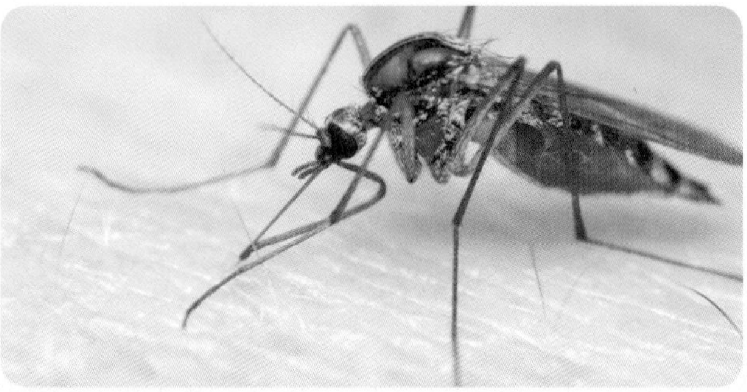

▲ Mosquito

▲ Whale shark

▲ Panda

▲ Potato aphid

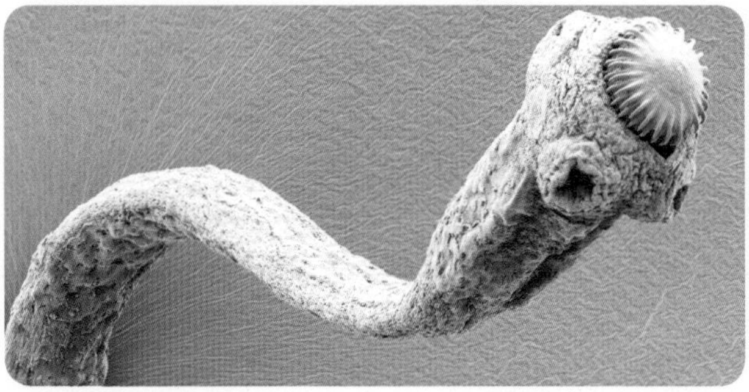

▲ Dog tapeworm

▲ Chimpanzee

Interactions between species due to feeding are explored more fully in Chapter 6.

How does energy enter and leave ecosystems?

You have already seen in this chapter that living organisms cannot live alone. They depend on other organisms for supplies of energy and much more. They also depend on their non-living surroundings of air, water, soil and rock. Biologists have therefore developed the concept of an ecosystem, which is an ecological system such as a lake or a forest. An ecosystem is composed of all the organisms in an area together with their non-living (abiotic) environment.

Systems are an important concept in biology. Here we introduce the concept and in the later chapters that take systems as the key concept we shall consider them more fully.

A system is a set of interacting or interdependent components. There are two main types of system:

- **Open systems** where resources can enter or exit, including both chemical substances and energy.

- **Closed systems** where energy can enter or exit, but chemical resources cannot be removed or replaced.

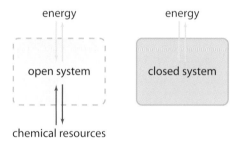

▲ Forest ecosystems are sustained by sunlight, but most river ecosystems are sustained by the energy in dead organic matter that enters the river

Making a mesocosm

◄ A glass jar was filled with water and mud from a pond and then sealed to create a closed system. Since then it has been kept on a sunny lab windowsill. When the photograph was taken it had been there for 18 years. Layers of differently coloured bacteria have developed including green and yellow photosynthetic types. This type of small experimental ecosystem is called a mesocosm. You could make up a mesocosm to investigate how closed systems function, but you must ensure that no organisms are harmed if you do this.

1. **a)** What is the only thing that has entered the mesocosm since it was set up?

    b) What is the only thing that was lost from the mesocosm?

2. Explain whether bacteria that rely on aerobic respiration for their energy could survive in the mesocosm.

3. Explain whether life could be sustained in the mesocosm for millions of years, or whether it will inevitably die out after a time.

4. Discuss whether larger organisms than bacteria could evolve in the mesocosm.

▲ Sunlight sustains shallow coral reefs, but does not penetrate far below the surface. What is the energy source there?

Most natural ecosystems are open, with some chemical substances entering and other substances leaving. In all ecosystems, living organisms generate thermal energy and cannot change this into any other more useful form of energy. You might expect the temperature of the organisms and indeed the temperature of the whole ecosystem to increase. This does not happen because the organisms lose heat to the surroundings and the ecosystem as a whole loses energy to other systems.

The amount of energy in an ecosystem will decrease and the organisms will die unless energy lost as heat is replaced by energy entering the ecosystem. In most ecosystems, energy enters as sunlight. There are also some ecosystems that are sustained by supplies of dead organic matter from other ecosystems or by inorganic chemical reactions.

Data-based question: Energy flow in a deep-water ecosystem

The diagram shows energy flow in deep water in the Bay of Quinte on the northern shore of Lake Ontario, Canada. There is little or no photosynthesis in this ecosystem. Micro-organisms feed on dead organic matter that sinks down from surface waters and that comes from organisms which defecate and die in the deep water. Detritivores feed on the micro-organisms mostly by filtering the lake water. Carnivores are larger organisms that feed on the detritivores. The numbers indicate energy flow in kilojoules per square metre per day (kJ m^{-2} day^{-1}). There are small energy losses from this ecosystem due to insect larvae maturing into flying adults and migrating from the lake. These losses are not shown on the diagram.

1. Suggest a reason for the lack of photosynthesis in this ecosystem.

2. State which group of organisms releases most energy in the form of heat from respiration.

3. **a)** Of the 4960 kJ of energy that the detritivores take in, 33.7% is lost as heat. Calculate the percentage of the energy taken in by carnivores that is lost from them as heat.

   b) Suggest reasons for the difference in the percentage of energy taken in that is lost as heat.

4. Deduce with reasons whether this is an open or a closed system.

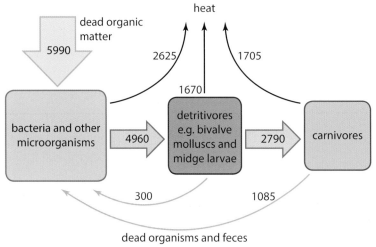

What prevents long food chains from developing?

A food chain is a series of organisms, each of which feeds on the previous organism in the chain. Food chains start with a producer and continue with a primary consumer, secondary consumer and so on. When real food chains are studied, they rarely extend beyond a tertiary consumer and very little food gets beyond that stage. A terrestrial food chain is shown below:

| grass | → | zebra | → | lion |

The marine food chain shown here gives the sizes and typical lengths of the organisms.

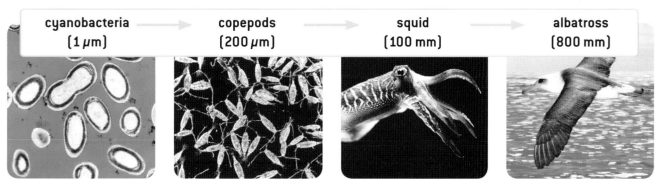

| cyanobacteria ($1\,\mu m$) | → | copepods ($200\,\mu m$) | → | squid ($100\,mm$) | → | albatross ($800\,mm$) |

To explain the reasons for food chains rarely extending beyond four stages, let us consider the lion and the zebra. The lion is dominant in the sense that it can catch and kill a zebra to obtain the chemical energy contained in its body. But the zebra has already used up much of the energy that was in the grass that it ate and this energy has been lost as heat. Less than 10% of the energy that was in the grass remains in the bodies of the zebras. Lions and other secondary consumers therefore inevitably get less energy than zebras and other primary consumers. If there are tertiary consumers in a food chain, they get even less of the energy. So, an animal can increase its supply of energy by feeding at an earlier stage in the food chain.

We could ask the question "Why don't lions increase their supply of energy by eating grass?". The answer is that they are not well adapted to do this—they are adapted instead to kill and digest prey. Zebras are far better at feeding on grass than lions and they therefore obtain much more energy from the ecosystem. Perhaps it is the zebra and not the lion that is dominant.

Which is my trophic level?

Humans can be primary, secondary or tertiary consumers, depending on what food we are eating. Find examples of foods that place us at each of these levels. Thinking globally, which trophic level is best for using energy efficiently, given that the human population is already higher than 7 billion?

▶ Select a food from this barbecue—what trophic level are you at if you eat it?

Data-based question: Pyramids of energy

The chart shows data from the Silver Springs River in Florida, USA. This type of chart is called a pyramid of energy. Each bar represents the amount of energy taken in by all the organisms in a trophic group. The units are kilojoules per square metre per year (kJ m^{-2} year^{-1})

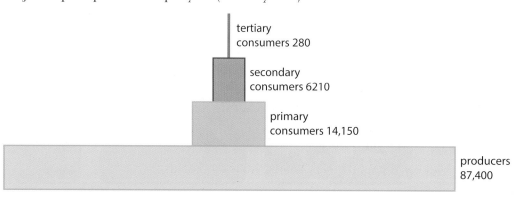

tertiary consumers 280

secondary consumers 6210

primary consumers 14,150

producers 87,400

1 **a)** Calculate the amount of energy taken in by producers that does not pass to primary consumers.

   b) Suggest two possibilities for what happens to this energy, assuming that the producers do not have more energy at the end of the year than at the start.

2 **a)** Of the energy taken in by primary consumers, 43.5% eventually passes to secondary consumers. Calculate the percentage of energy taken in by secondary consumers that passes to tertiary consumers.

   b) Explain how energy can pass from one consumer to another.

3. There are no quaternary consumers in this ecosystem. Explain the reasons for this.

Summative assessment

Introduction

This assessment is based principally on a report entitled *Oil palm plantations: threats and opportunities for tropical ecosystems*, published by the UNEP Global Environmental Alert Service (GEAS) in 2011 and available at
https://na.unep.net/geas/archive/pdfs/Dec_11_Palm_Plantations.pdf
To begin the assessment, read the report carefully.

 Energy in ecosystems

1. Energy cannot be created or destroyed but can change from one form to another. Deduce what change happens in these cases.

    a) Rainforest is cut down and burned to clear land for oil palm plantations. [1]

    b) Peat swamps are drained, allowing the peat to oxidize. [1]

    c) Sunlight is absorbed by palm leaves and oil is produced. [1]

    d) Palm oil is used as biodiesel in a vehicle. [1]

    e) Food containing palm oil is eaten by a person in Europe or the USA. [1]

2. The diagrams here show energy flows between trophic groups of animals in a natural rainforest (left) and an oil palm plantation (right). The animal groups are primary consumers (green), detritivores (yellow), carnivores (red) and omnivores (blue). The size of the circles indicates the biomass of the groups of animals and the width of the arrows indicates the amount of energy flowing from one group to another.

    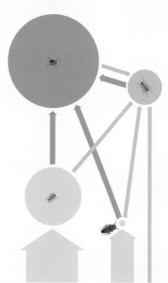

    a) Compare and contrast the source of energy for herbivores and detritivores in the natural rainforest. [2]

    b) What changes in energy flow happen when an area of natural rainforest is replaced by an oil palm plantation? [1]

    c) State the reason for the much lower biomass of carnivores in the oil plantation than in the natural rainforest. [1]

    d) Suggest a reason for a higher biomass of omnivores in the oil palm plantation than the natural rainforest. [1]

3. One hundred years ago there were probably more than 230,000 orangutan (*Pongo pygmaeus*) in their natural tropical rainforest habitats on Borneo and Sumatra. Population estimates by the World Wide Fund for Nature in 2016 were 41,000 on Borneo and 7,500 on Sumatra. The maps here show the parts of Borneo that orangutan inhabited in 1930 and the parts of the island where there was natural intact forest, logged forest, and plantations of rubber trees and oil palms in 2010.

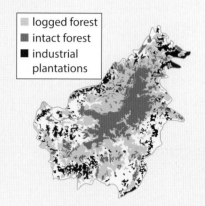

▲ Areas of Borneo inhabited by orangutan in 1930 (in green)
Source: The Ministry of Forestry, 2009

▲ Intact and logged forests, as well as industrial plantations in Borneo in 2010
Source: Gaveau DLA et al (2014), PLoS ONE 9(7): e101654. doi:10.1371/journal.pone.0101654

a) Analyse the information in the maps to assess whether or not:

i) orangutan originally inhabited all areas of forest on Borneo [1]

ii) plantations of rubber or palm oil have been established in areas formerly inhabited by orangutan [1]

iii) areas of intact forest remain where orangutan were living in 1930. [1]

b) Discuss whether logging or clearance of forest for plantations has had more harmful effects on orangutan. [2]

 Measuring the energy content of vegetable oils

4. The table shows how much oil is produced per hectare (100 m × 100 m) when four different crops are grown and also the total global area of their production.

Oil crop	Average oil yield (kg ha^{-1} year^{-1})	Planted area (million hectares)
Soybean	400	94.15
Sunflower	460	23.91
Rapeseed (canola)	680	27.22
Oil palm	3620	10.55

The yield of oil palm crops in kilograms per hectare is much higher than the other three crops, but to determine whether the energy yield per hectare is higher, the energy content of the different oils is needed.

a) Suggest a testable hypothesis for the relative amount of energy in palm oil and one other oil from the table. [2]

b) Design an experiment to test your hypothesis by measuring the energy content of the two oils. This should include:

   i) the types of oil that you will test [2]

   ii) how you will measure the energy content of the oil [5]

   iii) details of the variables you must keep constant in the experiment [3]

   iv) risks and how you will minimize them. [3]

 Analysis and evaluation

5. a) Present the results of your experiment to measure the energy content of oils in a clear and detailed results table. Remember to include row and column headings and SI units for quantitative variables. [3]

b) Display the results using a suitable type of graph or chart. [3]

c) Use calculations to evaluate the energy yields per hectare of palm oil and the other crop that you have investigated. [3]

d) Suggest scientific reasons for the differences in energy yield between the crops. [3]

e) The diagram shows a food calorimeter which is designed to measure the energy content of foods accurately. Suggest how it improves on your method in three ways. [3]

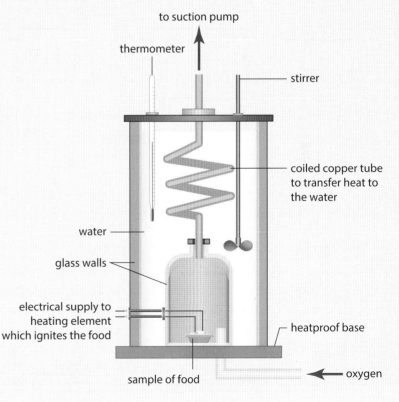

Sustainability of palm oil production

The article here was posted online in 2015 at http://theconversation.com/palm-oil-scourge-of-the-earth-or-wonder-crop-42165.

It was written by Denis J Murphy, who is Professor of Biotechnology at the University of South Wales, where he is an independent researcher and advisor to organizations that include the Food and Agriculture Organization of the United Nations and the Malaysian Palm Oil Board.

Read the passage and then answer the questions below.

Palm oil: scourge of the earth, or wonder crop?

If you happen to mention palm oil to most people outside of Asia you are unlikely to get a particularly positive reaction. Over recent years, media coverage of palm oil has typically included images of displaced orangutan and burning, degraded tropical forests. There has been a feeling that palm oil is an evil that needs to be stopped. Indeed, in some of the richer countries there have been attempts to organize consumer boycotts of palm oil products ranging from cosmetics to chocolate. Examples include France, the United Kingdom and Australia. But there is another story about palm oil that is much less frequently heard, especially in richer countries. This is a story about an ancient and bountiful African tree whose fruits provide a wholesome, vitamin-rich oil that feeds 2 billion to 3 billion people in 150 countries every day.

The oil palm tree has been cultivated as a source of food and fibre by people in western Africa for as much as 4,000 years and was harvested by our hunter gatherer ancestors for tens of millennia. Palm oil is a uniquely productive crop. On a per hectare basis, oil palm trees are 6–10 times more efficient at producing oil than temperate oilseed crops such as rapeseed (canola), soybean, olive and sunflower. The trees also have a productive lifetime of around 30 years. Soil in oil palm plantations is rich in organic content and is less disrupted compared to temperate, annual oil crops where highly destructive annual ploughing of the soil is required.

In 2014, the total estimated global production of palm oil was almost 70 million tonnes (Mt). Over 85% is exported from Indonesia and Malaysia, mostly to India and China, where the fruit oil is used in food, including as a cooking or salad oil, and in a wide range of processed food products. If oilseed crops were to replace palm oil, it would require at least 50 million additional hectares of prime farmland just to produce the same amount of edible oil.

The seed oil from palm is rich in lauric acid, a critical component in many cosmetics and cleaning products. Much of this type of palm oil is exported to Europe where it is used in toothpaste, washing up liquids, shower gels and laundry detergents. The only viable alternative oil that is rich in lauric acid comes from coconut, but the oil yield of this plant is less than 10% of palm oil. To completely substitute coconut for palm oil would require cultivating ten times as much tropical land. This is rarely realized by consumers who choose to use products containing coconut oil instead of palm oil.

Another misconception is that palm oil is overwhelmingly a "big business" crop. In fact, there are about 3 million smallholder growers, nearly all of whom farm individual family-owned plots. In Indonesia, which is the largest palm oil producing country, smallholder plots account for 40% of the total crop area. I have recently returned from a fact-finding visit to Sarawak where we saw some of the innovative ways that local people are growing oil palm alongside other crops.

Over the past year or so the pendulum of informed opinion has started to swing away from a simplistic view of palm oil as an unmitigated environmental scourge and towards a more nuanced approach that recognizes the genuine pros and cons of this bountiful tropical crop. One of the most encouraging developments has been the establishment of a reasonably robust and independent body to certify the environmental and social credentials of palm oil. The Roundtable on Sustainable Palm Oil, or RSPO, has a vision to "transform the markets by making sustainable palm oil the norm". The RSPO has over 2,000 members globally that represent 40% of the palm oil industry, covering all sectors of the supply chain.

There is also an increasingly active international research effort aimed at understanding the ecological and environmental impact of oil palm compared to other habitats such as rainforests and rapeseed or soybean farms. One example of this research is a recent analysis of tropical peat soils, some of which have been targeted for oil palm cultivation. When improperly farmed these soils can release large amounts of CO_2 and grow poor crops. But the analysis found some of types of peat can readily support oil palm crops without high CO_2 emissions, while others should be left un-farmed and conserved. They conclude that rather than a blanket-ban on farming peat soils, decisions should be made on a case-by-case basis depending on the type of peat.

Another study did a more rigorous life cycle assessment of oil crops, which is a measure of their overall environmental impact and found the overall ecological impact of palm oil is comparable, and sometimes superior to temperate crops. Two other studies examine the potential impact of land use and climate change on biodiversity in Borneo where a great deal of oil palm planting has occurred. The conclusions include the need to establish nature reserves in upland areas where climate change will be less severe and to improve connections between reserves and plantations with wildlife corridors.

There are undoubtedly many significant challenges facing oil palm, and further encroachment onto sensitive native forest areas should be minimized and eventually halted. But palm oil is also a uniquely efficient edible crop that is essential for food security in Africa and Asia. By working together as an international community that includes scientists, farmers, processors and consumers we aim to develop solutions to many of the problems faced by oil palm. Hopefully this will soon enable palm oil to regain its rightful place as one of the stars in the pantheon of global crops.

6. List examples mentioned in the article of science helping to address problems caused by palm oil production. [5]

7. Denis Murphy gives a strong argument in support of palm oil production. Write a counter-argument based on the harm that palm oil production has caused to tropical ecosystems in South-East Asia. Apply scientific language effectively in your argument. [5]

8. There are links in the online version of this article to the sources of information used, which are scientific papers published in journals. Explain the importance of giving sources of information. [5]

2 Transformation

◀ Claims were made in ancient Egypt that mice emerged out of earth moistened with water from the Nile; Greek philosopher Aristotle claimed that material from the guts of earthworms could be transformed into eels (photo); there have also been claims that dust can turn into fleas and dead flesh into maggots. These would all be examples of the transformation of non-living material into living organisms (spontaneous generation). Is it possible?

◀ The High Line is a public park in New York that is maintained by volunteers. It was formerly a raised railway line that served an industrial district of Manhattan. The line closed in the 1980s and after remaining derelict for many years it was transformed into gardens and paths that all can enjoy.

◀ Diamonds are one of the forms of the common element carbon. They are rare because other forms of carbon are only transformed into diamonds in special and very unusual conditions: extremely high pressures of 4.5–6.5 Pa and temperatures between 900 and 1,300°C. Nearly all diamonds are more than a billion years old. What does this suggest?

▼ The desert in central Australia rarely receives rain, but when it does a transformation occurs, with ephemeral plants germinating, growing and flowering in just a few weeks, in one of the world's great natural shows. Why do ephemeral plants in deserts have such showy flowers?

Introduction

A transformation is a radical change of form. Energy, chemical matter and living organisms can all undergo transformations. Energy transformations are described in Chapter 1; the other types of transformation are the subject of this chapter.

Chemical reactions are transformations in which bonds between particles are broken and new bonds are made, so the structure of molecules is changed. Living organisms simultaneously perform thousands of different chemical reactions inside their cells. Collectively, the reactions occurring in a cell are its metabolism.

Metabolism differs between cells, causing significant chemical and structural divergence. In humans, for example, cells can be transformed in over a hundred ways. Radically different cells are produced as a result, with each type specialized for particular roles. This process is called differentiation and is described in Chapters 3 and 4.

▼ The shoot tips of plants produce only stems and leaves for months or even years and then an irreversible transformation occurs leading to a reproductive phase in which only flowers are produced. In bamboos, the transformation may not happen until the plant is a hundred or more years old. After flowering and setting seed, the bamboo plant dies. In some bamboos, there is a mass flowering, with all members of the species carrying out this transformation at the same time, wherever they are growing in the world. What is the advantage of this?

Statement of inquiry:

Small chemical changes can transform our identity.

Transformations can also happen in the overall structure of living organisms. In many animals, such transformations turn a juvenile or larval stage in the life cycle into the mature stage that produces gametes for sexual reproduction. Gamete production starts with meiosis, the genetic transformation of cells that halves the number of chromosomes and breaks up combinations of genes inherited from parents. Without meiosis and sexual reproduction, the greatest transformation of all in biology, evolution by natural selection, would be extremely slow.

All of us undergo transformations during our lives. The transformations that occur during teenage years are probably the most significant, as they change us from being a child into an adult. Hand in hand with this change of identity are changes in relationships with family members and with others in the community. Transformations that occur during teenage years and at other times in our lives can all be traced ultimately to changes in the metabolism of our cells. The global context of this chapter therefore is identities and relationships.

▲ Testosterone causes adult male elk (*Cervus canadensis*) to start growing antlers in the spring, in preparation for breeding at the end of summer. A second transformation happens in late fall: when females stop releasing sex pheromones, testosterone levels in males drop, causing the antlers to be shed. What are the advantages to male elk of these two transformations?

▼ Teenage years are a time of change, with new interests and new relationships developing. Sometimes this is easy and fun, but it can also be challenging

What is a chemical reaction?

A chemical reaction is a transformation. Reactants, which are the chemical elements or compounds that a reaction starts with, are changed into products. The products have chemical properties that differ from those of the reactants. For example, a chemical reaction between oxygen and hydrogen, both of which are highly reactive, produces the much more stable compound water. Dissolving sugar in water is not a chemical reaction, because both the water and sugar are still the same chemical substances. Boiling water to produce steam is also not a chemical reaction as steam is simply water converted reversibly from a liquid into a gas.

The transformation of reactants to products involves energy changes, as chemical bonds are broken and formed. But a chemical reaction can also release or take in energy from its surroundings: an exothermic reaction is a reaction that releases heat to the surroundings; an endothermic reaction takes in energy from its surroundings, causing a temperature drop.

The transformation that happens in a reaction can be represented with an equation. Reactants are shown on the left and products on the right, with an arrow linking them to show the direction of change.

$$\text{reactants} \longrightarrow \text{products}$$

In a simple word equation the reactants and products are named. For example:

$$\text{hydrogen} + \text{oxygen} \longrightarrow \text{water}$$

We can give more information about a reaction if we use the chemical formula for each substance and the relative quantities. Let us use the example of the reaction that produces water again. The formula for hydrogen is H_2 and for oxygen is O_2 because molecules of each of these gases contain two atoms. A water molecule has one oxygen atom and two hydrogen atoms, so the formula is H_2O. If we write the equation thus, the equation is not balanced, because there is twice as much oxygen on the left as on the right:

$$H_2 + O_2 \longrightarrow H_2O$$

We cannot correct this by changing the formula of water to H_2O_2 because that is a different substance—it is hydrogen peroxide. Instead we must double the amount of water, which we show as $2H_2O$. However, the equation is still not balanced because there is now more hydrogen on the right than on the left:

$$H_2 + O_2 \longrightarrow 2H_2O$$

If we double the amount of hydrogen on the left, the equation is perfectly balanced:

$$2H_2 + O_2 \longrightarrow 2H_2O$$

The equation tells us that two water molecules are produced when two hydrogen molecules react with one oxygen molecule.

Is each of the following equations balanced and if not, can you balance them?

1. The reaction between carbon dioxide and water that happens inside red blood cells:

$$H_2O + CO_2 \longrightarrow H_2CO_3$$

2. The reaction that happens in all living cells to break down toxic hydrogen peroxide:

$$H_2O_2 \longrightarrow H_2O + O_2$$

3. The overall process of aerobic cell respiration (which is the sum of many individual reactions):

$$C_6H_{12}O_6 + O_2 \longrightarrow CO_2 + H_2O$$

4. The reaction in which urea from urine is hydrolysed by bacteria in the soil to produce carbon dioxide and ammonia:

$$(NH_2)_2CO + H_2O \longrightarrow CO_2 + NH_3$$

Light-induced changes

Light is absorbed in the retina of the eye by retinal, causing part of the molecule to rotate so that it is converted from cis-retinal to trans-retinal in just a few picoseconds. Has the molecule been changed by exposure to light? Is this a chemical reaction? Is it a transformation?

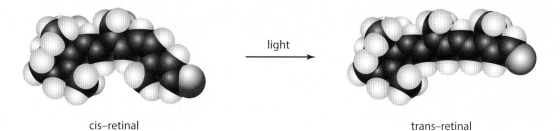

cis–retinal   trans–retinal

Experiment

Gather the materials that you need and carry out observations on the changes that occur in each of the following experiments. Organize your observations into a table of your own design.

What is the evidence that a new substance is being formed?

1. Cut a banana and an apple and observe the cut surfaces twenty minutes later.

2. Put some drops of iodine solution on the cut surface of pieces of banana and apple.

3. Add some dry yeast to a small amount of hydrogen peroxide in a test tube.

4. Add dry yeast to a solution of sugar and leave for twenty minutes or longer if possible.

5. Boil water in a test tube.

6. Boil water containing egg white in a test tube.

7. Add drops of vinegar to egg white.

BIOCHEMISTRY

What effect does an enzyme have on a chemical reaction?

The rate of a reaction can be increased by a catalyst. Catalysts increase reaction rates without being changed themselves, so they are placed above the arrow in a chemical equation.

$$\text{reactants} \xrightarrow{\text{catalyst}} \text{products}$$

A catalyst cannot change whether a reaction is exothermic or endothermic, but it can reduce the amount of energy needed to get the reaction started (activation energy). Even if a reaction is strongly exothermic, it will not happen unless the activation energy is available, but there is more chance of this if a catalyst is present.

An enzyme is a biological catalyst, so it speeds up a biochemical reaction without being altered itself. Enzymes are proteins, and like other proteins they can be damaged by high temperatures, or changes of pH. They are large and extremely complex molecules and can currently only be made by living cells. The reactants in a reaction catalysed by an enzyme are called the substrates.

$$\text{substrates} \xrightarrow{\text{enzyme}} \text{products}$$

Unlike most non-biological catalysts, enzymes do not catalyse a wide range of reactions. They show enzyme-substrate specificity. Each type of enzyme therefore acts as the catalyst in just one or a small group of biochemical reactions. For example, the enzyme catalase only speeds up this reaction:

$$\text{hydrogen peroxide} \xrightarrow{\text{catalase}} \text{water} + \text{oxygen}$$

ⒶⒷⒸⒹ Experiment

Note: Hydrogen peroxide solution is used in this experiment. It is corrosive, so it is important not to get any in the eyes or on skin or clothes. 1.0 mol dm⁻³ is a suitable concentration. The instructions here assume that potato tissue is being used as a source of catalase, but other live tissues can also be used.

1. Put 5 cm³ of hydrogen peroxide solution into a test tube.

2. Add 0.5 cm³ of liquid detergent and gently mix in with the hydrogen peroxide.

5. Add five 4×4×4 mm cubes of uncooked potato and at the same time start an electronic timer.

3. A layer of foam should develop above the solution. Measure the depth of foam every minute.

4. Stop taking measurements when the foam is not increasing in volume.

5. Calculate the maximum rate of oxygen production per minute.

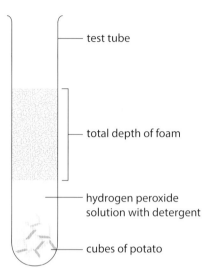

Further experiments

You can test the foam by plunging a glowing splint into it to confirm that it is oxygen. You can also try any of the experiments listed below. Make sure that you only vary one factor in each experiment (the independent variable) and that all other factors are kept constant (control variables). In each case the result you need (the dependent variable) is the maximum rate of oxygen production per minute. Try to predict the result before you do an experiment.

A. Repeat the experiment with a different number of potato cubes of the same size.

B. Use the same number and size of potato cubes, but chop each cube into smaller pieces or grind it to a pulp before adding it to the hydrogen peroxide.

C. Use potato cubes of the same size, but before putting them into the hydrogen peroxide solution, heat-treat in boiling water for 20 seconds and then let them cool to the ambient temperature of the laboratory.

D. Repeat the experiment using hydrogen peroxide solution and potato cubes warmed to higher temperatures.

E. Substitute the hydrogen peroxide with other liquids to which detergent has been added. You could try water, ethanol and sparkling water.

Conclusions

What properties of enzymes have you demonstrated in your experiments?

How do enzymes work?

Enzymes are proteins with a very distinctive three-dimensional structure. As part of this structure, they have a region where the reactants in a chemical reaction can bind. This region is the active site. The reactants are substrates of the enzyme. The sequence of events in an enzyme-catalysed reaction is shown in the diagrams below. In the example shown there is one substrate and two products, but the numbers of both substrates and products can vary—there may be two substrates and one product for example.

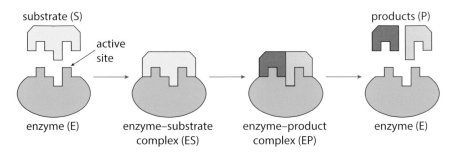

Binding of substrates to the active site causes a slight change in the shape and chemical bonding in both substrate and active site. This triggers weakening of bonds within the substrate, making it easier for them to break, which lowers the amount of energy needed to start the reaction. Soon after bonds in the substrates have broken, new bonds are formed and this is what creates the products of the reaction. They are released from the active site, which returns to its former shape and can then accept more substrates.

The substrates and active site of an enzyme have compatible shapes and chemical properties. Only an enzyme's substrates can bind to its active site and be changed into products. This explains the specificity of enzymes: each type of enzyme catalyses one chemical reaction only, or at most a particular group of chemical reactions where the reactants are all very similar.

Naming enzymes

A few enzymes have names with –in at the end, for example, pepsin and trypsin, but early on it was decided that enzymes should end in –ase, so all but the first few enzymes to be discovered follow this rule. Later on, the International Union of Biochemistry decided that the name of an enzyme should tell us what the substrate of an enzyme is, and the type of reaction catalysed. For example, malate dehydrogenase removes hydrogen from an organic acid called malate during aerobic respiration.

What do these enzymes do?

- Nitrate reductase
- Iodotyrosine deiodinase
- Phosphoglucose isomerase

What biochemical transformations happen inside our cells?

Cells perform many chemical transformations simultaneously in a tiny volume of cytoplasm. For example, a human hepatocyte (liver cell) has a volume of 3.4×10^{-12} liters (between three and four billionths of a cm^3), yet thousands of reactions happen in a controlled way inside it. No chemical plant designed by humans can achieve anything as complex as this.

These chemical transformations are typically accomplished in a series of small steps, collectively called a metabolic pathway. Most metabolic pathways consist of linear sequences of reactions, but some are metabolic cycles that transform molecules fed into them. Sometimes, a pathway can have branching points, where two products of a reaction are processed in different ways or where there is a choice over how a molecule is processed.

In a metabolic pathway, the substrate for the first reaction is transformed, via a series of intermediates, into the end product of the final reaction. All the substances between are both products of one reaction and substrates of the next. They are called intermediates. Because of enzyme-substrate specificity, a different enzyme is required for each reaction in a metabolic pathway.

initial substrate → enzyme A → first intermediate → enzyme B → second intermediate → enzyme C → end product

An example of a metabolic process is cell respiration, in which glucose is broken down to release energy; another is photosynthesis, which converts simple inorganic substances including carbon dioxide and water into glucose and other carbon compounds, but many more have been discovered by biochemists, such as the examples below.

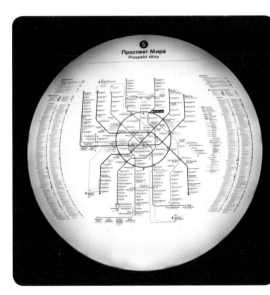

▲ What are the similarities between metabolic pathways and an underground railway system?

1. Phenylalanine to tyrosine

Proteins are made of subunits called amino acids. All amino acids have the same basic structure.

There are 20 different amino acids in proteins, each of which has a different R group. Of these 20, 9 amino acids are essential in the human diet because they cannot be synthesized in the body, for example, phenylalanine. The other 11 amino acids are non-essential for most people, because they can be made by changing one amino acid into another. Tyrosine, for example, can be made from phenylalanine.

amino group · carboxyl group · variable group

▲ The basic structure of an amino acid

phenylalanine

phenylalanine
hydroxylase

tyrosine

1. What is the difference between phenylalanine and tyrosine?

2. The enzyme that catalyses this reaction is called phenylalanine hydroxylase (PAH). What happens in a hydroxylation reaction?

3. The genetic disease phenylketonuria (PKU) results in very low levels of the enzyme PAH. What will be the effect on concentrations of phenylalanine and tyrosine in the body?

4. PKU has some harmful effects on the development of babies, so a blood test is routinely done a few days after birth.

   a) What treatment could be given to babies with PKU to avoid the harmful effects?

   b) Why is it not necessary to test babies, or start this treatment, before birth?

2. Lactose to glucose and galactose

Lactose is the sugar in milk. Lactose is a disaccharide because it consists of two monosaccharide sugars, glucose and galactose, linked together. It is digested in the small intestine by the enzyme lactase, in an exothermic hydrolysis reaction.

glucose

galactose

Babies and young children naturally secrete lactase. Some adults continue to secrete the enzyme, but in many human populations most adults do not, making them lactose-intolerant. Milk therefore tends not to be part of an adult diet.

1. Describe the difference in structure between the two monosaccharide sugars glucose and galactose.

2. Lactose synthase is the enzyme which catalyzes the production of lactose, using glucose and galactose as substrates. Explain the need for different enzymes to synthesize and digest lactose.

3. Predict what will happen to lactose in the intestines of adults who do not produce the enzyme lactase.

4. Explain how lactase secretion in adulthood could have become common in populations that keep cattle or other mammals and drink their milk.

▲ Milk and milk products are a traditional part of the diet in only some populations

3. Ethanol to ethanoic acid

Ethanol is the form of alcohol that is found in drinks such as beer and wine. Conversion of ethanol to ethanoic acid is a two-stage process that happens in hepatocytes. Ethanoic acid can be used in cell respiration to provide a source of energy. The conversion of ethanol to ethanoic acid is therefore an example of the transformation of a toxic substance into something that is harmless or even useful.

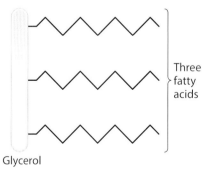

ethanol   ethanal   ethanoic acid

- If oxygen is added or hydrogen is removed from a molecule, it has been **oxidized**.

- If oxygen is removed or hydrogen added to a molecule it has been **reduced**.

Different enzymes are used for the two reactions: ADH (alcohol dehydrogenase) catalyses the first and ALDH (aldehyde dehydrogenase) the second. Ethanal is much more toxic than either ethanol or ethanoic acid and many of the harmful side effects of excessive alcohol consumption are due to it.

1. Deduce whether the reactions that change ethanol into ethanoic acid are oxidations or reductions.

2. Explain the reason for different enzymes in the two reactions.

3. Suggest a reason for not converting ethanol to ethanoic acid in just one reaction.

4. Glucose to fat

In humans the transformation of glucose into fat happens in several different types of cell: hepatocytes, adipose cells (which store fat) and milk-secreting cells in the mammary gland. Glucose is a simple sugar. The formula for glucose is $C_6H_{12}O_6$.

Fat molecules consist of three fatty acids linked to one glycerol molecule. Each fatty acid has a long chain of carbon and hydrogen atoms, with oxygens only at one end. The length of these chains can vary, giving a range of types of fat.

Glycerol

Three fatty acids

▲ Fat – simplified structure

The overall size of a fat molecule is much larger than that of glucose. The metabolic pathway that transforms glucose into fat therefore has these two properties:

- it is anabolic, because smaller molecules are converted into larger ones

- it includes reduction reactions that reduce the oxygen content or increase the hydrogen content.

Due to the significant differences in molecular structure, many changes are needed to transform glucose into fat, so the metabolic pathway is long and complex. A different enzyme is needed to catalyse each reaction in the pathway. Plants can transform fat back into glucose, but humans are unable to do this as the necessary enzymes are lacking. Instead, fat is stored in the body and at certain times it is used in cell respiration to provide a source of energy.

Data-based question: Alcohol flush

Humans have several different versions of ALDH, the enzyme that converts toxic ethanal into harmless ethanoic acid. ALDH1 works in the cytoplasm and ALDH2 works inside the mitochondrion. Both of these enzymes are needed for rapid removal of ethanal.

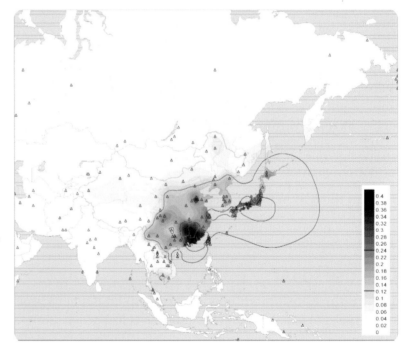

ALDH2*504Lys is a variant form of ALDH2. It works at a much slower rate than the normal form, so it takes longer for ethanal to be removed from the body after drinking alcohol. Symptoms such as facial flushing, palpitations, nausea and other features of a "hangover" are more pronounced and more persistent.

The frequency of ALDH2*504Lys has been measured in over 350 human populations. It is effectively absent in all parts of the world apart from populations in East Asia. Red triangles on the map indicate sampled populations and the key shows the shades of black used to indicate the frequency of ALDH2*504Lys.

1. Using an atlas if necessary, identify three countries with a high frequency of the ALDH*504Lys and three countries with a low frequency.

2. Almost all Japanese, Chinese and Korean people have ADH1C, a variant of the ADH enzyme.

This variant converts ethanol to ethanal much more efficiently than other forms of the enzyme. Explain the consequences of having a combination of both ADH1C and ALDH*504Lys.

3. Alcoholics are addicted to alcohol and tend to consume excessive amounts of it. In populations where ALDH*504Lys occurs, the frequency is much lower among alcoholics than non-alcoholics. Suggest a reason for this trend.

4. Average alcohol consumption in liters per year is much lower in China (6.7 l/year) than in the USA (9.2 l/year), Canada (10.2 l/year) or Russia (15.1 l/year). Suggest reasons for this, based on what you know about the enzymes metabolizing alcohol.

5 Do our enzymes affect our identity?

What chemical transformations can other organisms do for us?

The chemical industry produces a wide range of chemical substances, using various factors, such as heat, pressure and catalysts, to make particular transformations occur. The biotechnology industry uses living organisms or living systems to produce substances. In some cases, it is more efficient to use a biotechnological approach, and some substances can only be produced by living cells, including enzymes and all other proteins consisting of more than 50 amino acids.

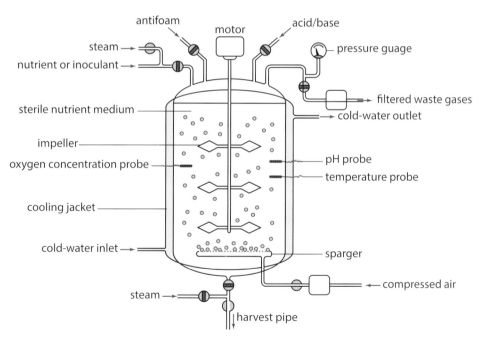

▲ Bioreactor used for culturing bacteria or fungi

Three groups of organisms are used in biotechnology:

- Bacteria are very widely used because they grow quickly, they are metabolically very diverse and they can be easily cultured in vessels called bioreactors.

- Plants make a huge range of different substances and they can be easily grown as crops in fields. As with bacteria, there are no ethical objections to growing plants and extracting chemicals from them.

- Animals are less commonly used mostly because of potential ethical problems with their use.

Until recently, the only substances that could be obtained from other organisms were the ones that they naturally produce. It is now possible to genetically modify organisms so they produce other substances. This is described in Chapter 10.

Biochemistry alphabet

Select any substance from the list and research what organism produces it, how it is produced and how humans use it. Can you find other examples for letters *k* to *z*?

antibodies	**f**ollicle stimulating hormone (FSH)
bioethanol	**g**rowth hormone (GH)
citric acid	**h**ydrogen
digoxin	**i**singlass
erythropoietin (EPO)	**j**asmolin

How does a cell transform amino acids into proteins?

Proteins are chains of amino acids, linked by peptide bonds. These bonds are made between the amine group (NH_2) of one amino acid and the carboxyl group (COOH) of another. The reaction can be summarized by this equation:

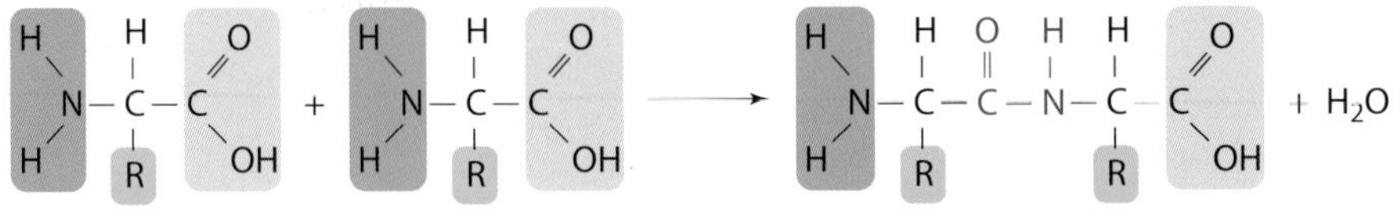

The equation shows that two bonds have to be broken, removing a hydrogen atom from the amine group of one amino acid and a hydroxyl (OH) from the carboxyl group of the other amino acid. This allows nitrogen and carbon in the two amino acids to bond together; this strong covalent linkage is called a peptide bond. Another new bond is made between the hydrogen and the hydroxyl group that were removed, producing water. Linking together amino acids is therefore a condensation—a chemical reaction in which water is released.

To make any particular protein, amino acids have to be linked together in the correct sequence. There are 20 different amino acids in proteins, each with a different R group. Most proteins consist of hundreds or even thousands of amino acids, so it is a significant challenge to get the sequence 100% correct. Apart from very small proteins, it still cannot be done artificially—only cells can synthesize these proteins. Even more remarkably, all cells store amino acid sequence data for making thousands of different proteins.

The information needed to make proteins is stored using genes, made of DNA. A gene contains a linear sequence of the four DNA bases: adenine (A), cytosine (C), guanine (G) and thymine (T); the particular sequence of amino acids in a protein is stored, in coded form, in the base sequence of a gene.

The first stage in protein synthesis is copying the base sequence of a gene in a process called transcription. The copy is made of RNA which will have a base sequence identical to that of the gene, with one exception: RNA has U (uracil) where there is T (thymine) in DNA. Because the RNA copy takes the genetic information to another part of the cell, it is called messenger RNA (mRNA).

The second stage of protein synthesis is a transformation of the base sequence of mRNA into the amino acid sequence of a protein. The special name for this process is translation. It requires another type of RNA, known as transfer RNA (tRNA), which helps the cell "translate" the information on the gene into the amino acid sequence of a protein.

Translation is coordinated by complex nanostructures found in the cytoplasm of cells, called ribosomes. Ribosomes have a catalytic site on the surface where a peptide bond between amino acids is formed. Amino acids that have already been joined together form a peptide chain, which lengthens by one amino acid at a time. When a group of three bases that acts as a stop signal is reached in the mRNA, translation ends and the protein is released.

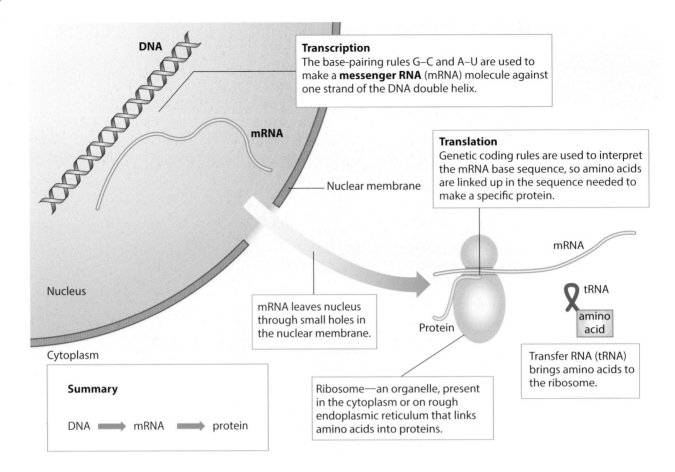

DNA

Transcription
The base-pairing rules G–C and A–U are used to make a **messenger RNA** (mRNA) molecule against one strand of the DNA double helix.

mRNA

Nuclear membrane

Translation
Genetic coding rules are used to interpret the mRNA base sequence, so amino acids are linked up in the sequence needed to make a specific protein.

mRNA

tRNA

amino acid

Nucleus

mRNA leaves nucleus through small holes in the nuclear membrane.

Protein

Transfer RNA (tRNA) brings amino acids to the ribosome.

Cytoplasm

Summary

DNA ➡ mRNA ➡ protein

Ribosome—an organelle, present in the cytoplasm or on rough endoplasmic reticulum that links amino acids into proteins.

The linking together of amino acids is a remarkable transformation, because the completed protein can have emergent properties that would be very hard to predict. In most proteins, the chain of amino acids folds up into a distinctive shape as it is made by the ribosome, with only some R groups exposed on the protein's surface. Amino acids that are not adjacent to each other in the chain are brought together, meaning that their R groups can interact with each other in a variety of ways, such as making up the active site of enzymes. Proteins are an amazingly diverse group of molecules and this allows them to do a huge range of tasks inside living organisms.

Investigating the diversity of proteins in membranes

Cell membranes contain many different proteins and perform a wide variety of functions. Search the PDB Molecule of the Month website (https://pdb101.rcsb.org/) for images of these membrane proteins:

- sodium-potassium pump
- acetylcholine receptor
- cadherin
- mechanosensitive channel

How does the structure of each protein help it to perform its function in the membrane?

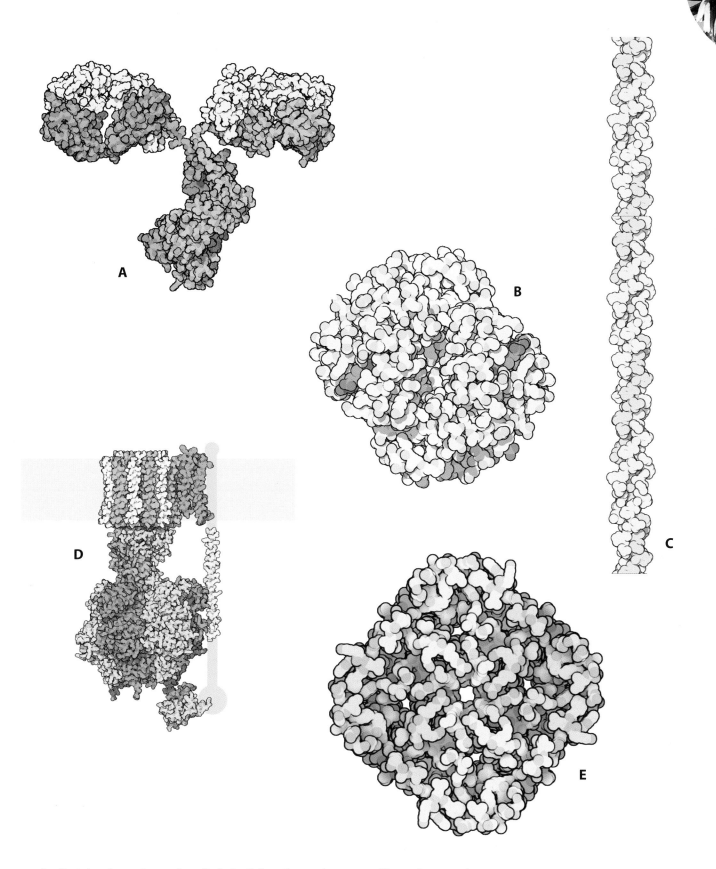

▲ Proteins show a huge diversity in both function and structure. Shown here are the structures of an antibody (A), a hemoglobin (B), a collagen (C), an ATP synthase (D) and an aquaporin (E) molecule

Generate metaphors and analogies

- The digestion of proteins into single amino acids is exothermic, so energy has to be put in to link amino acids together to make a protein.

- Linking an amino acid to ATP (made by respiration) is exothermic.

- Transfer of this amino acid to tRNA is exothermic.

- Linking together amino acids attached to tRNAs is exothermic.

The analogy of a rock being rolled up a hill is used in the diagram shown here to help understand how cells provide the energy for linking together amino acids. Can you think of a better metaphor or analogy?

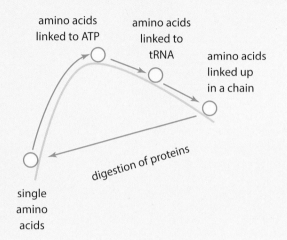

amino acids linked to ATP

amino acids linked to tRNA

amino acids linked up in a chain

digestion of proteins

single amino acids

REPRODUCTION

What changes occur at puberty?

During the life cycle of humans, a newborn baby grows in size to become a toddler, then a child and then an adolescent. During adolescence, a transformation occurs in the bodies of boys and girls. This stage of human life is known as puberty. The changes that occur prepare the body for sexual reproduction. Primary sexual characteristics are structures that are directly necessary for reproduction. Although present from birth, these parts of the male and female reproductive systems grow and develop during puberty. Secondary sexual characteristics are not directly necessary for reproduction, but they do emphasize differences between males and females that are less obvious during childhood; these characteristics are summarized in the table below:

Females	Males
Pubic hair growth	Pubic hair growth
Underarm hair growth	Underarm hair and facial hair growth
Female pattern changes in voice (slight deepening)	Male pattern changes in voice (greater deepening)
Female pattern adipose tissue development	Male pattern muscle development
Increased width of the pelvis and thus of the hips	Bone growth to give wider shoulders and larger jaw

Data-based question: GnRH

GnRH is one of the smallest proteins. It is only made in miniscule amounts by one part of the human body, yet it causes a major transformation. GnRH is made by cells in the hypothalamus of the brain and acts as a hormone. The GnRH molecule is a short chain of amino acids and the full name is gonadotropin-releasing hormone.

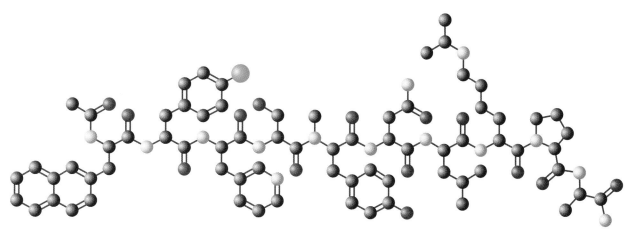

▲ The structure of the GnRH molecule

1. A gene called *GNRH1* on chromosome 8 is transcribed in the first stage of GnRH production – what are the other stages?

2. How many amino acids are there in the chain – eight, ten or twelve?

3. A chain of amino acids as short as this is usually called an oligopeptide, rather than a protein. What is an advantage of using oligopeptides or small proteins as hormones, rather than large proteins?

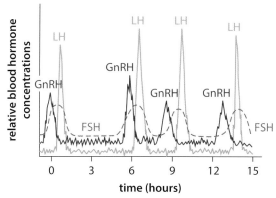

▲ Levels of GnRH and two other hormones over 15 hours in an adult human male

4. What are the similarities and differences in the data for the three hormones shown in the graph?

5. GnRH causes secretion of LH and FSH. What evidence for this is there in the graph?

6. One of the effects of LH is to cause the testes to secrete more testosterone. Testosterone causes production of sperm and also secondary sexual characteristics such as pubic hair. At approximately what age do you expect the hypothalamus to start secreting GnRH?

7. What would happen if a boy was lacking the *GNRH1* gene?

What is metamorphosis in animals?

Over the life of all animals, the body grows and develops. There can be periods when particularly significant changes occur. During puberty in humans, for example, the body gradually changes from that of a child to an adult over a period of several years. In some animals, including insects, marine invertebrates and amphibians, a much more sudden or radical change, known as metamorphosis, occurs.

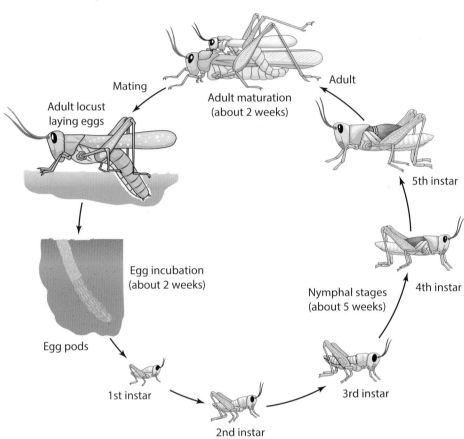

▲ Incomplete metamorphosis in the life cycle of a locust

Insects such as locusts, grasshoppers and dragonflies undergo a series of abrupt changes to their body form. As with all animals, these insects begin their life as a fertilized egg. When the egg hatches, a nymph emerges. Repeated phases of growth followed by shedding of the exoskeleton then occur, with the new exoskeleton having a modified form every time. Each nymph stage is closer in form to the adult, until the final shedding of the exoskeleton. An adult then appears, with wings and functional reproductive organs. Adult males and females mate and females lay the fertilized eggs that start the next generation. This type of life cycle is called incomplete metamorphosis.

Insects such as bees, beetles and butterflies also start life as a fertilized egg, which hatches out into a larva. The larva grows and sheds its exoskeleton repeatedly, but without any significant changes in form. There is then a very radical transformation, called pupation. The larva encases itself in a protective covering to form a pupa. Inside the

Adult
(butterfly)

Pupa
(chrysalis)

Eggs

Larva
(caterpillar)

▲ Complete metamorphosis in the life cycle of a butterfly

immobile pupa, nearly all the tissues of the larva are digested and remaining groups of cells grow and develop into the body of an adult. When this process is completed, the adult emerges from the pupal case. Male and female adults mate and females lay fertilized eggs to start the next generation. This type of life cycle with just one major change of body form is called complete metamorphosis. The timing of stages in the life cycle of butterfly species is considered in Chapter 9.

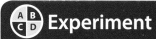 **Experiment**

How does the pupal stage differ from the larval stage?

Obtain some insect larvae. Mealworms *(Tenebrio molitor)* are sold in pet stores as a source of food for pet lizards and birds. Alternatively, fly larvae may be found on the inside of rubbish bins in warm weather. Depending on the conditions that they are kept in, fly larvae can advance to the pupal stage within 10 days. Mealworm larvae take longer. A mealworm colony can be maintained in the school laboratory on a supply of oatmeal, with very little care required.

- Make careful observations of the insect larvae including length measurements. Date each entry.

- Look for evidence of shedding of the exoskeleton (moulting). Remove from the container and examine the shed exoskeletons.

- Look for pupae. They will be stationary individuals. The colour of these individuals will often differ from the mobile larvae.

- Using a magnifying lens or a dissecting microscope, construct a diagram of both the larval and pupal stages.

- Create a two-column chart to distinguish pupae from larvae.

1. What are the advantages of a life cycle that involves complete metamorphosis?

2. What are the dangers of the pupation stage?

3. In some insects with complete metamorphosis the adult males feed little or not at all, whereas the females may feed voraciously. What are the reasons for this difference?

ATL Communication skills

Use a variety of organizers for writing tasks

A Venn diagram can be used to organize information to make a comparison. Two overlapping circles are drawn, large enough to contain the writing. The overlapping area is used to outline shared features. Unique features of the two things being compared are then described or listed in the non-overlapping areas.

Use a Venn diagram to compare and contrast the processes of puberty and pupation.

Data-based question: Metamorphosis in the western spadefoot toad

Female toads and frogs lay eggs in water and males deposit sperm over them, so fertilization happens externally. The fertilized eggs develop into an aquatic larval stage known as a tadpole. Metamorphosis subsequently occurs, changing the tadpoles into adults. This is how metamorphosis is triggered:

- Corticosterone causes the production of proteins that act as thyroid hormone receptors in target cells in tadpoles.

- Thyroid hormone receptors are activated by binding of thyroid hormone.

- Activated receptors bind to specific genes in the nucleus and activate them.

- These activated genes cause metamorphosis.

The western spadefoot toad (Spea hammondii) lives in desert areas in California and lays its eggs in pools formed by rain. Sometimes the pools where the eggs have been laid shrink due to a lack of rain. In an investigation of metamorphosis, tadpoles were all initially raised in a tank containing 3 dm³ of water, which gave them a high-water environment. Half of them were then transferred to a tank of the same size containing only 0.35 dm³ of water, which provided a low-water environment. The table shows differences that had developed between the two groups when they reached the same stage in metamorphosis.

	High water	Low water
Time taken to reach same stage of metamorphosis (days)	133	90
Body mass at metamorphosis (grams)	1.9	1.2
Corticosterone concentration (pg/cm³)	210	380
Thyroid hormone concentration (pg/cm³)	3.5	16.5
Thyroid hormone receptor levels (arbitrary units)	225	325

1. **a)** Calculate the difference in body mass between the groups raised in high and low water.

   b) Explain the difference in body mass.

2. Using all the data in the table, explain how western spadefoot toad tadpoles respond to a low-water environment.

3. Suggest advantages to the western spadefoot toad of being able to metamorphose at different times in response to water levels.

What stages occur in all sexual life cycles?

There are many different types of life cycle in plants and animals, but three events always occur at some stage in the cycle:

1. **Gametogenesis** which is the production of male and female gametes (sex cells). The female gamete is always larger because it contains stored food. The male gamete is smaller, making movement to reach the female gamete easier. Male gametes in humans are sperm produced by the testes and female gametes are ova (egg cells) produced by the ovaries. In flowering plants the male gametes are nuclei inside pollen grains and female gametes are egg cells inside ovules.

2. **Fertilization** which is the fusion of male and female gametes to produce a zygote. During fertilization the nucleus of the male gamete fuses with the nucleus of the egg cell. This doubles the number of chromosomes. For example, human gametes contain 23 chromosomes, so the zygote produced by fertilization has 46. It is therefore essential to halve the number of chromosomes at some stage in a sexual life cycle.

3. **Meiosis** which is the special type of cell division used to halve the chromosome number. When human cells with 46 chromosomes divide by meiosis, cells with 23 chromosomes are produced. The number of chromosomes in the gametes is called the haploid number (n). Zygotes have the diploid number of chromosomes ($2n$). Usually meiosis happens as a part of gametogenesis, but in some plant species it happens much earlier.

In the life cycle below there are separate male and female parents, but some plants and animals are hermaphrodite—they produce both male and female gametes.

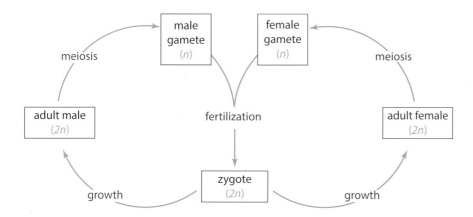

How does meiosis halve the number of chromosomes?

PHYSIOLOGY

Chromosomes are long DNA molecules, which in plants and animals are associated with proteins. Every chromosome in a gamete contains a separate DNA molecule, with a different sequence of genes arranged along it. In humans, there are 23 chromosomes in a sperm or an egg cell. All plant and animals species have a characteristic haploid number of chromosomes in their gametes: 24 in chimpanzees, 37 in polar bears and 8 in garlic, for example.

When two gametes fuse to produce a zygote during fertilization, the number of chromosomes doubles from the haploid to the diploid number. In a diploid cell, there are two chromosomes with each sequence of genes, one inherited from the mother and one from the father.

Special staining procedures allow chromosomes with different sequences of genes to be distinguished. In the image below, the spherical structure is a human nucleus. To the right are stained chromosomes that have been spread out by bursting a diploid cell. To the left are the same chromosomes rearranged so that chromosomes with the same gene sequence are next to each other. It is clear from this image that diploid cells have two of each numbered type of chromosome.

▶ Numbers have been assigned to human chromosomes, going from chromosome 1, which is the largest, to 22 which is the smallest. The 23rd chromosome type determines whether a person is male or female. There are two possible sex chromosomes, which have been assigned the letters X and Y

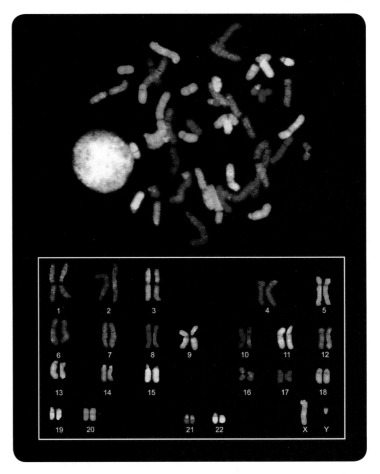

Before meiosis begins, all the DNA molecules in the nucleus are replicated, so each chromosome consists of two identical DNA molecules, together with the associated proteins. DNA replication is described in Chapter 9. Because of this replication, there are enough DNA molecules for one diploid cell to divide twice during meiosis, producing four haploid cells. It is during the first of these two divisions that the number of chromosomes is halved.

▼ Cell at the start of meiosis with chromosomes paired up

Each of the cells produced by the first division must get one of each of the numbered types of chromosome. To help ensure this, the numbered types of chromosome pair up with each other in the middle of the cell. The nuclear membrane breaks down, so the chromosomes are free to move. The diagram to the left shows this pairing up of chromosomes, but just three chromosome types have been included (chromosomes 1, 5 and 11). In a full human cell there would be 23 pairs of chromosomes.

Protein fibres called microtubules are constructed that connect each chromosome to one of the ends (poles) of the cell. These microtubules then pull the chromosomes to the poles, after which the cell divides. The chromosomes in each pair are connected to opposite poles, ensuring each of the two cells produced by the first division of meiosis receives half the total number of chromosomes and one of each pair of chromosomes.

The two cells produced by the first division of meiosis immediately prepare for the second division. Microtubules are again constructed and connected to all the chromosomes. Each chromosome consists of two DNA molecules, one of which becomes connected by microtubules to each pole. This ensures that both poles receive one DNA molecule from each chromosome. As soon as this movement towards the poles begins we think of the individual DNA molecules as separate chromosomes.

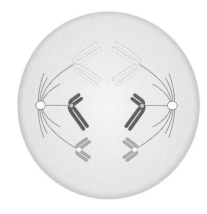

▲ Cell during the first division of meiosis with chromosomes moving to opposite poles

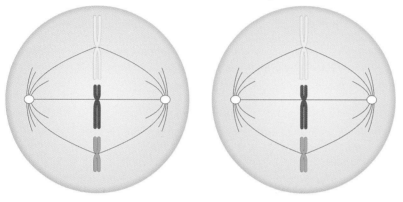

▲ Two cells produced by the first division of meiosis preparing to divide again

The movements of chromosomes during the two divisions of meiosis ensure that each of the four cells produced are haploid, with one full set of the chromosomes of the species.

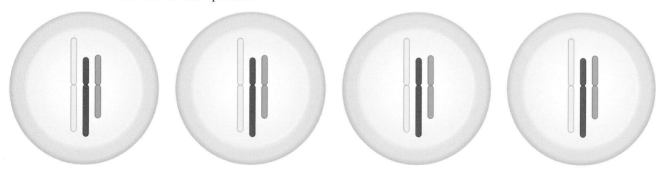

▲ Four cells at the end of meiosis

How does sexual reproduction change combinations of genes?

REPRODUCTION

However many children are produced by two parents, all of them are different from each other, unless they are identical twins. This is a characteristic feature of sexual reproduction—it is a potent source of genetic diversity.

A key event in sexual reproduction is the fusion of male and female gametes. Genes from the mother and the father come together, producing a combination that has probably never existed before. Each parent contributes one of each chromosome type and so passes on one copy of each gene. The zygote produced by fusion of gametes therefore has two copies of each gene (apart from genes located on X and Y chromosomes in males). The zygote's combination of genes is passed on unchanged to all the body cells that are produced by repeated cell divisions. This is done by the process of mitosis, which has similarities with meiosis but also significant differences. Mitosis is described in Chapter 9.

Meiosis is another key event in sexual reproduction. Cells produced by meiosis only have one copy of each gene, not two. Some of the 25,000 or so genes in humans are the same in all of us, so the two copies in a cell undergoing meiosis are identical and it does not matter which of them is passed on. However, there are alternative versions of many genes and if two different versions are present in a cell that carries out meiosis, it is a matter of chance which one passes into each of the haploid cells produced.

Let us take an example: a person who is in blood group AB has the genes I^A and I^B; 50% of the cells produced by meiosis will receive I^A and 50% I^B. If two versions of the eye colour gene are also present, B and b, there are four possible combinations of genes in cells produced by meiosis and they are all equally likely, as shown in the table:

B and I^A	B and I^B
b and I^A	b and I^B

A small proportion of genes are linked because they are close to each other on the same chromosome type, but most pairs of genes move independently when they pass into one cell or another during meiosis. This is known as independent assortment.

If we add another gene with alternative versions, there are eight possible combinations and if we factor in all the genes with different versions in a cell entering meiosis, the number of possible combinations is immense. However many gametes we produce in our lifetime, it is unlikely that any two of them will have precisely the same combination of genes.

1. If a cell with different versions of two genes carries out meiosis, there are four possible combinations of genes in the cells produced. Calculate the number of possible combinations for each of these numbers of genes with different versions:

   a) 3   b) 4   c) 10   d) 1,000

2. Identical twins have the same combinations of genes as each other. Consider this hypothesis: identical twins are the result of two sperms with identical combinations of genes fertilizing two eggs with identical combinations of genes. Is this likely? If not, can you suggest a better hypothesis?

3. If identical twin men married identical twin women, would all their offspring be the same?

4. Explain the reasons for greater genetic diversity among children of mixed-race parents, compared with same-race parents.

▲ Meiosis and fertilization generate great genetic diversity

Summative assessment

Statement of inquiry:

Small chemical changes can transform our identity.

Introduction

The theme of this assessment is differences between humans – how do they arise and how extensive are they?

The genetic basis of gender

In humans, the 23rd pair of chromosomes determines whether we are male or female. Males have one large X and one small Y chromosome. Females have two X chromosomes. In females, the two X chromosomes pair up in the early stages of meiosis. Despite being different in structure along most of their lengths, X and Y chromosomes have the same structure at their ends, allowing them to be paired when meiosis happens in males. X chromosomes carry far more genes than Y chromosomes, but the gene *SRY*, carried by the Y chromosome, sets off a significant transformation.

1. The diagram below shows the sex chromosomes in a testis cell at the start of the first division of meiosis. Draw diagrams to show where these chromosomes would be at

   a) the end of the first division of meiosis [2]

   b) the end of the second division of meiosis. [2]

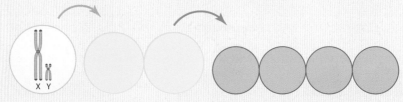

2. *SRY* codes for a protein of 204 amino acids called TDF (testis determining factor).

   Outline the processes that transform the base sequence of SRY into the amino acid sequence of TDF. [5]

3. Until human embryos are four to six weeks old there are no visible differences between males and females. The embryonic gonads could develop into ovaries or testes. TDF is a transcription factor that binds to DNA in specific places to activate certain genes. These genes prevent the embryonic gonads from developing into ovaries and instead cause them to develop into testes. The developing testes secrete the hormone testosterone.

   a) Deduce what causes the embryonic gonads in a female embryo to develop into ovaries. [2]

   b) Suggest some of the changes that testosterone will cause during the development of a male embryo. [4]

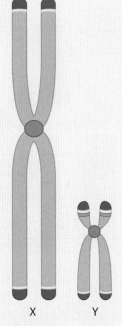

▲ The X and Y chromosomes have the same structure at their ends (red) but elsewhere they are different (grey). The location of the gene SRY is shown with a blue band

X   Y

Investigating amylase

This reaction happens in the mouth:

$$\text{starch} \xrightarrow{\text{salivary amylase}} \text{maltase}$$

The amount of amylase in saliva can be assessed by testing how long it takes for a sample of saliva to digest all the starch in a measured quantity of starch solution. You can use the following protocol:

- Obtain a sample of liquid saliva from one person.

- Put 5 cm³ of 1% starch solution in a test tube.

- Put 1 cm³ of saliva in another test tube.

- Heat both tubes to 37 °C.

- Put iodine solution into the depressions on a spotting tile, so you can repeatedly test for starch.

- When the fluids are both up to temperature, pour the starch solution into the saliva and mix.

- Test a drop of the mixture for starch at 30-second intervals for a few minutes until all the starch has been digested. If this takes longer than two or three minutes, you can extend the time intervals between tests. If it takes less than 30 seconds, repeat the procedure but use diluted starch solution or test at shorter time intervals.

- Calculate the rate of starch digestion in milligrams per minute.

4. **a)** Choose one of these hypotheses:

- There is more amylase in the saliva of girls than boys.

- There is more amylase in the saliva of boys than girls.

- There is no difference between the amount of amylase in the saliva of girls and boys (null hypothesis).

Explain the reasons for your choice of hypothesis. [3]

b) Describe how you plan to test your hypothesis, including control of variables. [3]

c) Either using your actual results, or results supplied by your teacher, calculate average rates of starch digestion, showing your working clearly. [3]

d) Use whatever chart or graph you think is most appropriate to display the rates. [3]

e) Evaluate your hypothesis using the results of the experiment. [3]

The genetic basis of amylase activity

5. a) The gene that codes for salivary amylase is *AMY1*. This gene is located on chromosome 1. Explain why we might expect there to be two copies of this gene in all humans. [3]

b) Many humans inherit more than two copies of *AMY1*. This is because of tandem repeats of the gene on a chromosome passed in a gamete from one or both parents. Tandem repeats are sequences of bases in DNA that are repeated, with the repeats adjacent to each other.

The scatter graph below shows the number of copies of *AMY1* in a sample of 50 European-American individuals and also the concentration of amylase (*AMY1* protein) in their saliva.

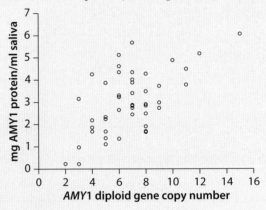

i) State the minimum, maximum and median number of *AMY1* copies. [3]

ii) Outline the relationship between the number of copies of *AMY1* and the concentration of amylase. [2]

iii) Explain the reasons for this relationship. [2]

c) The European-American population traditionally eats a high starch diet. Six other populations were investigated, three that traditionally eat low starch diets and three that eat high starch diets. The cumulative frequency graph below shows the results.

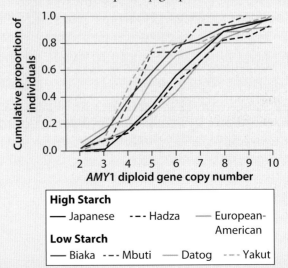

i) What trend does the data in the graph show? [2]

ii) Suggest an explanation for this trend. [3]

 ## Genetic counseling and color blindness

6. Red-green color blindness is the condition where a person has difficulty in distinguishing between red and green wavelengths of light. The commonest form is deuteranomaly, in which the pigment that normally absorbs green light instead absorbs yellow, orange or red light. The frequency of deuteranomaly can be as high as 6% of males and 0.4% of females in some populations.

a) Suggest reasons for testing a person to see if they have red-green color blindness. [4]

b) The two genes required for normal red and green vision are located next to each other on the X chromosome. These genes are very similar in base sequence. They code for different versions of the protein opsin. This protein binds to retinal to form a light-absorbing pigment. Three differences in base sequence cause three differences in amino acid sequence in opsin, which cause the pigment to absorb either red or green light.

Deuteranomaly is due to the presence of a changed version of the gene coding for the green-absorbing opsin.

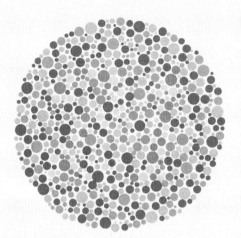

▲ This image is called a transformation plate and is used to test vision. The number that a normal person would see is transformed into another number with red-green color blindness. Further images are available at http://www.vischeck.com.

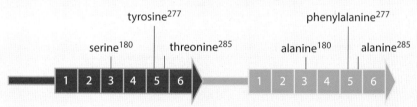

◀ The genes coding for the red- and green-absorbing versions of opsin have six regions. The amino acid differences that affect light absorption are indicated.

From the information that you have been given, write an explanation of the probable causes of deuteranomaly for a young boy with this condition. Try to use clear and simple language that he would understand. [4]

c) Genetic counselling is offered to parents who might have a child with a genetic condition. If a husband has deuteranomaly and his wife has normal vision, explain advice that should be given about the chances of

i) a son inheriting the condition [2]

ii) a daughter inheriting it. [2]

d) Discuss the effects on identity that having a genetic condition such as deuteranomaly might have. [3]

3 Form

To make sense of the world around us we rely on recognizing familiar shapes, whether from descriptions or by directly observing them. Can you solve the riddle?

> **"**
>
> I come in different colors and shapes.
>
> Some parts of me are curvy, some are straight.
>
> You can put me anywhere you'd like,
>
> But there's only one place that's right.
>
> What am I?
>
> **"**

▼ Two twigs?

▼ Two leaves?

Endless forms most beautiful and most wonderful have been and are being evolved.

Charles Darwin, *On the Origin of Species*

▼ Rhinoceros beetle (*Oryctes nasicornis*)

▼ Two-flowered orchid (*Bulbophyllum biflorum*)

▲ Blue poison arrow frog (*Dendrobates tinctorius*)

▲ Red starfish (*Echinaster sepositus*)

It is not possible for form to do without matter because it is not separable, nor can matter itself be purged of form.

Robert Grosseteste

(A jigsaw puzzle piece)

Key concept: Relationships

Related concept: Form

Global context: Identities and relationships

Introduction

Observing, describing, identifying and classifying the forms that appear in nature stands at the core of science, as does understanding the relationships between them.

Form is the shape and structure of an organism. We are all very familiar with the human form and we can notice small differences in form between individuals.

There is a tremendous amount of diversity of life on Earth. It is natural for humans to try to order their world by generalizing as well as by recognizing what is novel. Across human societies, distinctive features have been used to name organisms and shared features have been used to classify organisms into groups.

Our own form is an important part of our identity. Knowledge of human form also allows us to assess how closely related we are to other species. The global context of this chapter is therefore identities and relationships.

▼ How do you know who you are? Identity in humans develops from an early age. Choice of a hair style or hat is just a small sign of this, but identity itself resides in our own minds.

Statement of inquiry:

Relationships between organisms are revealed by similarities and differences between the myriad of forms.

How is form used in classification?

Similarities and differences in form between species were the original basis of the natural classification of organisms. One commonly used classification system recognizes the kingdoms of life, for example, animal, plant and fungus. This system further divides kingdoms into groups called phyla. An individual phylum is divided into groups of similar classes; classes are divided into groups of similar orders; orders are divided into similar families; and families into genera. The lowest level of classification is the species.

This system of classification, in which similar species are put into successively larger and larger groups, is called the hierarchy of taxa. A taxon (singular form of taxa) is any type of group in the hierarchy, for example, kingdom or class. Some examples are shown in the table, with a new taxon of domain added above kingdom.

	Taxon	Humans	Neanderthals	Chimpanzee	African elephant
Largest and most diverse groups ↑	Domain	Eukaryota	Eukaryota	Eukaryota	Eukaryota
	Kingdom	Animalia	Animalia	Animalia	Animalia
	Phylum	Chordata	Chordata	Chordata	Chordata
	Class	Mammalia	Mammalia	Mammalia	Mammalia
	Order	Primates	Primates	Primates	Proboscidea
	Family	Hominidae	Hominidae	Hominidae	Elephantidae
↓ Smallest and least diverse groups	Genus	*Homo*	*Homo*	*Pan*	*Loxodonta*
	Species	*sapiens*	*neanderthalensis*	*troglodytes*	*cyclotis*

ATL Communication skills

Use and interpret a range of discipline-specific terms

What is the difference between a puma, a cougar, a panther and a mountain lion? There isn't one! In popular culture we use these different names to refer to the same animal, whose scientific name is *Puma concolor*.

To address issues that may arise across cultures from using different names for the same organism, scientists have developed a standardized naming system (nomenclature) that avoids confusion about which organism is being discussed. This system relies on the use of Latin and Greek words because these were the languages of academics when the nomenclature system was developed.

Despite attempts to standardize naming, variation still exists. The creation of databases such as the Encyclopedia of life, The tree of life and The catalogue of life has assisted in the effort to address this variation.

Understand and use technology systems

A database is a collection of information that is organized in such a way that it can be easily accessed, managed and updated. When you first visit a database, there are often some procedural steps that have to be learned to "query" the database, that is, determine the answer to your question.

Tracking down taxonomy

Access the database called Catalogue of Life (www.catalogueoflife.org). Enter the species name of any organism mentioned in this chapter. Record the complete taxonomy of the organism (kingdom, phylum, class, order, family, genus, species).

Even within one species there can be varieties that are distinctly different. These are called forms of the species. From the earliest times, humans have studied the form of organisms so that beneficial and harmful species can be distinguished and useful forms can be selected.

The field mushroom *Agaricus campestris* is delicious to eat, but it is similar in form to the destroying angel *Amanita virosa*, which is so toxic that it usually causes liver failure and death if ingested. Only experts who can identify wild fungi by their form should risk eating them.

▲ *Agaricus campestris*

▲ *Amanita virosa*

How can we use form to identify plants?

Each species of plant is different in form from all other plant species. Closely related species may be very similar but even so there are differences that can be used to identify them.

Cedarwood has been used for thousands of years around the Mediterrean to construct ships, buildings and furniture. It is light but strong and durable because of its resistance to pests, decay and fire. Cedar trees growing in Lebanon (*Cedrus libani*) and in the Atlas Mountains (*Cedrus atlantica*) were overexploited, but trees that had produced similar timber were discovered in other parts of the world: Western red cedar (*Thuja plicata*), Deodar cedar (*Cedrus deodara*), Port Orford cedar (*Chamaecyparis lawsoniana*), Japanese cedar (*Cryptomeria japonica*) and Northern white cedar (*Thuja occidentalis*).

Humans have an inbuilt ability to recognize familiar plants and animals. You can identify unfamilar cedars by either reading through descriptions of each possible species or using a dichotomous key.

A dichotomous key consists of a sequence of numberered stages. In each stage, we consider a pair of statements about specific features of form and choose the one that best describes the species we would like to identify. This will either lead us to the name of the species or to the next stage in the key.

The features of form used in the key should be conspicuous—they are easy to see. The features should also be constant—shared by all members of a species.

The key shown here will let you identify different species of cedar by looking at the leaves from side branches on mature trees.

▲ Cedar trees on Mount Lebanon

1. Leaves are elongated needles that spread out from the stem 2
   Leaves are shorter scales that are pressed against the stem..5

2. Needles 15–50 mm long, ovoid in transverse section and clustered in whorls of 10–40 on short side shoots (spurs) on older stems..3
   Needles 5–15 mm long, rhombic in transverse section ....*Cryptomeria japonica*

3. Needles 35–50 mm long ....*Cedrus deodara*
   Needles shorter than 30 mm 4

4. Needles in whorls of 30–50, shorter than 25 mm ....*Cedrus atlantica*
   Needles in whorls of 10–20, 15–30 mm long ....*Cedrus libani*

5. Tips of leafy shoots smooth, stout and fleshy, scales do not have translucent glands, foliage smells fruity..6
   Tips of shoots thin and harsh, scales have a translucent gland, foliage smells of sour parsley..*Chamaecyparis lawsoniana*

6. Foliage uniformly yellowish green below, smelling of cooked apples ....*Thuja occidentalis*
   Foliage with white streaks below, smelling of pineapples ....*Thuja plicata*

Conifers (Class Pinopsida)

Trees and shrubs with roots, stems and leaves. They produce pollen in male cones and female gametes and then seeds in female cones. They do not produce flowers or fruits.

Species discovered so far: 630

Using a dichotomous key

1. Use the dichotomous key to recognize the different types of cedar shown in the photos A–D. Note that these photos are all ⅔ life size.

2. Every species of organism is given a binomial, consisting of a genus and a species name. What is the genus and the species name for Western red cedar?

3. Some species included in the key have the same genus name. Give an example and explain the reasons for this.

4. All the species in the key are types of cedar according to their English name. Explain the reasons for:

    a) them being regarded as types of cedar

    b) them being classified in several different genera and not all together in the same genus.

5. This key includes smells as distinguishing features. Suggest reasons for smells of plants not usually being used in identification keys.

Make your own identification key

Find out what types of trees grow on your school campus or in a local park and make a dichotomous key for identifying them. You could base the key just on leaf characterstics or on all parts of the tree.

Same or different?

Predict whether the five species shown in the photographs are placed in the same or different groups and then test your prediction by finding the classification using the Catalogue of Life website.

▲ *Varanus komodoensis* (Komodo dragon)

▲ *Pseudonaja textilis* (Eastern brown snake)

▲ *Caiman crocodilus* (spectacled caiman) and *Podocnemis sextuberculata* (Amazon river turtle)

▲ *Chelonia mydas* (green turtle)

Reptiles (Class Reptilia)

A class of vertebrate animals with a dry scaly skin and lungs. Most species have four legs and females lay eggs with soft shells.

Species discovered so far: 10,300

How do we decide if organisms are different forms of a species or different species?

BIODIVERSITY

All members of a species share features of their form. These constant features are used in dichotomous keys for species identification. Members of a species also vary. The variations may be small and insignificant, or bigger. It is often debatable whether the forms of a species are different enough to be split into separate species. Darwin famously invented terms for biologists who were on the two sides of such a debate: "Those who make many species are the splitters, and those who make few are the lumpers".

To help us decide whether to lump together recognizably different forms within one species or to split them into two or more species, we need to agree what a species is. The key to this is understanding what makes members of a species similar. Two factors hold a species together:

- interbreeding—if a group of organisms breed with each other and produce viable offspring they will remain similar

- adaptation—if a group of organisms have the same lifestyle, they will need the same adaptations.

This leads us to a definition of species: a group of interbreeding organisms that are similar in form.

Bony ray-finned fish (Class Actinopterygii)

A class of vertebrate animals with scales, fins and a skeleton made of bone rather than cartilage. They have gills with a single gill covering (operculum) and a swim bladder for buoyancy.

Species discovered so far: 28,000

Data-based question: Lough Melvin trout

Lough Melvin is a lake in north-western Ireland that has three populations of brown trout. These populations are sufficiently different in form to have separate local names: gillaroo, sonaghen and ferox. Gillaroo have golden flanks with large red spots; sonaghen are silvery with black fins, many black spots and a few red spots; ferox are silvery with few spots.

Each of the forms has particular feeding preferences. Gillaroo feed principally on snails on the lake bed, mostly in shallow water, whereas sonaghen filterfeed on zooplankton in deep water, and ferox are predators of other fish—including smaller trout—in open water. Gillaroo move downstream to breed in the river that carries water from Lough Melvin to the sea and the offspring move back upstream to the lake. Sonaghen and ferox do the reverse and breed in one of the inlet rivers to the lake, with ferox choosing larger slower-flowing inlet rivers and sonaghen smaller faster-flowing ones.

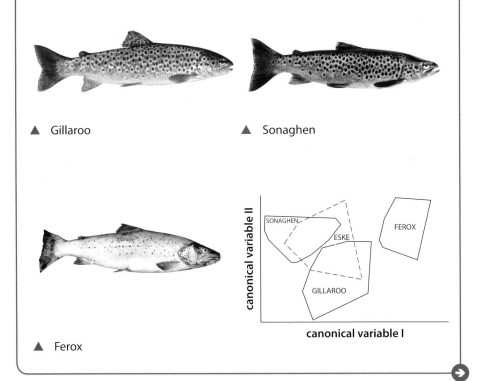

▲ Gillaroo

▲ Sonaghen

▲ Ferox

Samples were obtained of the three forms of trout from Lough Melvin and also brown trout from Lough Eske. Thirty aspects of form were measured. Analysis of the data resulted in a graph known as an ordination, which combines the differences between the forms.

1. Describe the similarities in form between gillaroo, sonaghen and ferox shown in the illustrations of them.

2. Deduce whether there has been interbreeding between the three forms of trout in Lough Melvin.

3. Discuss whether the three forms of Lough Melvin trout are separate species or not.

4. Discuss the significance of the ordination of brown trout from Lough Eske.

Data-based question: Asymmetric form

The photographs here all show the face of Abraham Lincoln. One shows a normal view and the others each show the left or right side of the face with a mirror image alongside.

1. Which is the normal photo and which show the left side and right sides of the face?

2. Give three examples of differences in form between the left and right sides of Lincoln's face.

3. What conclusion can you draw about Lincoln's face?

4. Suggest other parts of the body where the left and the right sides are different in:

   a) external form

   b) internal form.

Our face is a significant part of our identity. Some people prefer one side of their face to the other and try to have it showing more in photographs. If you manipulate a digital image of your own face you can find out how symmetrical it is and what you would look like if you had exact symmetry.

How much do humans differ in form?

All humans belong to the same species so should be very similar in form, but we tend to notice differences. Perhaps this is because we spend so much time looking at other humans and become adept at seeing differences that we would miss in other species. It is also possible that humans do indeed differ more in form than other species.

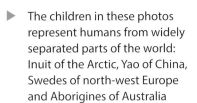 The children in these photos represent humans from widely separated parts of the world: Inuit of the Arctic, Yao of China, Swedes of north-west Europe and Aborigines of Australia

The two factors that make members of a species similar in form are interbreeding and adaptation to the same lifestyle. Over the past 50,000 years or so, humans have migrated out of Africa and then spread to almost all parts of the world. This geographical separation has prevented interbreeding between the separated populations. Also, because conditions vary greatly around the world, humans have developed many different types of lifestyle. It is therefore easy to see how significant differences in form could have developed.

1 Are there significant differences in form between humans? Remember that skin and hair colour are not usually considered to be part of form because they are not differences of structure.

2 Are there more differences or more similarities in form between humans?

3 Our physical form is part of our identity. What other parts of our identity are there?

Which animals are most similar in form to humans?

The small group of animals to which humans are most similar in form are the great apes. To use more scientific language, they are species in the family Hominidae. Currently, seven species are recognized in this family:

Pongo pygmaeus (Bornean orangutan)

Pongo abelii (Sumatran orangutan)

Gorilla gorilla (Western gorilla)

Gorilla beringei (Eastern gorilla)

Pan troglodytes (common chimpanzee)

Pan paniscus (bonobo)

Homo sapiens (humans)

▲ These photos show human hands with the hands of orangutan (top left), bonobo (top right) and gorilla (above)

1. What are the similarities in form between human hands and the hands of orangutan, bonobos and gorillas?

2. What are the differences in form between these hands?

3. Considering other aspects of the external form of orangutan, bonobos and gorillas, are there more similarities or more differences between them and humans?

4. The great apes are currently classified in four different genera: *Pan*, *Pongo*, *Gorilla* and *Homo*. How do we decide whether some of the species should be classified together in the same genus?

Thumbless

Humans have an opposable thumb and four fingers rather than five fingers. Discover the advantage of an opposable thumb by trying to do these tasks without using either of your thumbs:

1. Write with a pen.

2. Compose a text message on your cell phone (mobile phone).

3. Tie a shoelace or a necktie.

4. Open a bottle with a screwcap.

Can you find a task that is even more difficult to do without using your thumbs?

Data-based question: Splitting and lumping

The number of species per genus varies from 1 to over 1,000. For example, the bee genus *Andrena* consists of over 1,300 species The table shows current estimates for how many species have been described and how many different genera they are classified into.

Group	Number of genera	Number of species	Mean number of species per genus
Birds	2,280	10,600	4.65
Anthophila (bees)	425	16,230	38.2
Primates (lemurs, monkeys and apes)	72	463	6.43
Cetaceans (whales, dolphins and porpoises)	39	88	2.26
Flowering plants	14,000	350,000	

1. Calculate the mean number of species per genus of flowering plants.

2. Suggest reasons for a high number of species per genus in the Anthophila.

3. Suggest reasons for a higher mean number of primates per genus than cetaceans.

4. Suggest reasons for the larger mean number of species per genus in the flowering plants than in the birds.

BIODIVERSITY
What type of classification is best?
Consider these four animals:

▲ Sperm whale (*Physeter catodon*)

▲ Whale shark (*Rhincodon typus*)

▲ Manatee (*Trichechus manatus*)

▲ Elephant (*Loxodonta africana*)

Which is the odd one out? If you used a single feature to decide, such as the environment where these animals live, you have produced an artificial classification. This type of classification risks grouping together organisms that are not closely related. For example, you might think that the whale, the shark and the manatee all belong to the same family, that of underwater organisms. This would be wrong because the whale and the manatee are mammals, as is the elephant. Which makes the shark—a cartilaginous fish—the odd one out.

Bats, birds and insects all have wings, so they could be placed together in an artificial classification, but this would be unhelpful because there are many differences between them.

To avoid artificial classification, biologists aim to reflect the closeness of the relationships between species, so they need to consider many different features before they can group organisms together. In this way, they produce natural classifications that allow us to predict, with reasonable confidence, the characteristics of species. For example, we can predict that a newly discovered species of mammal will feed its young with milk produced by the mother's mammary glands.

Artificial classification does not have a predictive value.

Mammals (Class Mammalia)

A class of vertebrate animals with mammary glands for feeding young offspring. Mammals have hair, three bones in their middle ear and a double circulatory system with four chambers in their heart.

Species discovered so far: 5,520

Cartilaginous fish (Class Elasmobranchii)

A class of vertebrate animals with placoid scales, fins and a skeleton made of cartilage rather than bone. They have gills with multiple gill slits and no swim bladder.

Species discovered so far: 1,150

Data-based question: Sperm whales and whale sharks

The diagrams here show the bone structure of a flipper and a fin:

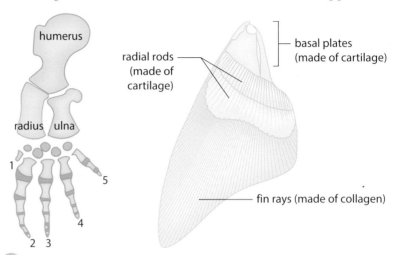

1. What are the similarities between the flipper of a sperm whale and the pectoral fin of a whale shark?

2. Compare and contrast the form of the skeleton in the fin and the flipper.

3. Compare other aspects of form in sperm whales and whale sharks by finding out whether each animal has the following structures: diaphragm, gills, intestines, kidneys, lungs, mammary glands, nostrils, navel, toes and vertebrae. You could show your findings in a table using ticks or crosses to indicate whether a structure is present or not.

4. Discuss whether sperm whales and whale sharks should be grouped together in a natural classification.

The diagrams here show the bone structure of the front limb of a manatee and of an elephant.

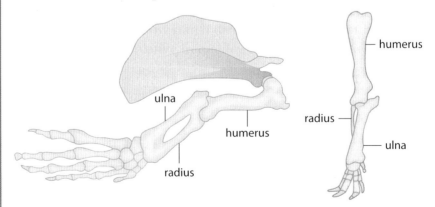

5. Considering the limb bone structure of elephants, manatees and sperm whales and other features of the form of these animals, discuss which of them should be classified together.

6. Predict with a reason whether manatees and elephants have navels.

What are the main groups of flowering plants?

The flowering plants are a huge group that are more abundant than any other plant group in most habitats on land. In the traditional hierarchy of taxa they are a phylum, so are divided into classes. Two classes have been recognized in the past: monocotyledons and dicotyledons. The table shows the typical form in these two groups.

Monocots	Dicots
Leaves long and narrow, or oblong	Leaves broad and very varied in shape
Base of leaf wrapped round stem	Leaf attached to the stem with a petiole (leaf stalk)
Parallel leaf veins	Leaf veins in a branched network
Unbranched roots attached to the stem	Primary root attached to the stem with other roots branching from it
Stamens and other parts of the flower in multiples of three	Stamens and other parts of the flower in fours or fives
One cotyledon (seed leaf)	Two cotyledons

This is a natural classification because many aspects of form are included, not just one. If you use this table to determine whether a plant is a monocot or a dicot you should look at as many aspects of the plant's form as you can, because some monocots and dicots are atypical in certain respects.

Research has thrown into doubt the division of the flowering plants into two classes. There is evidence that the monocotyledons are a natural group, but the dicotyledons should be divided into seven separate groups. Some of these groups are more closely related to the monocotyledons than others, as in the tree diagram shown here. The relationships between the eight groups of flowering plant make it impossible to decide objectively how many classes there should be. Because of this problem with the classification of flowering plants and problems with many other groups, some biologists recommend simply calling all groups of organisms clades instead of phyla, classes or any other of the taxa within the traditional hierarchy.

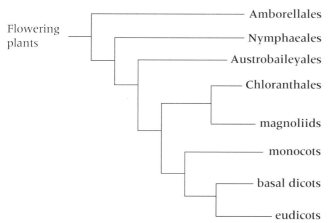

Flowering plants
- Amborellales
- Nymphaeales
- Austrobaileyales
- Chloranthales
- magnoliids
- monocots
- basal dicots
- eudicots

Flowering plants (Phylum Angiospermophyta)

Plants with stems, roots and leaves and also flowers with stamens producing pollen, and with ovaries. Enclosed within the ovary are ovules containing female gametes. Ovules develop into seeds and ovaries into fruits.

Species discovered so far: 268,000

Monocot or dicot?

Are the the four plant species in the photos monocots or dicots?

What other monocots and dicots can you find growing near your school?

▲ *Tradescantia virginiana* (spiderwort)

▲ *Syringa vulgaris* (lilac)

▲ *Hibiscus waimeae* (aloalo)

▲ *Erythronium grandiflorum* (glacier lily)

PLANTS

Does mathematics help us understand form?

One of the most famous books in the history of biology is *On growth and form* by D'Arcy Wentworth Thompson, published in 1917. In this book, Thompson describes many instances where he saw mathematical relationships in plant and animal forms. He also pointed out parallels between engineering structures and the form of living organisms. Mathematicians and engineers continue to find inspiration in living organisms that already incorporate solutions to many design problems in their form.

Thompson pointed out that there is a link between the arrangement of leaves and flowers and the Fibonacci series. In this series, each number is the sum of the two preceding numbers: 1, 1, 2, 3, 5, 8, 13, 21, 34, 55, 89 and so on. The nth number in the Fibonacci series can be calculated using this equation:

$$F_n = \frac{1}{\sqrt{5}} \cdot \left(\frac{1 + \sqrt{5}}{2}\right)^n - \frac{1}{\sqrt{5}} \cdot \left(\frac{1 - \sqrt{5}}{2}\right)^n$$

In a pineapple, for example, the subunits are arranged in radiating spiral rows. Two directions of rows can be seen. There are eight spiral rows in one direction and thirteen in the other direction—adjacent numbers in the Fibonacci series. You can check this next time you see a whole pineapple.

▲ A romanesco cauliflower is a remarkable structure that conforms to the Fibonacci series, both in the numbers of spiral rows of subunits and in the spiral rows of florets within each subunit. What are the numbers of rows?

▲ Count the number of spiral rows near the edge of the flower head. How many are there in each direction? Are the two numbers adjacent in the Fibonacci series?

If leaves are attached singly to a stem—rather than in pairs or in whorls—the positioning of the leaves also follows the Fibonacci series. To test this, start with a lower leaf on a stem (Leaf 0) and find the next leaf that is attached to the stem directly above this leaf (Leaf 1, 2, 3 or more). How many times does the spiral rotate around the stem between Leaf 0 and the leaf directly above it? You can then produce a fraction where the numerator is the number of rotations around the stem and the denominator is the number of the leaf above Leaf 0.

The fractions found in plants are $\frac{1}{2}$, $\frac{1}{3}$, $\frac{2}{5}$, $\frac{3}{8}$, $\frac{5}{13}$, $\frac{8}{21}$, $\frac{13}{34}$ and so on. The numerator and demoninator are always next but one to each other in the Fibonacci series.

▲ In bay (*Laurus nobilis*), Leaf 5 is directly above Leaf 0 and the spiral of leaves rotates twice round the stem between these two leaves

How are organisms grouped into kingdoms?

▲ *Obelia longissima*

Many organisms can easily be recognized as a plant or an animal, but others can confuse us. To check which kingdom a species is in, we sometimes have to look at the structure of the cells. For example, the photograph here shows part of an *Obelia* colony, which looks superficially like a plant, but if its cells are examined, it is obvious that *Obelia* is an animal. Biologists therefore need to know how to recognize plant and animals cells and how to distinguish them from fungi and bacteria.

A B C D Experiment

A Method for examining human cheek cells

1. Obtain a sample of cells from the lining of your cheek by swabbing it with a cotton bud.

2. Dab the cotton bud onto the middle of a microscope slide to transfer your cells.

3. Add a drop of stain, such as methylene blue.

4. Leave for at least a minute to allow the stain to penetrate your cells.

5. Put on a cover slip and remove any excess stain with a paper towel.

6. Put the slide on the stage of your microscope and examine at low power.

7. Search the slide to find the cells that show most clearly.

8. Move the slide so that these cells are in the middle of the field of view.

9. Change to high power and study the structure of your cells.

10. Draw some of your cells and add labels for the structures that you can see, including cell membrane, cytoplasm and nucleus.

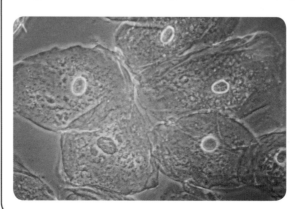

◀ Human cheek cells

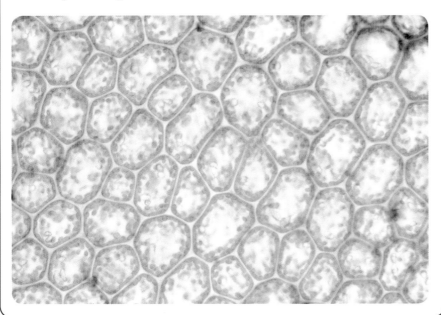 Experiment

B Method for examining moss leaf cells

1. Obtain a leaf of a moss or leafy liverwort that is one cell thick.

2. Cut off a few leaves using dissecting scissors and place them in a drop of water on a microscope slide.

3. Carry out stages 3 to 10 as for cheek cells.

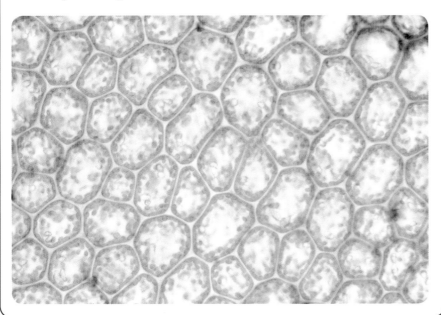

Mosses and liverworts (Phylum Bryophyta)

Plants with rhizoids but no true roots. Some have simple stems and leaves; others have only a flattened thallus. There is no specialized transport tissue (xylem or phloem) and no pollen or seeds. Produces spores in sporangia.

Species discovered so far: 16,240

When you have studied plant and animal cells you can compare and contrast them using a table. The table should have three columns: one for the structures that may or may not be present and one each for plant and animal cells.

You should consider whether each of these structures is present: nucleus, cell membrane, cellulose cell wall, chloroplasts and large permanent vacuole.

Although not clearly visible in the cells that you have examined with a light microscope, you can add to your table the presence of mitochondria in both plant and animal cells and different forms of stored carbohydrate: starch in plant cells and glycogen in animal cells.

CELLS

How are cells arranged in multicellular organisms?

Most plants and animals that are larger than a millimetre are composed of many cells, not just one. There are usually different types of cells in an organism. They are not randomly arranged; cells performing the same function are organized into tissues. Some multicellular organisms have just two tissues, for example, animals in the phylum Cnidaria, which includes corals, sea anemones and jellyfish. Most plants and animals have more tissues than this.

There is another level of organization in most plants and animals. Groups of tissues are organized into organs. Stems, roots and leaves are examples of organs in plants. The lungs, kidneys and heart are examples of animal organs.

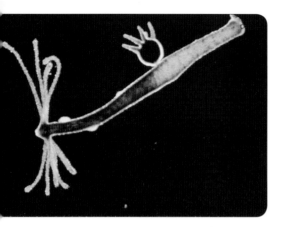

▲ *Hydra viridissima*, seen in this micrograph, has stinging tentacles and a single opening to the gut, showing that it is in the phylum Cnidaria. The body wall appears white in this micrograph and contains just two tissues: endoderm and ectoderm

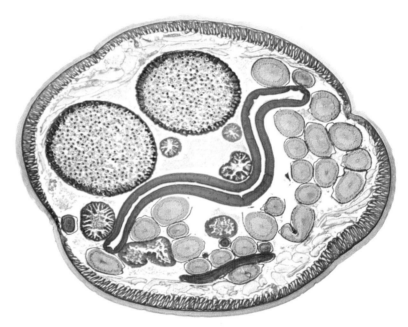

▲ Transverse section through *Ascaris lumbricoides*, a parasite of the gut, showing its reproductive organs. The intestine (not containing food) is the large flattened tube in the center. The ovaries appear as yellow spheres and the two uteri as large red spheres. *Ascaris* is in the phylum Nematoda and has an outer cuticle made of protein (yellow) with a muscle wall (red) adjacent to it

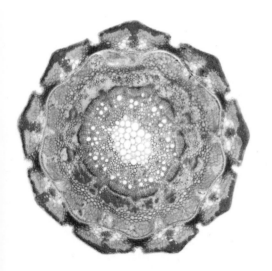

▲ How many tissues can you distinguish in this transverse section of a stem and the surrounding scaly leaves of *Casuarina equisetifolia*? Colour has been added to the image to make the differences between the tissues clearer. The diameter of the section is 1 mm

Adding groups

In this chapter, the number of species and typical form of three plant and four animal groups have been given. To increase your knowledge of biodiversity you could research other groups and add them to your list. Among plants you could add ferns or divide Angiospermophytes into smaller groups. You could add amphibia and birds to your list of vertebrate groups and add any of the many groups of invertebrates.

Why are domains needed in classification?

Until relatively recently, the highest taxon in classification was the kingdom, but in 1990 a higher taxon called domain was proposed. It was already known that all organisms can be classified either as eukaryotes or prokaryotes based on their cell structure. Although prokaryotes are very diverse in their metabolism, they show very little variation in form, so they cannot be classified on this basis. The new evidence about relationships came from DNA base sequences. It showed that prokaryotes divide into two distinct groups that are in some ways as different from each other as they are from eukaryotes. These two prokaryote groups were named Archaea and Bacteria, with Eukaryotes as a third group. Because eukaryotes are divided into kingdoms, the three groups must be at a higher level in the hierarchy of taxa. This explains the need for domains in classification.

Differences in cell structure between the three domains are shown in the table.

	Archaea	**Bacteria**	**Eukaryotes**
Cell wall	Made of pseudopeptidoglycan	Made of peptidoglycan	Made of cellulose or chitin if present
Chromosome	Circular	Circular	Linear
Nucleus	Not present	Not present	Present
Cytoplasm	No mitochondria or other membrane-bound organelles	No mitochondria or other membrane-bound organelles	Mitochondria and other membrane-bound organelles are present
Cell shapes	Unicellular with a limited range of cell shapes, mostly spheres, rods and spirals	Unicellular with a limited range of cell shapes, mostly spheres, rods and spirals	Unicellular or multicellular with a huge range of cell shapes.

▲ Archaea from a hot spring in Yellowstone National Park

▲ Bacteria from plaque on teeth

▲ Eukaryote cells (diatoms) in plankton from a lake

Summative assessment

Statement of inquiry:

Relationships between organisms are revealed by similarities and differences between the myriad of forms.

Introduction

This assessment is based on the theme of the hand. Humans have hands with five digits: four fingers and a thumb. In most humans the right hand is dominant. The digits contain a high density of nerve endings, making them very sensitive to touch. There are also many joints in the hand and muscles to control movement in them.

 ## Human form – hands and relationships

1. The X-ray shows the bones in a human hand. There are 27 bones in the hand including 8 in the wrist. Use the X-ray to count how many bones are in the palm of the hand (metacarpals) and in each digit (phalanges). [3]

2. Discuss whether the hand is a tissue of the body, an organ, or a system. [3]

3. A small number of other animal species have opposable thumbs including the other great apes, gibbons, African and Asian monkeys, and also koalas. Discuss whether all animals with opposable thumbs should be classified together in one group. [3]

4. Fingerprints are due to ridges on the last segment of each finger. They are so variable that every human is assumed to have fingerprints with a different form, even identical twins.

   A few other species have fingerprints including gorillas, chimpanzees and fishers (*Martes pennanti*) which are carnivorous relatives of weasels. Koalas have fingerprints that are so similar in form to human ones that they are difficult to distinguish.

   Using this information, evaluate whether fingerprints can help to assess closeness of relationship. [3]

5. Explain the difference between the form of an organism and forms of a species. [3]

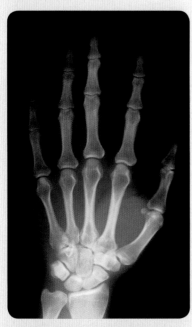

▲ X-ray of a human hand

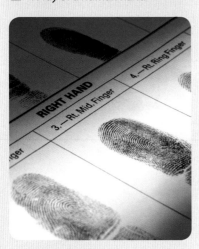

▲ Fingerprints are used to establish identity

Investigating the development of the hand

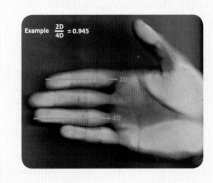

6. The relative length of the various fingers of the hand is variable in humans. The 2D/4D ratio is calculated by dividing the length of the 2nd (index) finger by the length of the 4th (ring) finger. Many hypotheses have been suggested for correlations between 2D/4D ratio and other human traits such as ability in sport. Carry out an investigation in these stages:

   a) Formulate a testable hypothesis. [3]

   b) Design a scientific investigation to test your hypothesis. [10]

   c) Collect data and analyse it. [10]

   d) Evaluate the validity of your hypothesis based on your data. [4]

   e) Explain how you could improve or extend your methods. [3]

7. Human hands start to develop at an early stage of embryonic development. By day 32 of normal development, 8 mm long paddle-shaped hand plates have formed with no signs of a thumb or fingers. By day 52, there are separate digits and the hand is 23 mm long. Digit formation is accomplished by the programmed death of some cells and the growth and division of other cells.

   Sometimes babies are born with a deformity of the hands. Gene mutations can affect development of the digits. Polydactyly is having an extra finger or thumb. Syndactyly is the condition where two or more digits are fused together.

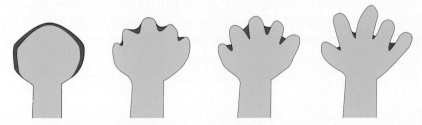

▲ Stages in the development of the hand showing regions of cells that die (red) and regions that continue to grow and divide (green).

   Draw diagrams, based on those shown above to explain how polydactyly and syndactyly could develop in an embryo. [5]

8. The drug thalidomide was used in some countries between 1957 and 1961 to treat nausea and morning sickness in pregnant women. Thalidomide caused abnormal development of the arms and hands in over 10,000 children whose mothers took the drug during pregnancy.

In Germany, the sale of thalidomide was unrestricted. In the UK, it was available only with a prescription from a doctor. In the United States of America, the manufacturers of the drug repeatedly requested a license from the Food and Drug Administration (FDA). Each time the FDA refused a license until drug safety trials had been done on pregnant women, but the manufacturers repeatedly refused to do these trials. There was a view that a drug such as thalidomide could not cross the placenta and reach a developing fetus so tests were unnecessary. The FDA refused a total of six requests for a license and the number of children born with deformities due to thalidomide was far smaller than in Germany or the UK.

Explain the mistakes that were made that led to so many children being harmed by thalidomide in Germany and the UK. [5]

ATL Information literacy skills

Preview and skim videos to build understanding

On the MYP eAssessment, you will have access to a library of resources and stimulus material. Sometimes, there will be a short video for you to watch from which you are expected to extract information. There are a number of strategies you can employ to preview and skim videos quickly so that you don't end up under time pressure during the exam.

At the start of the eAssessment you have five minutes to review the contents of the resource library and to preview the questions. If the resource library contains a video, the examination authors have selected it for a reason.

During your five minutes preview time you should note any common themes among the questions and the resources. If a video is present, note the question that requires you to watch it. This will provide you with the purpose for watching this video and will help you prioritize ideas and information from least to most important.

Once you start watching the video, pause it often to take notes. Note the position of the timer on the slider in your notes. You might want to reference the video's content in your answer.

To practice watching a video while taking notes, locate the video: "The Shadow of the thalidomide Tragedy/Retro Report/The New York Times". After viewing it, discuss whether the drug *thalidomide* should still be prescribed. If so, for what purpose? Reference the point in the video that provides support for your position.

Hands and identity

9. Countless images of hands have been produced. Two are shown here: a drawing of praying hands by Albrecht Dürer and hands that are part of a sensory homunculus in which parts of the body are sized according to the area of cortex in the brain that receives sensory information from them. Discuss how well each of the two images helps us understand our identity. [5]

▲ Praying hands by Albrecht Dürer

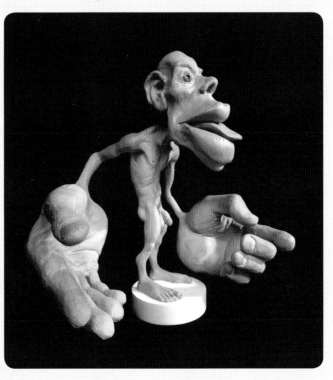

▲ Sensory homunculus

4 Function

Functions, purposes and roles are related but are not quite the same. What are the differences?

▼ The jaw of *Homo neanderthalensis* was long and held two premolars and three molar teeth with the function of grinding fibrous plant foods. In modern humans, the jaw is shorter and the third molar (wisdom tooth) seems to cause more problems than benefits, if it develops. Does our third molar have a function?

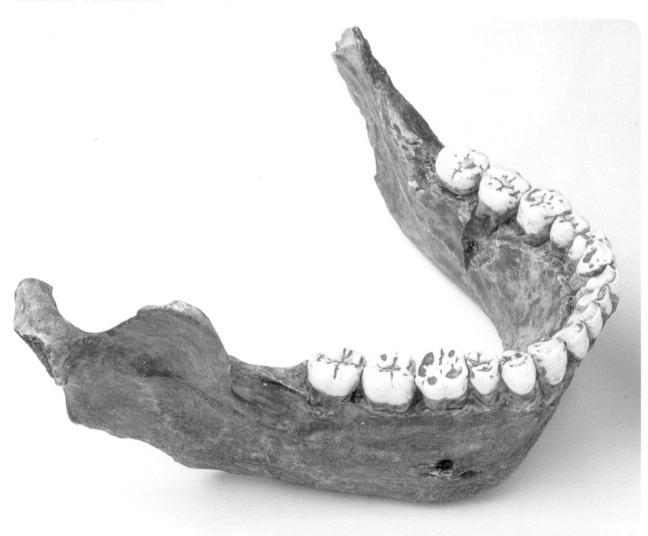

Roundhouses with turntables were used for turning steam locomotives at the end of a journey. Modern trains have control cabs at each end and power units that run equally well in both directions, so the original function of roundhouses has been lost. New functions have been found for some, including offices, factories and theatres. Is there a building near your home that has been "repurposed"?

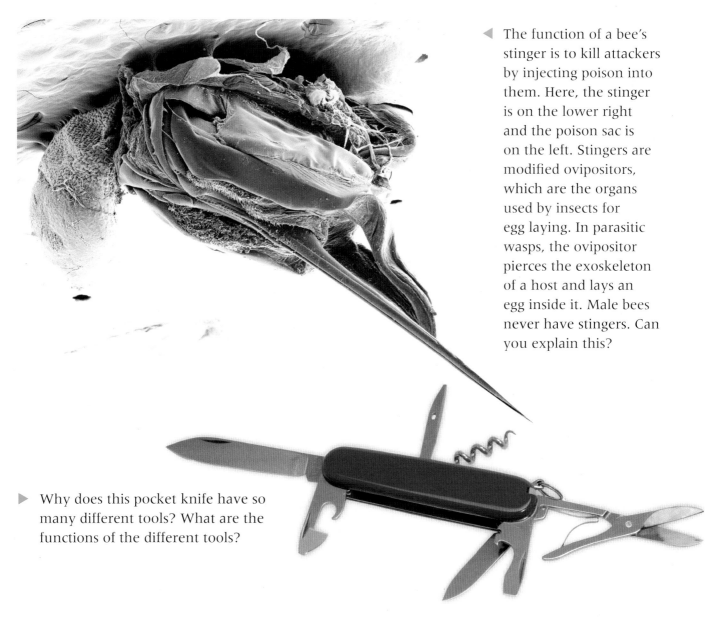

The function of a bee's stinger is to kill attackers by injecting poison into them. Here, the stinger is on the lower right and the poison sac is on the left. Stingers are modified ovipositors, which are the organs used by insects for egg laying. In parasitic wasps, the ovipositor pierces the exoskeleton of a host and lays an egg inside it. Male bees never have stingers. Can you explain this?

Why does this pocket knife have so many different tools? What are the functions of the different tools?

Key concept: Systems

Related concept: Function

Global context: Orientation in space and time

▼ The overall function of a digital watch is to tell the time. As in the human body, each of the component parts has a vital function, without which the overall function could not be performed

Introduction

In simple terms, the function of something is what it does. The heart pumps blood; a clock tells us the time. Humans design objects so that they can perform a function. The function is the purpose of the object. The parts of living organisms have evolved to perform their functions. Each component part of a living organism interacts with other parts, carrying out its function within a system. In this chapter, function is therefore studied in relation to the key concept of systems.

Human physiology is the study of some of the most complex systems ever investigated. To carry out its normal activities successfully, the human body relies on each of its components—from individual molecules to cells, organs and body systems—working together seamlessly. To understand how this is achieved, we will turn to the global context of orientation in space and time.

Statement of inquiry:

Each component in a system must perform its specific function at the right time and place for the system as a whole to be successful.

As in a drama, each part of a living organism has a role and all vital roles must be performed. The biologist and philosopher Herbert Spencer wrote in 1851: "A function to each organ, and each organ to its own function is the law of all organization." In biology we rarely speak of laws because life is so varied and exceptions to proposed laws are often found. In this case, vestigial organs would be exceptions—organs that have lost their former role.

Herbert Spencer expanded on the theme of specialization: "separateness of duty is universally accompanied with separateness of structure". This is telling us that the different parts of an organism have different structures because they are specialized to carry out different functions. We expect specialists to perform their functions better than generalists. In this chapter we shall look at how molecules, cells and organs are specialized for particular functions, featuring the digestive and nervous systems. We can also test Spencer's law by trying to find examples of organs that perform a wide range of functions and organs that do not have a very specialized structure.

▲ "What is the point of a mosquito?" Questions like this are frequently asked about parasites. The many body parts of a mosquito clearly have functions, but does an animal have an overall function?

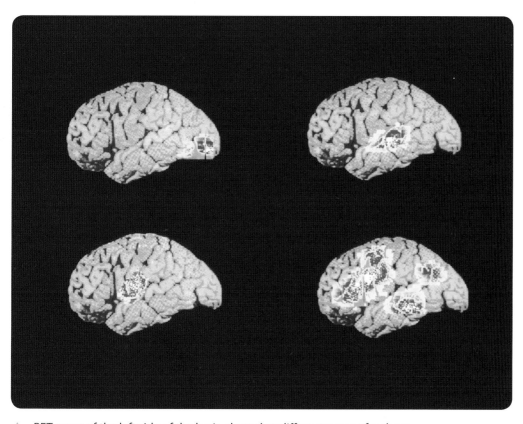

▲ PET scans of the left side of the brain show that different types of task are performed by different parts of the brain. Clockwise from upper right: sight (visual cortex in the occipital lobe); hearing (auditory area in the temporal lobe); thinking about verbs and saying them (hearing and speaking areas of the temporal and parietal lobes); and speech (centres in the frontal, temporal and parietal lobes)

What are the functions of the parts of a cell?

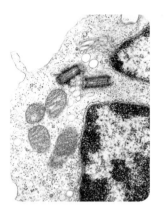

▲ Electron micrograph of part of an animal cell

Cells make up the structure of living things. The interior of a living cell is a miniature and very orderly system. The structure of each part of a cell allows it to carry out its role or function efficiently and helps the cell to function as a whole.

A light microscope allows the shape of cells and also relatively large features such as the nucleus to be seen, but usually the cytoplasm just looks slightly grainy. No structures in it show clearly because they are so small. An electron micrograph can reveal structures in the cytoplasm because the magnification is much greater. It also reveals more details of the nucleus and the cell membrane.

Five structures that are needed to perform functions within eukaryotic cells are described in the table.

Name	Structure		Function
Membrane	The membrane on the outside of the cell is very thin (10 nm which is a hundred thousandth of a millimetre across) but it is continuous—there aren't any gaps in it.		Prevents useful parts of the cell's contents from leaving and prevents unwanted or harmful substances from entering. As the cell is an open system, the membrane must allow entry of substances that the cell needs and exit of waste products.
Nucleus	The nucleus is a part of the cell that is separated from the cytoplasm by a double membrane with pores in it. Nuclei contain large amounts of DNA and protein.		Stores genes. Working copies of genes are made inside the nucleus and then prepared so that they are ready to be translated into proteins by ribosomes in the cytoplasm. These edited copies pass out through nuclear pores.
Cytoplasm	The cytoplasm was once thought to be just water with substances dissolved in it but the electron microscope shows that it contains many small structures called organelles. Most of these are separated from the rest of the cytoplasm by either one or two membranes.		Acts as the chemical processing factory of the cell. Organelles with membranes around them are compartments that are separated from the rest of the cytoplasm so particular reactions that need special conditions can be carried out.

Mitochondrion	The mitochondrion is an example of an organelle that has two membranes separating it from the rest of the cytoplasm. The inner membrane is folded inwards to increase its surface area.		Supplies the cell with energy in a usable form (ATP) by aerobic respiration, which is the release of energy from carbon compounds using oxygen.
Ribosomes	The ribosome is an example of an organelle that is not surrounded by a membrane. It is roughly spherical and very small—only about 0.00002 mm in diameter.		Ribosomes make all the proteins that the cell needs. Many different proteins can be made using copied genes sent out from the nucleus.

Balloon debate

Evaluate information about one cell structure (cytoplasm, cell membrane, mitochondrion, nucleus or ribosome), then argue for keeping it.

▲ In a balloon debate you imagine that there are too many people flying in a hot air balloon and one must be thrown out to prevent it sinking and crashing. In this debate you imagine that there are too many cell structures and the cell must get rid of one, then another, and so on…

How do cells specialize for particular functions?

Within the human body there is an amazing range of cell types specialized for a wide range of different functions. Many cell types contain extra structures in addition to the five basic ones described earlier. Some of these extra structures are represented below.

Lysosomes: sacs with enzymes inside, which are used to digest and therefore destroy bacteria or other organisms taken in by a cell

Glycogen granules: clusters of many molecules of the polysaccharide glycogen, to which glucose molecules can be easily added or removed

Microtubules: hollow protein fibres that resist bending and compression and act as microscopic scaffolding poles

Keratin fibres: tough proteins that repel water, so groups of cells shrink, die and turn into hard body parts

Actin and myosin filaments: contractile proteins that pull the cell into different shapes

Pseudopodia: outgrowths of the cell in various forms but often becoming cup-shaped so they can enclose something in a vesicle or vacuole

Vesicles: small, spherical, movable sacs that consist of a single membrane with substances inside such as enzymes, neurotransmitters or hormones

Microvilli: multiple finger-like projections of the cell membrane where it is in contact with surrounding fluid

Cilia: narrow projections of the cell that beat with a whip-like action

1. Formulate a hypothesis regarding which of these extra structures are needed in the cells below so they can perform their functions:

   a) Cells forming the lining of the small intestine, where digested foods are absorbed.

   b) White blood cells that fight disease by moving into infected tissue and engulfing the organisms causing the infection.

   c) Neurons that transmit nerve impulses and send signals across synapses from one neuron to another.

   d) Cells that develop into hair or nail.

2. The photos (I–IV) shown here are electron micrographs of the four cell types in the previous question. Apply your scientific knowledge to deduce the cell type in each photo and what cell structures are visible.

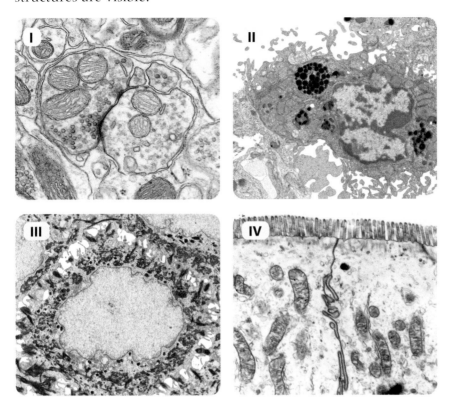

Research one of your cell types

Pick a specialized cell type in your body that you want to know more about and investigate the structures that enable it to perform its function.

▲ This baby boy, busy investigating his toes, does not yet know that there are over 100 different cell types in his body, each with a different function

What is the function of a cheek lining cell?

In Chapter 3 there is an opportunity to look at the structure of human cheek lining cells with a light microscope. Though they might look like average cells without any unusual features, they have a specialized structure. This allows them to perform their function efficiently, which is protecting tissues in the cheek wall.

▲ Cells that have been rubbed off the cheek lining

1 Which features (I–V) help cheek lining cells to perform various functions (a–d)?

I. They are very thin cells that overlap adjacent cells.

II. They are flat cells with a thin flattened nucleus.

III. Their cell membrane is impermeable to most substances.

IV. They are easily rubbed off, so the cheek lining is replaced every day or so.

V. They contain keratin which is a tough fibrous protein.

a. Protecting the mouth from damage by acids and other chemicals in food

b. Providing a smooth surface inside the mouth so food can be moved easily during chewing

c. Protecting the mouth from damage by hard foods when they are chewed

d. Preventing bacteria in the mouth from causing an infection by getting into cheek tissues

How do cells communicate with other cells?

Read this text carefully and then answer the questions.

Cell to cell communication is needed within our bodies to coordinate the functions of the various cells. Cells are able to send and receive signals. Chemical signals are commonly used, with one cell releasing the chemical and another cell receiving it. Chemical signals are received by special proteins called receptors. Each receptor has a site on its surface where one specific type of molecular signal can bind. When the signal molecule is attached to the binding site, other parts of the receptor change the activity of the cell. Small numbers of signal molecules binding to just a few receptors can set off major changes in a cell.

Neurotransmitters are molecular signals used for communication between neurons. The junction between two neurons is called a synapse. The gap between neurons at a synapse is only about 20 nanometres wide. Neurotransmitters are released into the synapse by one of the neurons; the neurotransmitters travel across the junction and bind to receptors on the membrane of the other neuron. After binding, neurotransmitters can either trigger or stop a nerve impulse, depending on the type of neurotransmitter. Many different types are used in the nervous system, though only one is used at each synapse and there is a specific receptor for each neurotransmitter.

Hormones are another example of molecular signals used in cell to cell communication. They are carried via the bloodstream from the cells that secrete them to target cells in other parts of the body. The cells that secrete hormones are endocrine gland cells. Receptors for a specific hormone are only present in that hormone's target cells.

Some hormones such as insulin are proteins. The receptors for protein hormones are located in the membrane of target cells, with the binding site exposed on the outside of the cell. Steroid hormones, such as testosterone and estrogen, are smaller and can pass through the plasma membrane of cells. Their receptors are in the cytoplasm or the nucleus.

When a hormone binds to its receptor, the cell's activities are changed in some way. Some receptors cause a cascade of reactions that amplifies the effect of the hormone. Some, for example, rapidly activate enzymes. Other receptors bind to particular genes in the nucleus and switch them on or off, changing the types of protein that are being produced in the cell.

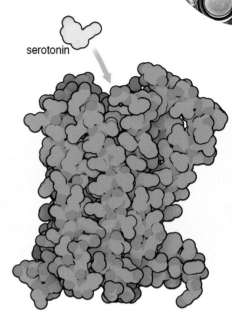

serotonin

▲ Receptor for the neurotransmitter serotonin. Muscle movements in the digestive system are controlled using serotonin. Synapses in the brain that control our emotions and moods also use this neurotransmitter

▶ When the hormone estrogen (pink) enters cells and binds to the estrogen receptor (blue) it causes estrogen receptors to pair up to form a dimer. This dimer then binds to any of 12 specific sites in the DNA (orange and pink), activating adjacent genes that code for proteins needed during female growth and development. Blue dotted lines on the image are parts of the receptor that were omitted to make the associated DNA visible. Estrogen receptors activate these genes during early embryonic development and from puberty onwards

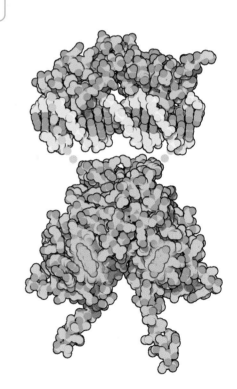

1. Explain the reasons for a different receptor being needed for every hormone and neurotransmitter.

2. Explain whether neurotransmitters or hormones have a more rapid effect on the body.

3. Explain whether neurotransmitters or hormones have a more widespread effect on the body.

4. Every receptor has a special site to which only certain molecules can bind. Which other group of proteins has a binding site to which specific molecules bind?

5. Proteins such as receptors have functions. Does anything smaller than a protein molecule have a function within the human body?

Data-based question: Life reduced to the minimum

The text below is part of an online article from the *Independent* newspaper from 27 March 2016.

Scientists have long pondered over the "minimal genome" required for a free-living cell to exist and reproduce successfully, and now they have answered the question by creating one—by tinkering with the existing genome of a bacterium called *Mycoplasma mycoides*. The scientists, led by veteran genome researcher and synthetic life enthusiast Craig Venter, selectively eliminated the genes of the *Mycoplasma* chromosome until they got down to the minimum set required for a cell to survive and replicate. They then re-synthesized the genes into a single strand of DNA and "rebooted" a genetically empty cell until it sprang into life once more.

With just 473 genes and 531,000 DNA bases, the synthetic microbe is smaller than the smallest known natural genome of a related bacterial species called *M. genitalium*, which has 525 genes and 600,000 DNA bases. The "supercharged" microbe can double in volume every three hours instead of the several weeks needed for *M. genitalium*.

"Our goal is a cell so simple that we can determine the molecular and biological function of every gene," said the scientists, writing in the journal *Science*. The latest microbe is called JCVI-Syn-3.0. About two-thirds of the genes in its minimal genome have known functions.

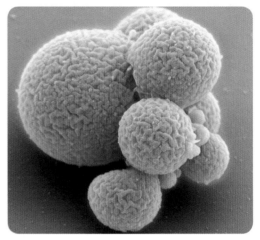

▲ JCVI-Syn-3.0

1. The researchers have discovered the functions of 324 genes in JCVI-Syn-3.0. Calculate the percentage of the genes in this synthetic bacterium that currently have an unknown function.

2. Explain how the researchers could discover whether a gene was needed for the bacterium to survive and reproduce successfully in the laboratory.

3. Discuss whether the 473 genes in JVCI-Syn-3.0 must all have a function.

4. Naturally occurring bacteria have more than 473 genes. For example, *Mycoplasma mycoides* taken from its natural habitat in the stomach of cattle has about 900 genes. Is it reasonable to expect none, all or some of these extra genes to have a function?

Living or non-living?

The difference between living and non-living is sometimes explained by listing seven functions of life: nutrition, respiration, growth, response, excretion, reproduction and movement. The mysterious white lumps in the photo are sometimes found in natural habitats and have been called "star jelly". How could you find out whether they are living or non-living?

▲ Star jelly found in January 2016 in Shropshire, England, in an area where geese had been feeding

Assigning life functions to organs and systems

Biologists have defined a small number of processes that we expect to occur in all living organisms, so they are called "functions of life" or "life functions".

Draw the table below and complete it by adding where each life function is performed in the body. List both organs and systems that are involved. See if you can get above 10 organs in any of the columns.

Life function	Nutrition	Respiration	Response	Excretion	Reproduction	Movement
System						
Organs						

What type of organization works best?

We are likely to become unhappy and unproductive if we are part of a disorganized system. In everyday life, managers try to make businesses and other organizations as productive and efficient as possible but do not always succeed. Key question words for managers at work are "where" and "when". If we understand how living organisms organize themselves, there might be useful insights for managers.

▶ Mintzberg's organigram—an example of an organizational model. Can you devise an alternative management structure for an organization such as a school or a business and represent it with an organigram? Can you draw an organigram to represent the organization of the human body?

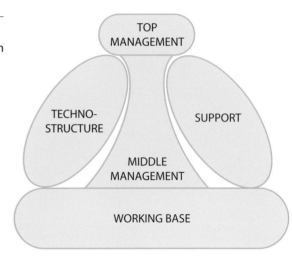

The English saying "Jack of all trades and master of none" tells us that it is better to assign each function to a specialist, rather than let a generalist try to perform them all. In the body, many organs specialize in one or two functions. By contrast, the liver has many functions, even though 80% of it is just one cell type. These multifunctional cells are hepatocytes, which have a cuboidal shape and are about 25 μm in diameter. The following are some of the functions of hepatocytes:

- synthesis of plasma proteins including serum albumin, fibrinogen and prothrombin

- synthesis of lipoproteins and assembly of LDL and HDL complexes

- synthesis of cholesterol and bile salts as a part of the secretion of bile

- storage of vitamin D and iron

- transformation of carbohydrates into lipids

- regulation of blood sugar level by reversible transformation of glucose into glycogen

- detoxification of drugs and toxins absorbed by the body

- transformation of ammonia into urea.

1 What are the advantages of specializing in one function?

2 What are the advantages of performing a wide range of functions?

3 What examples of specialists and generalists can you find in the wider world?

Two extremes of business organization are open-plan offices where many different functions are performed together and "silos", which are separated parts of an organization with restrictions on intercommunication. There is a parallel with cell organization. The cytoplasm of a bacterial cell is one undivided space that performs all cell functions. In contrast, hepatocytes in the liver have one or two nuclei, 500–4,000 mitochondria, 200–300 lysosomes and also many compartments in their smooth and rough endoplasmic reticulum.

4. What is the advantage of having separate functions performed in separate compartments?

5. What is the advantage of having many small compartments which carry out the same function, rather than one large compartment?

6. What is the advantage of having all functions carried out in one undivided space?

7. What examples can you find in the wider world of open-plan organization and division into silos.

8. Discuss the reasons for the type of organization seen in these photos.

▲ Storage tanks at an oil refinery in Singapore

▲ Enclosed fields in the valley and open grazing on the hills in Swaledale, Yorkshire, UK

▲ Cells at Kingston Penitentiary, Ontario, Canada

▲ Dormitory in a pilgrim's hostel at Santiago de Compostela, Spain

Data-based question: Total parenteral nutrition

Nutrition is one of the major life processes that all living organisms must perform, including humans. Parenteral nutrition is feeding a person with a sterile solution of nutrients via a needle inserted into a vein. With total parenteral nutrition (TPN), all nutrients are supplied intravenously and no food passes through the gut.

The pie charts show the composition of fluid used for TPN and also daily nutritional goals (FDA diet) for 14- to 18-year-olds published in *2015–2020 Dietary Guidelines for Americans*. For both diets the elements sodium, potassium, calcium, magnesium, chloride and phosphorus are required, together with smaller quantities of trace elements. Twelve different vitamins are needed in each diet. The mass in grams of each group of nutrients is shown.

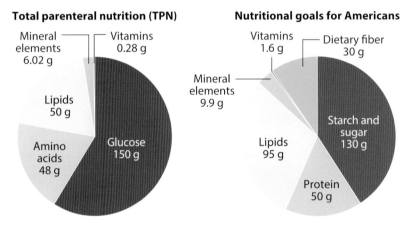

1. Compare the TPN and FDA diets by giving three similarities.

2. Explain the differences between TPN and FDA-recommended diet in:

    a) starch

    b) amino acids

    c) vitamins

    d) dietary fiber.

3. The TPN fluid must be sterile but this is not necessary with food ingested by mouth. What is the reason for this difference?

4. Suggest three conditions that might result in a patient in hospital needing TPN.

5. Of the 20 amino acids used to make proteins by human cells, 12 are usually included in TPN. How can the other 8 amino acids be obtained if they are not included in the diet?

6. Discuss whether nutrients such as amino acids have a function in cells or are merely needed.

Why are the organs of the digestive system in sequence rather than in parallel?

Animals such as coral polyps and jellyfish digest their food using a single gut cavity lined with one type of tissue. A single opening to the gut cavity is used for ingesting food and egesting undigested wastes. All stages in the digestion and absorption of food therefore happen at the same time in the same place.

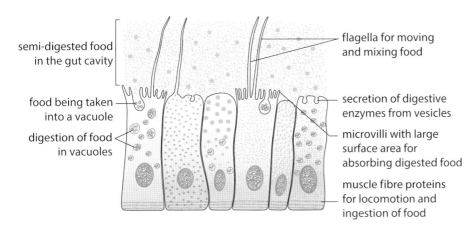

semi-digested food in the gut cavity

flagella for moving and mixing food

food being taken into a vacuole

digestion of food in vacuoles

secretion of digestive enzymes from vesicles

microvilli with large surface area for absorbing digested food

muscle fibre proteins for locomotion and ingestion of food

◀ Endoderm of a cnidarian – a single layer of cells that carries out all the functions of digestion and absorption of foods

In humans, food passes through a series of organs that link the mouth to the anus: mouth cavity, esophagus, stomach, small intestine (duodenum and ileum), colon and rectum. There are also associated organs: the salivary glands that secrete saliva into the mouth cavity, the pancreas that secretes pancreatic juice into the small intestine and the liver that secretes bile into the small intestine.

◀ Healthy digestive system

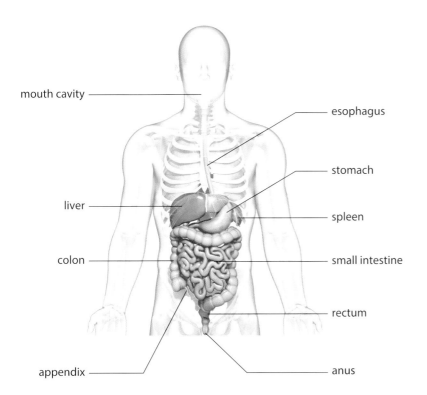

mouth cavity

esophagus

stomach

liver

spleen

colon

small intestine

rectum

appendix

anus

The tables below show in alphabetical order 10 specific functions of nutrition and 10 organs that are part of the digestive system.

Function
Absorption of digested foods such as amino acids and glucose
Absorption of water
Chewing of food to break up larger lumps and increase the surface area
Digestion of carbohydrates such as starch by enzymes that require a pH close to neutral
Digestion of lipids such as fats and oils by enzymes that require a pH close to neutral
Digestion of proteins by enzymes that require acid conditions
Digestion of proteins by enzymes that require a pH close to neutral
Killing bacteria to prevent gut infections (food poisoning)
Temporary storage of food that cannot all be digested immediately
Swallowing and vomiting

Organ
Appendix
Colon
Esophagus
Liver and gall bladder
Mouth cavity
Pancreas
Rectum
Salivary glands
Small intestine
Stomach

1. For each of the 10 functions in the table, find out which organ or organs performs it.

2. When you have assigned each function to an organ, deduce the sequence in which the functions are performed as food passes through the digestive system.

3. Try to explain the reasons for the sequence in which the functions of the digestive system are performed.

4. Discuss whether there are any organs in the digestive system that have:

   a) the same functions as each other

   b) no functions at all.

▶ Rabbits have a structure that is equivalent to the very small human appendix, but it is much larger and performs an essential function for the rabbit—it holds bacteria that digest cellulose in plant cell walls

Data-based question: CT scans of abdominal organs

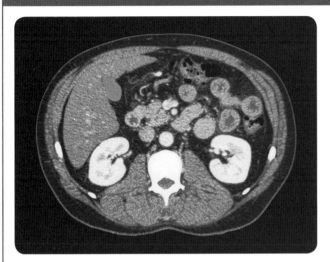

Computerized tomography (CT or CAT) scanners consist of a ring that rotates around a small part of the body. X-rays are passed through and a computer analyses them to make detailed images of structures inside the body. The CT scan above shows normal organs at one level in the abdomen. No health problems were diagnosed in this patient.

1. Identify these organs:

   a) the organ colored red and the green organ adjacent to it

   b) the two bright yellow organs.

2. Bone tissue is shown pale yellow on this CT scan. Identify the five bones that are visible.

3. The small intestine is visible in the centre and right of the CT scan. Describe and explain its appearance in the scan.

4. Muscle tissue has the same appearance wherever it occurs in the scan. Identify four organs with muscle tissue that are visible.

5. a) Identify, with reasons, the ventral side (front) and dorsal side (back) of the person.

   b) Identify, with reasons, the left and right sides of the person.

How is the nervous system organized?

PHYSIOLOGY

The two body systems featured in this chapter are the digestive system and the nervous system. The organization of the digestive system can be likened to an assembly line where a product is manufactured from its parts and the nervous system to a telephone system.

▲ What are the similarities and differences between an automobile assembly line and the digestive system?

▲ What are the similarities and differences between a telephone system and the nervous system?

What is the function of a sensory receptor?

The nervous system includes many sensory receptors. They are cells that all have the same essential function: they detect a stimulus and transform it into an electrical signal, which is then transmitted to the central nervous system.

The table shows the functions of specific sensory receptors.

Type of sensory receptor	Where are the receptors located?	What type of stimulus is detected by the receptors?
Baroreceptors	Walls of blood vessels	Blood pressure
Chemoreceptors	Tongue	Five different chemical groups (tastes)
	Nose	Many different odorants (smells)
Photoreceptors	Retina of the eye	Rods detect low intensity (dim) light
		Cones detect red, green and blue light
Mechanoreceptors	Skin	Touch, pressure and hair movement
	Inner ear	Sound vibrations
	Muscles	Stretching of muscles
Osmoreceptors	Hypothalamus of brain	Solute concentration of body fluids
Thermoreceptors	Skin	Hot or cold temperatures

1. Propose a hypothesis to explain how a chemoreceptor might work.

2. Design an experiment to investigate the functions of one type of sensory receptor.

▲ What message are the sensory receptors on this child's tongue conveying?

▲ Who has more sensory receptors in the nose, the airport sniffer dog or its handler?

▲ What is the function of a cat's whiskers and where are the sensory receptors associated with the whiskers located?

▶ What type of sensory receptor does the glassblower use to avoid injury?

What is the advantage of locating all the main sense organs in the head?

Some animals have a head and some do not. The development of a head is called cephalization.

1. Which groups of animals develop a head and which do not?

2. What is the function of a head?

▲ Sea anemones

▲ Ant

▲ Marine flatworm

▲ Macaws

Sensory receptors are widely distributed in the human body, but there are particularly high concentrations of them in the sense organs: the eye, ear, nose and tongue. All of these organs are located in the head.

3. Discuss the reasons for the main sense organs being located in the head.

4. Suggest disadvantages of sense organs being located elsewhere in the body.

Where are sensory receptors located in the eye?

The overall function of the eye is vision. It has a complex structure that adjusts for distance and light intensity, to produce a clear and focused image on the retina.

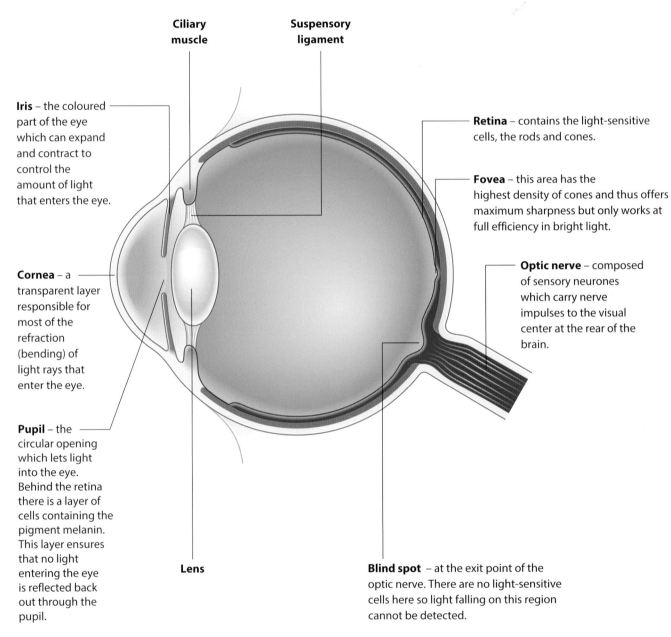

Ciliary muscle

Suspensory ligament

Iris – the coloured part of the eye which can expand and contract to control the amount of light that enters the eye.

Cornea – a transparent layer responsible for most of the refraction (bending) of light rays that enter the eye.

Pupil – the circular opening which lets light into the eye. Behind the retina there is a layer of cells containing the pigment melanin. This layer ensures that no light entering the eye is reflected back out through the pupil.

Retina – contains the light-sensitive cells, the rods and cones.

Fovea – this area has the highest density of cones and thus offers maximum sharpness but only works at full efficiency in bright light.

Optic nerve – composed of sensory neurones which carry nerve impulses to the visual center at the rear of the brain.

Lens

Blind spot – at the exit point of the optic nerve. There are no light-sensitive cells here so light falling on this region cannot be detected.

▲ Structure of the eye (in horizontal section)

The retina is a hemispherical screen at the back of the eye onto which images are projected. There are two types of photoreceptors in the retina: rods and cones. Both take their name from the part of the cell that absorbs light, which is either rod-shaped or cone-shaped.

1. Rods and cones are useful at different times. When are rods and cones most useful?

2. Rods and cones are not distributed evenly through the retina. Where are there most rods and most cones?

3. Rods and cones form a tissue layer in the retina but there are many other tissues in the eye. What is the function of these other tissues? Would it be possible to have the sense of vision without any of them?

4. What is the difference between a sensory receptor and a sense organ?

The diagram of the tissues in the wall of the eye shows a layer of ganglion cells, which are a type of neuron (nerve cell). Most of the ganglion cells process signals from rods and cones and then convey the signals to the visual centres of the brain where they are used to form images. About 1% of ganglion cells are photoreceptors. When stimulated by light they send signals to other parts of the brain that coordinate various responses to the intensity of light:

- adjustments to the size of the pupil

- setting the "biological clock" that controls when we do things in relation to day and night

- secretion of the hormone melatonin which promotes sleep.

What is the function of the eye and the structures around it?

1. Find each of these structures in the photograph of the baby and then draw a labelled sketch diagram to show their relative positions: pupil, iris, sclera, opening of tear (lacrimal) gland ducts, eyelashes, eyelid and eyebrow.

2. What is the reason for the pupil appearing black?

3. Explain where the baby was when the photo was taken—in a brightly illuminated or dimly lit room.

4. Blue eyes are common in some human populations but are absent from others. Identify some parts of the world where all of the indigenous population has brown eyes and explain the reasons for this.

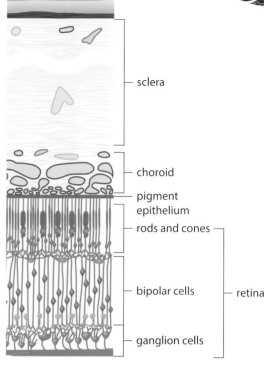

▲ Structure of the wall of the eye

▲ Photoreceptors in the eye help us to decide when it is time to go to sleep

PHYSIOLOGY

5. Muscles in the eyelids allow the eye to be closed. When does the eye close and what are the reasons for closure?

6. There are eyelashes above and below the eye, but an eyebrow only above it. Suggest hypotheses to explain where the eyelashes and eyebrow are located.

7. What are the advantages of having two eyes rather than just one? You could formulate a hypothesis in answer to this question and then design an experiment to test your hypothesis.

ATL Critical thinking skills

Making reasonable predictions

Question 7 above asks for the formulation of a hypothesis. Hypotheses are commonly expressed as "If....then...because..." statements, such as "If the (manipulated variable) is changed in this way, then the (responding variable) will be observed to change in this way". Hypotheses are based on an ability to offer an explanation for observations suggesting possible causes. Hypotheses are not just guesses, but are based upon evidence and a reasonable possibility of a cause and effect relationship.

PHYSIOLOGY

Where are the sensory receptors that we use for hearing?

It seems obvious that in order to hear sounds from the world around us, the necessary receptors would be close to the outer surface of the body. This is indeed where they are located in many invertebrates. For example, spiders have fine hairs on their legs that pick up vibrations from the air via receptor cells. Varying in length between 0.1 and 1.4 mm, these fine hairs respond to different frequencies of sound (40–600 Hz), all of which are in the range generated by flying insects.

In contrast, the sensory receptors used for hearing in humans are in the inner ear, deep inside the skull. They are called hair cells and are located in the cochlea. This consists of a hollow spiral bony chamber looking rather like a snail shell, containing a fluid-filled tube, also coiled into a spiral. The tube is divided into three canals by membranes that can vibrate. The hair cells are positioned between two membranes inside the cochlea and are of two types: inner hair cells, which are responsible for transforming vibrations into nerve signals, and outer hair cells, which amplify sounds.

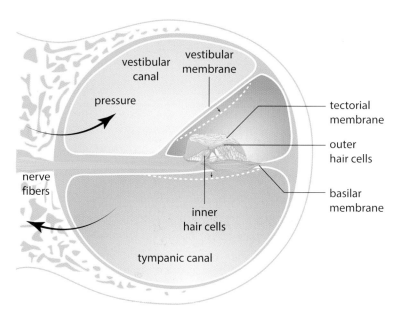

▲ Cross-section through the cochlea

Sound consists of a series of pressure waves. Inside the cochlea these waves pass inwards through the fluid in the vestibular canal, which is connected at its inner end to the tympanic canal. The sound waves then pass outwards through the tympanic canal. The canals in the cochlea are separated by membranes. One of these, the basilar membrane, varies in width and in stiffness. As a consequence, it vibrates in response to different frequencies in different parts of the cochlea, with the outermost parts vibrating in response to the highest frequencies of sound and the innermost to the lowest frequencies.

Hair cells close to the basilar membrane detect vibrations in their hairs caused by particular frequencies of sound waves. When this happens in a hair cell it releases a neurotransmitter that crosses a synapse to a sensory neuron. The sensory neuron responds to the neurotransmitter by transmitting a nerve impulse to auditory centers in the brain.

Find a diagram of the structure of the whole ear including the outer, middle and inner ear and then answer these questions.

1. **a)** What is the sequence of structures through which sound waves pass from the air outside until they are dissipated inside the ear?

   b) Discuss whether the sound waves are passing through a solid, liquid or gas at each stage in this sequence.

2. Explain the functions of the round and oval windows.

3. The loudness of a sound is due to the amplitude of the sound waves. How are we able to hear sounds with low amplitude and also avoid ear damage from sounds with high amplitude?

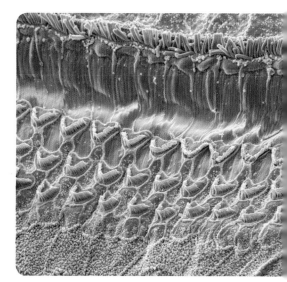

▲ The scanning electron micrograph shows the hairs that project from the inner and outer hair cells. The tectorial membrane has been removed. The function of the outer hair cells is to amplify sound vibrations of the frequency that adjacent inner hair cells detect, making human hearing much more sensitive

Tuning the orchestra

Either attend an orchestral concert or watch an online broadcast of one, then do some experiments using a sound generator.

At the start of the concert the musicians must tune their instruments. Usually an oboist plays an A note (often having used an electronic device to make sure they play the A with a standard pitch of 440 Hz) and all the other instruments are tuned to this.

Why do the other instruments tune to the pitch of the oboe? How can instruments that cannot play an A at 440 Hz still tune their instruments to the same pitch as the rest of the orchestra? How accurately can musicians tune their instruments with low notes and with high notes—try to give your answers in Hz (hertz). If you do not know the answers to these questions you could ask a musician.

▲ Learning to play in tune can be a challenge for young violinists

ATL Affective skills

Practicing resilience

How do people deal with difficult events that change their lives, such as cancer leading to a person having to live life with a ileostomy bag or a parent receiving a diagnosis in their child of cystic fibrosis or a medical condition leading to the onset of dialysis treatment? Many people generally adapt well over time to life-altering situations due to resilience.

One circumstance that supports a resilient response to life altering circumstances is close personal relationships with family members, friends or community members. Accepting help supports a resilient response. Supporting a resilient response involves such things as discussing what has been lost, expressing and resolving the grief, gaining an enabling perspective on the situation, encouraging exercise, maintaining optimism and practicing empathy.

Summative assessment

Statement of inquiry:

Each component in a system must perform its specific function at the right time and place for the system as a whole to be successful.

Introduction

In this summative assessment you investigate the need for a gut in humans, when and where certain functions are performed in the gut and the consequences if functions are not performed effectively.

 Cystic fibrosis

1. Cystic fibrosis (CF) is the most common genetic disease in Canada, the United States of America and north-west Europe. Chloride channels in certain cells do not function resulting in very viscous mucus that causes lung problems and blocks the pancreatic duct.

   a) State the function of the pancreatic duct. [1]

A percentile (centile) is a measure used to indicate the value below which a given percentage of observations in a population occur. For example, 50% of people in the population have a height lower than the 50th percentile. The bar chart (right) shows the percentage of female CF patients in the United States and Canada that are in each of six different height percentile classes. If their heights matched the distribution for the general population, then 25% of them would be above the 75th percentile.

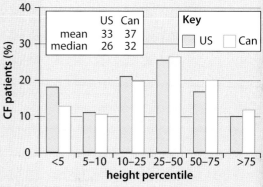

Source of data: http://ajcn.nutrition.org/content/69/3/531.full

   b) Using the US data in the bar chart, deduce the effect of CF on growth. [3]

   c) Suggest reasons for the effect of CF on growth. [3]

   d) The data suggests that where a CF patient lives affects their chance of growing at a normal or a reduced rate. Deduce where in North America patients seem to have a higher chance of normal growth rates and suggest possible reasons for this. [3]

2. Some patients have an ileostomy bag fitted. Material from the gut can pass into it at the end of the small intestine. An opening (stoma) through the abdomen wall is created surgically and the bag is connected to this and concealed under clothing.

a) Suggest one reason for fitting an ileostomy bag. [1]

b) Compare the functions of an ileostomy bag and the large intestine by giving one similarity and one difference. [2]

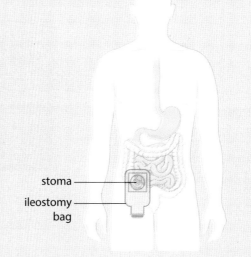

stoma

ileostomy bag

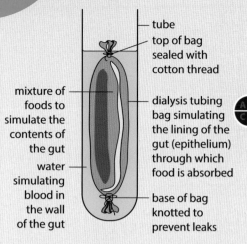

tube

top of bag sealed with cotton thread

mixture of foods to simulate the contents of the gut

dialysis tubing bag simulating the lining of the gut (epithelium) through which food is absorbed

water simulating blood in the wall of the gut

base of bag knotted to prevent leaks

c) What change in diet would you recommend to a patient after they have had an ileostomy bag fitted? [1]

d) What change in the volume of urine would you expect after the fitting of an ileostomy bag? [1]

Investigating food absorption

Dialysis tubing is manufactured for use in kidney machines. It can be used to simulate absorption of food by diffusion in the gut, because it is similar in permeability. The diagram shows how such a simulation could be contrived.

Possible foods to test:

Digested foods	Undigested foods
glucose	starch
aspartic acid (an amino acid)	casein (milk powder)

The presence of such foods can be detected using these methods:

- glucose—with urine test strips or with Benedict's test
- starch—with the iodine test
- amino acids—with universal indicator or a pH probe
- casein—with the biuret test.

3. Formulate a hypothesis for the function of the gut (to digest food) and explain it using scientific reasoning. [3]

4. Design an experiment to test your hypothesis, including how you will control the variables. [8]

5. Explain how you will collect data in your investigation. [4]

Analysis and evaluation

6. Present the results of your investigation in a results table. [3]

7. Interpret the data and explain your results using scientific reasoning. [3]

8. Evaluate the validity of your hypothesis based on the outcome of your investigation. [3]

9. Evaluate your method. Was it a valid test of your hypothesis? [3]

10. Explain how you could extend or improve your method. [3]

Researching the risks of GM foods

The following text is from Netherwood, T. *et al.* 2004. *Nature Biotechnology.* Vol 22. Pp 204–209. Read the passage and work through the tasks that follow.

Assessing the survival of transgenic plant DNA in the human gastrointestinal tract

If we ingest genetically modified foods, new genes enter our gut that are absent in equivalent non-GM foods. Antibiotic resistance genes which are often used as markers in genetic modification are a potential concern, because they might be transferred to bacteria in the gut. Research has been done to investigate whether new genes persist in the gut or are destroyed, and whether new genes can be transferred to gut bacteria to create novel and potentially dangerous strains. The researchers used seven volunteers with ileostomy bags (who can easily provide samples of gut contents at the end of the small intestines) and twelve volunteers with a normal intact gut.

The volunteers were all fed GM soya containing a gene called *epsps*. At time intervals after this the contents of the ileostomy bags were collected from the seven volunteers and egested feces was collected from the twelve volunteers. These materials were tested for the presence of the *epsps* gene. None of the feces from the twelve volunteers showed any trace of it. The material from the ileostomy bags did contain the *epsps* gene, with between 3.7% and 0.0001% of the ingested copies of the gene recovered in the seven volunteers.

At the start of the experiment tests had been done to check whether bacteria in the intestines of the volunteers already had the *epsps* gene. None of the bacteria in the feces collected from the volunteers with a normal gut contained the *epsps* gene either before or after the experiment. In the material collected from the ileostomy bags very small numbers of bacteria contained the gene before and after the experiment. There was no evidence of an increase during the experiment, suggesting that transfer of this gene to gut bacteria had occurred before the experiment started.

11. a) Explain why it was essential for scientists to get permission from the volunteers before carrying out this research. [3]

b) Few scientists consider the ingestion of new genes in GM foods to be a significant risk. Explain why research into this issue is still worthwhile. [3]

c) Explain the conclusions that can be drawn about what happens to the DNA of the *epsps* gene as it passes through the small and large intestines. [3]

d) Write a brief newspaper article explaining the research into the risks of ingesting GM foods, for readers who have little biological knowledge but strong views on this subject. [6]

5 Movement

Movement happens at every level, from subatomic particles to galaxies within the universe.

▲ Many birds travel huge distances when they migrate. Although weighing only 113 grams, the Arctic tern has the longest route of any species, flying 71,000 kilometres each year between Greenland and Antarctica. What is the reason for migrations?

◄ As the moon moves around the Earth, the pull that it exerts on sea water causes tidal movements. The greatest vertical rise and fall occurs in the Bay of Fundy, Nova Scotia, where it can be as much as 16 metres.

▲ The maple syrup industry takes advantage of the seasonal movement of sap in the conducting tissues of maple trees. In cold climates, maple trees store starch in their roots before the winter. The starch is converted into sugar in the late winter and rises in the tree trunk. Taps are hammered into the trees and the sap drips out into collecting containers. The syrup is then concentrated by evaporating the water

▲ Much warfare is based on ballistics - the launch of projectiles. The projectile in this case is an arrow, with the stretched bowstring providing kinetic energy and an archer establishing the trajectory. What other examples of ballistics can do you know? Do living organisms use this type of movement?

▲ Huge quantities of rock can be moved by hydraulic excavators. Pumping of hydraulic fluid into or out of a cylinder barrel causes the piston inside the barrel and an attached piston rod to move. This transmits a unidirectional force in one of two directions. Different hydraulic cylinders are needed for movement in other directions. What are similarities and differences are there between hydraulic systems of movement and muscle action in animals?

Key concept: Change

Related concept: Movement

Global context: Fairness and development

Introduction

Movement is a change in position with respect to other things in an environment. Within a biological context, materials can flow, like blood through vessels or air through lungs. At the molecular level, materials can be moved across cell membranes by pumps or diffuse in response to concentration differences. Muscle contractions can move arms and legs in relation to one another to achieve locomotion. Energy can move through systems like the waste heat rising from compost heaps or sunlight moving through the atmosphere to be intercepted by forest canopies.

Movement relates to the key concept of change, in this case a change of position. Inquiry into the concepts of movement and change involves understanding and evaluating how and why things move in relation to other elements of the environment. Indeed, movement can be detected by comparing the position of something at different times. This change could be something like a change in the position of one structure in relation to another, such as the changes in relative position of a jumping monkey and the tree it jumps from, or over time, such as with the opening and closing of flower buds.

Changes in the movement of water in the atmosphere due to forest clearance may impact rainfall patterns. Changes in the movement of water in the oceans due to climate change affect weather patterns, causing drought or abundant rainfall in areas of the world that would not normally experience these phenomena. Overall, such changes may severely impact the future of the planet, so in this chapter we explore the global context of fairness and development.

▼ Although flower buds don't seem to move at all, if you take a time-lapse film of them, it will reveal very slow movements when the flowers open. Can you think of something in the living world that does not move at all?

Statement of inquiry:

The changes in the weather patterns caused by current economic activity may not be fair to future generations.

In the living world, movement can occur on a range of scales:

- Substances can move in and out of cells across the cell membrane. Water molecules, for example, enter or leave cells by osmosis. In a similar way, individual molecules can move between tissues.

- Liquids, such as the blood in veins and arteries, and gases, such as air in the windpipe, are pumped around the body in a process known as mass flow.

- Different parts of an organism can be moved in relation to each other, through growth or muscle action.

- Whole organisms can move from one location to another—this is locomotion.

Particle theory states that atoms and molecules are constantly in motion. The direction of movement of individual particles is random. This random movement causes particles to become evenly spread, because more move from areas of high concentration to low concentration than in the opposite direction. The net movement of particles from an area of high concentration to an area of low concentration is known as diffusion.

The movement of gases between body cells and the blood in capillaries is an example of diffusion in living things. Carbon dioxide is a waste product of aerobic respiration so it is at a higher concentration in cells than in blood passing through capillaries in tissues. Oxygen is used up by aerobic respiration so it is at a lower concentration inside cells than in nearby blood. For this reason, gases are exchanged in tissues through diffusion by oxygen moving into the tissues and carbon dioxide moving out.

▲ This experiment demonstrates the diffusion of a gas. On the left, two gas jars are arranged with their open ends together, but their contents, gaseous bromine (brown) and air, are kept separate by a glass lid. When the lid is removed, diffusion occurs, and bromine can be seen gradually spreading into the upper jar (apparatus on the right). How can this be explained using particle theory?

Exploring diffusion through simulations and animations

An animation is a dynamic visual model of a process. A simulation allows the viewer to alter variables within an animation or to follow investigative procedures as the animation plays. Animations and simulations help us to visualize events happening on a molecular level that are otherwise not directly visible.

In the interactive simulation of diffusion across a membrane produced by the University of Colorado, Boulder (https://phet. colorado.edu/en/simulation/membrane-channels), you can control the insertion of channels into a membrane and observe the particles that can pass through by diffusion. In a different activity, produced by the Concord Consortium (https://concord. org/stem-resources/diffusion), you can investigate how the random movement and collision of particles result in diffusion.

Write a script for an animation that shows how random movement and collisions between particles results in diffusion. Your animation should also take into account how external factors, such as temperature, influence the rate of diffusion.

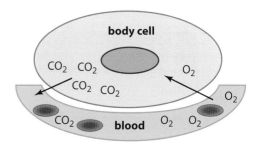

▲ Gas exchange between the body cells and blood

What movement occurs in osmosis?

A solution is a mixture that contains dissolved material, known as a solute, in a solvent. For example, in a salt water solution, salt is the solute and water is the solvent.

If two solutions are separated by a barrier that doesn't let the solute through, then the solvent moves from the area of lower solute concentration to the area of high solute concentration. In the living world, where water is almost always the solvent, the solute–solvent interaction limits the movement of some water molecules, effectively lowering their concentration. The net movement of water through a selectively permeable membrane is known as osmosis.

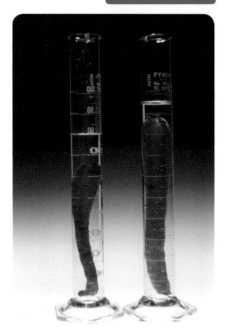

▲ The vial on the left contains a carrot in a solution of sodium chloride (table salt) and water. The vial on the right contains a carrot in water only. If both carrots were initially the same size at the start of the experiment, how can the difference in their size be explained?

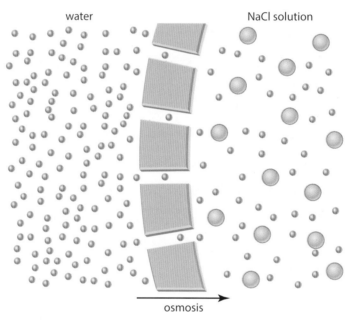

water   NaCl solution

osmosis

▲ Osmosis is the movement of water through a selectively permeable membrane from a lower to a higher solute concentration. Here, because the membrane is impermeable to sodium chloride, water diffuses into the side with the sodium chloride solution

---

(ABCD) Experiment

Aim

In this experiment we will use potato tissue to investigate the process of osmosis in cells.

Method

1. Prepare six different concentrations of sodium chloride solution, as indicated in the table.

Concentration of NaCl solution (mol L^{-1})	0.00	0.10	0.20	0.30	0.50	0.80
Volume of distilled H$_2$O (cm^3)	100	90	80	70	50	20
Volume of 1 M NaCl (cm^3)	0	10	20	30	50	80

2. Place 20 cm³ of each solution into three separate test tubes; this will result in three sets of six test tubes, with each of the sets containing a full concentration range of NaCl, from 0.0 molar to 0.80 molar.

3. Using a core borer, create 18 cylinders of potato tissue; remove the potato peel and place them onto a tile or a paper towel. Then using a scalpel and a ruler (calibrated in millimetres), cut the cores into 30 mm lengths.

4. Place one potato core into each of the test tubes and store for two hours at room temperature.

5. After two hours, remove the cores from the test tubes and measure them. Record your measurements for each set of test tubes.

Using the data you collected, determine the percentage change in length and then graph it against sodium chloride concentration of the solutions. What is the significance of the point where the trend line on the graph crosses the x-axis?

Describe how this method can be modified using a percentage mass change instead of a percentage length change. Would using mass or length as a reporter be more accurate?

Extension

Repeat the experiment using boiled potato cores: are your results any different and if yes, how do you explain this?

What is the relationship between gas exchange and transpiration?

PLANTS

The diagram (right) shows a leaf from a flowering plant. Photosynthesis occurs in chloroplasts in the mesophyll. Carbon dioxide is used and oxygen is produced. This creates concentration gradients which cause carbon dioxide to diffuse into the leaf and oxygen to diffuse out. The exchange of gases occurs via stomata, which are microscopic pores in the epidermis.

Whenever the stomata are open, water vapour molecules can pass through them. Water evaporates from moist cell walls inside the leaf creating a high concentration. If the concentration of water vapor in the atmosphere outside is lower, it diffuses out through the stomata in a process called transpiration.

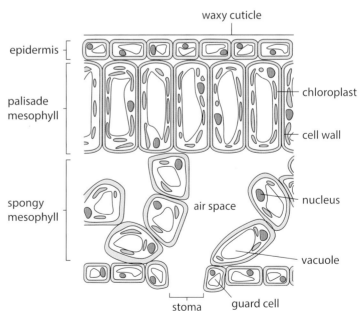

waxy cuticle
epidermis
palisade mesophyll
chloroplast
cell wall
spongy mesophyll
air space
nucleus
vacuole
stoma
guard cell

▲ A plastic bag has been secured over the branches of a potted plant. The inside of the bag has condensation on it from water transpired from the plant's leaves. How can this be explained?

⊕ Experiment

The diagram below shows a potometer. This apparatus consists of a leafy shoot fitted tightly through a hole in a rubber stopper, a reservoir (to the right of the shoot) and a graduated capillary tube. A bubble in the capillary tube marks the zero point. As the plant takes up water, the bubble will move along the capillary tube. The progress of the bubble can be monitored by recording its position over time. The tap below the reservoir allows the bubble to be reset to carry out replicates.

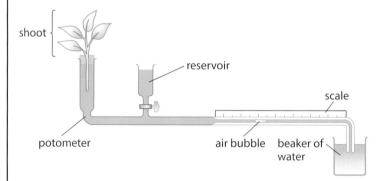

Design an experiment to measure the effect of wind speed on transpiration. You can simulate wind using a fan; you can measure wind speed using an anemometer.

1. What are the units of wind speed?

2. Discuss the concept of movement in relation to this experiment.

3. Transpiration rates are not as high as expected when fans blow air at very high speeds: have you noticed this? Suggest a testable hypothesis that could be investigated to explain this observation.

PHYSIOLOGY

How does water move from roots to leaves?

Transpiration causes a loss of water from cell walls inside the leaf. These walls regain the lost water from vessels within a tissue called xylem. No leaf cell is more than a few cells away from the nearest xylem vessel. The water is drawn through the walls of leaf cells by a type of capillary action. It depends on the attraction between water molecules and cellulose in cell walls; this attraction is known as adhesion.

Adhesion of water to leaf cell walls can be modelled by placing the edge of a dry piece of blotting paper or paper towel in water. These types of paper consist almost entirely of cellulose. Water is quickly drawn through the paper, even if it has to rise vertically to do so.

No matter how much water cell walls inside the leaf lose by transpiration, they do not dry out because of adhesion. When the walls lose water, it is replaced with an equal amount sucked out of the nearest xylem vessel. Transpiration therefore causes a pulling force (suction) inside xylem vessels. We might expect this powerful force to cause water molecules in the xylem to be pulled apart from each other and change to water vapor. This does not usually happen because water molecules are held together by hydrogen bonds. This property of water is cohesion. Water rises in the stem through the combined pull of transpiration and the cohesion of water molecules.

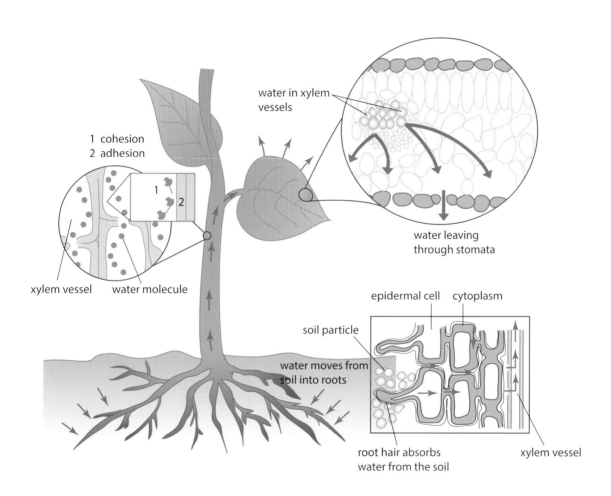

1 cohesion
2 adhesion

xylem vessel   water molecule

water in xylem vessels

water leaving through stomata

epidermal cell   cytoplasm

soil particle

water moves from soil into roots

root hair absorbs water from the soil

xylem vessel

◀ This piece of celery was placed in water that had blue food coloring added to it. Transpiration from the celery leaves (now removed) created suction, causing the blue coloring to be drawn into the xylem vessels and moved upwards. The position of xylem tissue can be deduced from the pattern of blue coloration. The celery sticks that we eat are leaf stalks (petioles) not stems. What pattern of blue coloration would you expect if a true stem had been used in this experiment?

We can use a leafy shoot of *Pelargonium* (geranium) to investigate movement of liquids through the xylem. Vascular bundles leading to the larger leaves will have greater velocity of sap movement, so the blue dye penetrates higher up the stem in a given time.

Method

- Prepare a very concentrated solution of methylene blue dye in water (you want the color of your solution to be almost black).

- Cut a leafy stem of *Pelargonium* and stand it in the dye solution.

- After an hour, remove the stem from the solution and cut serial sections through it using a clean scalpel. Record whether the dye is visible through the sections you cut.

Based on your understanding of how liquids move through the vascular bundles of plants, propose a formula for the rate of movement, then use this formula to quantify the rate of movement in the *Pelargonium* stem.

METABOLISM

How do sugars move in plants?

Plants make sugars (carbohydrates) by photosynthesis in leaves and other organs that contain chloroplasts. These sugars can be moved throughout the plant, either to storage organs or for use in other plant tissues. Plants have a specialized tissue for the transport of carbohydrates known as phloem.

The pressure-flow hypothesis is used to explain the movement of sap within phloem. A high concentration of sugar in the phloem near the source of production in the leaf draws water from the nearby xylem. This creates pressure within the phloem. At the same time, sugar is withdrawn at other locations within the plant, either at storage organs or in tissues that will use the sugar. These are known as sinks. This causes water to leave the phloem by osmosis and so creates low pressure. The phloem sap therefore moves from the source where there is high pressure to the low pressure sinks.

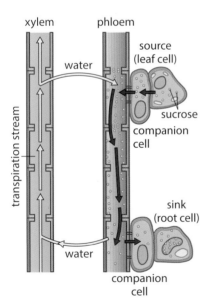

It is not certain whether trees could grow to a greater height than the tallest tree currently known, which is about 110 m. This tree is found in the wet temperate forests of northern California. As trees grow taller, gravity increasingly restricts the movement of water upwards towards the leaves of the tree. This limits both the growth in height and the expansion of the leaf area, which will impose a maximum rate of photosynthesis even when sufficient soil moisture is present.

The following graph shows the variation in leaf length (l) with tree height (h) of 1,925 tree species. Grey triangles represent individual leaf samples. Red dots represent the mean of the five longest leaves for that tree height for a certain tree and green dots represent the mean of the five shortest leaves for that height for a certain tree.

1. Estimate the mean length of the:

   a) longest leaves for a 90 m tree

   b) shortest leaves for a 90 m tree

   c) longest leaves for a 20 m tree

   d) shortest leaves for a 20 m tree.

2. As the height of the tree increases, outline what happens to:

   a) the maximum leaf length

   b) the minimum leaf length

   c) the variability in leaf length.

3. Explain what limits the rate at which carbohydrates can be carried away from the leaves.

4. With reference to photosynthesis and transpiration, state one advantage and one disadvantage of a large surface area leaf.

5. Does the data in the graph suggest that there is a limit to tree height?

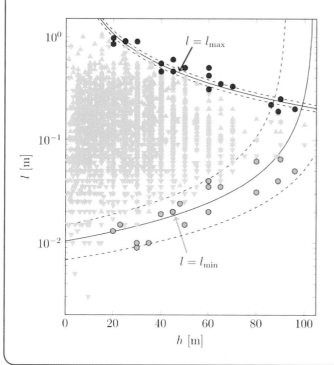

How are materials moved inside multicellular organisms?

PHYSIOLOGY

Multicellular organisms often have specialized systems for the transport of materials throughout the organism. Vascular plants have phloem tissue specialized for the movement of carbohydrates and xylem tissues which are specialized for the transport of water and nutrients.

Humans have a circulatory system that consists of blood vessels, a heart and blood. The blood is moved around the body by the

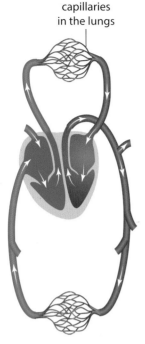

capillaries
in the lungs

▲ This diagram represents the flow of blood through the chambers of the heart and around the body, with the arteries carrying oxygenated blood (red) and veins carrying deoxygenated blood (blue). Gas exchange occurs in the capillaries of the lungs and the tissues

contraction of the heart. The blood carries nutrients and oxygen to the tissues and picks up carbon dioxide and other waste products and carries them to the lungs and to the kidneys.

The heart is a double pump with the right side pumping blood to the lungs and the left side to all other organs. Blood vessels include veins which carry blood toward the heart, arteries which carry blood away from the heart and smaller vessels known as capillaries where materials are exchanged between the blood and surrounding tissues across the thin layer of cells forming the capillary walls.

Blood movement in the circulatory system

The function of several blood vessels is described below. Read the descriptions and deduce the location of the vessel in the diagram to the left.

- **Vena cava:** a vein which brings deoxygenated blood to the right atrium of the heart

- **Aorta:** an artery which carries oxygenated blood away from the left ventricle to the tissues of the body

- **Pulmonary artery:** carries deoxygenated blood to the lungs from the right ventricle

- **Pulmonary vein:** carries oxygenated blood from the lung to the heart

PHYSIOLOGY

What is the role of muscle cells in moving blood through the heart?

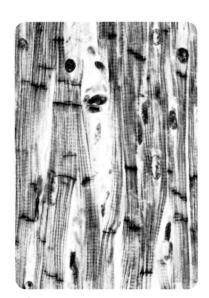

▲ A micrograph of heart (cardiac) muscle cells

Cardiac muscle cells are unique to the heart. Their function is to contract and exert force on blood inside the heart chambers. Within the chambers known as the atria, the coordinated contraction of these cells causes a volume decrease that pushes blood into the ventricles. Similarly, the coordinated contraction of cardiac muscle cells in the wall of the ventricles decreases the volume of these chambers. This causes the movement of blood, including blood cells, around the body.

In the human body, there muscles that cause movements within our internal organs which are not consciously controlled. For example, the radial and circular muscles in the iris of the eye, move the iris to adjust the size of the pupil without our direct input. Muscle that contracts without conscious control is involuntary. Cardiac muscle is another example of involuntary muscle. The frequency and power of our heart beat is controlled throughout our lives without us being aware of doing it. What ensures that cardiac muscle pumps blood in the right direction?

How does the structure of arteries and veins affect the movement of blood?

With each heartbeat, blood enters the arteries under high pressure. This causes the artery walls to be stretched. The elastic fibers in the artery wall then return the artery to its original diameter. This expansion and contraction of arteries can be detected in the wrist and in the neck by holding fingers over the artery and feeling a pulse. Blood propelled by the next heart beat continues to push blood along in the circulatory system so that blood flows in one direction.

After the exchange of materials in capillaries, blood collects in veins. Veins have valves that prevent the backward flow of blood. They also depend on the contraction of skeletal muscles to increase pressure on the veins which returns the blood back to the heart.

Referring to the micrograph, compare the structure of arteries and veins.

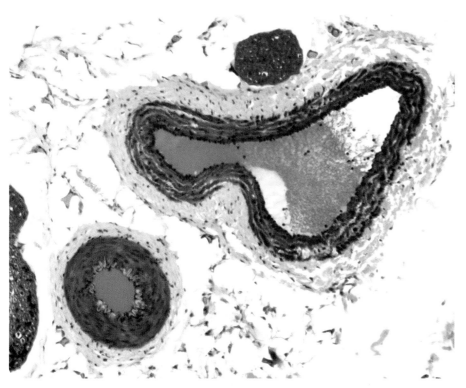

▲ The light micrograph is a section through tissue containing an artery (bottom left) and a vein (top right). Within the wall of the artery and the vein is a layer of smooth muscle and elastic fibers (purple) and a layer of connective tissue (light brown). Arteries carry blood away from the heart, while veins carry blood back to the heart from the rest of the body

How do skeletal muscles effect movement?

Movement such as running is achieved by extending and flexing (bending) limbs in a voluntary fashion. Voluntary muscles work in conjunction with the skeletal system to make the body move. Skeletal muscle consists of elongated structures called muscle fibers.

Each muscle fiber contains many parallel structures known as myofibrils. Every myofibril consists of a series of separate contractile units called sarcomeres. It is the combined action of millions of sarcomeres within a muscle that causes the muscle as a whole to contract with great force.

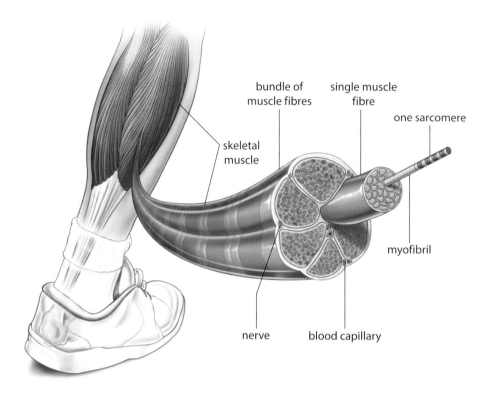

▲ The structure of human skeletal muscles

For example, the biceps and triceps muscles work to flex and extend the human arm. Muscle is attached to bones by tendons. The biceps is attached by tendons to the scapula (shoulder blade) and to the radius, which is the smaller of the two bones in the forearm. When contracted, the biceps flexes the arm.

The triceps is attached at its upper end to the scapula and also to the humerus, which is the single bone in the upper arm. At its lower end, the triceps is attached to the ulna, the larger of the bones in the forearm. When the triceps contracts, it extends the arm by strengthening the elbow.

The biceps and the triceps are referred to as an antagonistic pair of muscles as they exert force in opposite directions. Antagonistic pairs of muscles create movement when one contracts and the other relaxes. Another example of an antagonistic pair is the quadriceps and hamstrings in the leg.

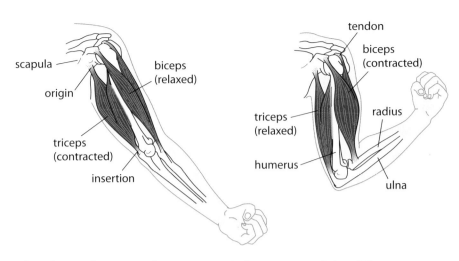

The biceps and triceps muscles are antagonistic; their concerted movement enables the movement of the whole arm. Why are separate muscles needed for flexing and extending the arm?

The place where two bones meet is known as a joint. There are several types of joint, each permitting a certain range of movement. For example, at the elbow is a hinge joint which permits extension and flexion. Bones are held together at a joint by tough cords or sheets of tissue called ligaments.

🅐🅑🅒🅓 Experiment

Safety note: Raw chicken may be contaminated by the bacteria Salmonella. Keep your hands away from your face and mouth throughout this investigation; if available, use gloves.

Materials

- A chicken wing

- Dissecting equipment: tray, scalpel, blunt probe, forceps

Recording results

- Design a data table that will allow you to note observations about the various structures found in your chicken wing, including muscles, tendons and ligaments.

- As you work, draw and label a simple diagram of your chicken wing, which should show the location and distribution of various tissues.

Method

1. Rinse the chicken wing under cool, running water and thoroughly dry it with a paper towel.

2. Pick up the wing and imagine it is still on the chicken. Do you think your wing is from the right or left side of the bird? Explain.

3. Move the joints. Describe the range of movement of the joints.

4. Carefully cut the skin along the entire length of the chicken wing, trying not to cut through the muscles below the skin. Remove the skin by first sliding your finger under it to break some of the connective tissues then grabbing it, pulling hard and cutting from top to bottom.

5. Observe the muscles on the wing. Use a blunt probe to separate the individual muscles from each other without tearing them. How many different groups of muscles are attached to the "elbow" joint?

6. Straighten the chicken wing and hold it horizontally above the tray. Pull on each of the muscles and note the movement it causes. Turn the wing upside down and bend the joints. Again pull on each muscle and note how the bones move. On your diagram, label each muscle that flexes a joint and each muscle that extends a joint.

7. Observe the shiny white tendons at the ends of muscles, then remove them, along with the muscles, to expose the bones of the chicken wing. Observe the white ligaments. How many ligaments hold a joint together?

8. Bend and straighten the joint and observe how the bones fit together. The shiny, white covering of the joint surfaces is made of cartilage.

PHYSIOLOGY

What is the role of muscle movement in the ventilation of the human lungs?

It is muscle contraction that causes ventilation of the lungs by the twin processes of inhalation and exhalation. Two muscle types increase the volume of the thorax and therefore lower the pressure when they contract, to cause inhalation. Shallow exhalation occurs by elastic recoil, but two muscle types can be used if forced exhalation is needed. What is the role of each of these muscle types:

- radial muscle fibres in the diaphragm, which is the sheet-like structure that separates the thorax from the abdomen?

- external intercostal muscles between the ribs, which move the rib cage up and out?

- internal intercostal muscle between the ribs, which move the rib cage down and in?

- abdomen wall muscles, which can push organs in the abdomen in and up?

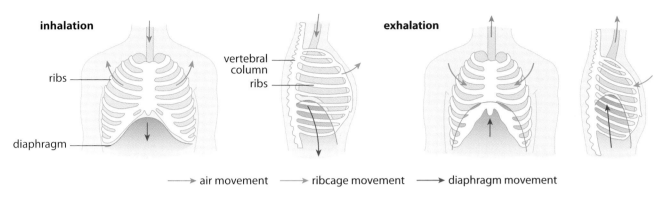

inhalation   exhalation

ribs

vertebral column

ribs

diaphragm

→ air movement   → ribcage movement   → diaphragm movement

▲ Inhalation and exhalation in humans

What movements are required for gas exchange in the alveolus?

Inhaled air passes into the lungs through a rigid tube called the windpipe or trachea. The trachea branches left and right into tubes known as bronchi. Bronchi divide further into smaller tubes: bronchioles. The smallest bronchioles end in groups of alveoli, which are tiny sacs. In the human lung, alveoli are the sites of gas exchange.

These movements occur in alveoli:

- during inhalation the alveolus expands and air is drawn in from the bronchioles

- during exhalation the alveolus decreases in volume and air is forced out into the bronchioles

- blood flows through the capillaries adjacent to the alveolus wall.

How does each of these movements increase the rate of gas exchange in alveoli? You should include the concept of concentration gradients in your answer.

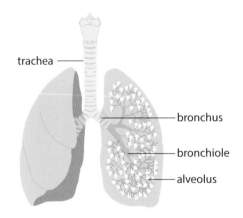

trachea

bronchus

bronchiole

alveolus

▲ The trachea branches into the right and left bronchi. Bronchi subdivide several times into narrower bronchioles. At the end of bronchioles are alveoli, the sites of gas exchange

oxygen-rich blood returns to the heart and is then distributed around the body

inhaled air

alveolus

deoxygenated blood carrying carbon dioxide

carbon dioxide

oxygen

capillary

▲ In the human lung, gas exchange occurs in structures called alveoli

Experiment

Design an experiment to determine the effect of the rest position on variables such as heart rate and ventilation rate.

Ventilation rate can be counted by placing a hand on the rib cage. Stand still for one minute and then measure both ventilation rate and heart rate. Repeat the procedure after one minute in these rest positions: sitting still, lying prone on the ground and lying back at a 45° angle. Other possible positions can be explored.

Discuss possible implications of your results.

PHYSIOLOGY

How does air pollution affect gas exchange?

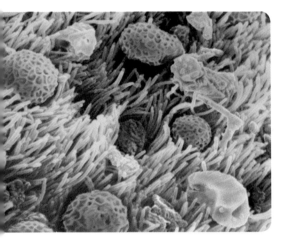

▲ Micrograph of the surface of the trachea with pollen (pink) and dust captured by hair-like cilia (yellow)

Asthma symptoms

Based on the illustration of a normal bronchiole (left) and an inflamed, constricted one with mucus build-up (right) in a person suffering from asthma, predict what the symptoms of asthma might be. Why do people suffering from asthma find it difficult to recover after exercise? How does asthma restrict the movement of air?

Smoking, cooking on stoves that burn wood and the burning of fossil fuels for transportation elevates the level of particulates in inhaled air. Inhaling these airborne particles may cause lung diseases, including cancer, emphysema and asthma.

The surface of the trachea is made up of cells with hair-like cilia. Together with mucus, these cilia serve to trap airborne particles; then, by beating upwards in a wave-like movement, they remove foreign matter from the air ways and lungs. Air pollutants can stop the movement of the cilia, so they do not continue to expel harmful materials.

Asthma is a long-term lung condition in which the bronchioles are inflamed and narrowed, making it harder to breathe normally. An estimated 300 million of the world's population have asthma and in some countries it is the most common long-term disease affecting all age groups. During an asthma episode, inflamed bronchioles react to environmental triggers such as smoke, dust or pollen, which can lead to an immune reaction that causes breathing difficulties.

How do macrophages move?

The large, irregularly shaped cell that has been colored yellow is a macrophage—a type of white blood cell. The smaller cells colored orange are bacteria. The function of the macrophage is to engulf bacteria and other cells that are identified as foreign. It does this by movement to these foreign cells, then movement of the cell membrane to form a cup-shaped structure that closes up around them. How might the macrophage be guided to move towards the bacteria when they are still some distance away?

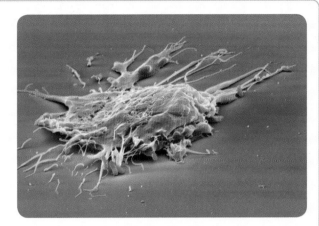

The macrophage is exhibiting amoeboid movement. Find and watch a video of this type of movement and write a description of it.

Data-based question: The impact of exposure to traffic on indicators of asthma

In a study published in the *New England Journal of Medicine*, a team of researchers explored the effects of roadside traffic exposure on people with asthma. The participants in the study were asked to walk for two hours through Hyde Park, a large traffic-free park in central London, on one occasion, and walk along Oxford Street, one of the busiest streets in central London, on a separate occasion. The researchers measured the pH of the participants' exhaled breath two hours before each walk and three hours and six hours after the start of each walk. The lower the pH, the more carbon dioxide is being exhaled. Researchers also measured the level of myeloperoxidase, which is a chemical indicator of swelling.

1. Compare and contrast the changes in exhaled breath pH caused by walking through Hyde Park and along Oxford Street. Explain these results.

2. Calculate the percentage increase of myeloperoxidase between Hyde Park and Oxford Street for participants.

3. Explain the myeloperoxidase results and deduce a conclusion that is supported by this data.

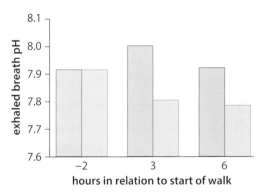

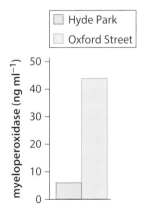

Do plants move?

Four responses of plants are shown in the table below. In each case discuss whether the plant has responded by growth, movement, locomotion or a combination of two or more of these processes.

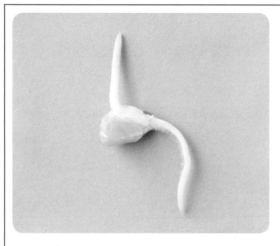

This recently germinated corn seedling is illustrating gravitropism—also known as geotropism. The seed was germinated in a sideways orientation in the dark. Nevertheless, the root is curving and growing downwards (positive gravitropism) and the shoot upwards (negative gravitropism). The emerging plant oriented itself correctly without any cue from the sun—it moved in response to gravity.

Red bryony (*Bryonia dioica*) is a climbing vine that illustrates a type of response known as thigmotropism, or growth in response to touch. It uses tendrils to wrap around fixed objects and other plants to help it climb.

These seedlings growing towards a window illustrate phototropism. Plant hormones cause cells on the side of the stem that is furthest from the light to elongate. This causes the stem to bend towards the light.

The "sensitive plant" (*Mimosa pudica*) illustrates a type of movement that is a touch response: its leaves close inward after being touched. They flush water out of cells in a hinge-like structure and can put it back again to regain their original form. A similar mechanism exists in carnivorous plants.

Data-based question: Darwin's phototropism experiment

Charles Darwin conducted an experiment on phototropism in the 19th century. He placed canary grass (*Phalaris canariensis*) seedlings in a box open on one side in front of a south-west window. Curvature towards the light was traced and accurately measured.

1. The diagrams shown below illustrate the curvature of three seedlings after eight hours. Explain why Darwin measured three shoots rather than one.

2. The graph shows average shoot curvature over time.

   a) What was the time delay before the shoots start to curve towards the light?

   b) At what time was the shoot curving most rapidly?

   c) Describe the pattern of shoot curvature shown in the graph.

d) Explain the reasons for shoot curvature not rising to more than 90°.

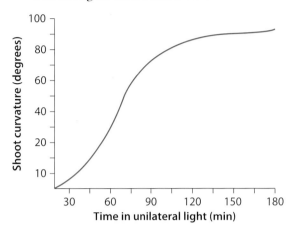

3. a) If a small aluminium foil cap is placed over the top of the shoots, they do not respond to unilateral light. What do you conclude from this?

b) Predict the response if the shoots were kept in the dark.

c) If Darwin's experiment is repeated with different wavelengths of unidirectional light, there is little or no response with some wavelengths but a strong response with blue (450 nm) wavelengths. What conclusions can you draw from this?

Ⓐ Ⓑ Ⓒ Ⓓ Experiment

Invertebrates move using a wide variety of methods. You can investigate these if you make careful observations either in the laboratory or in natural environments. You could also propose hypotheses and devise appropriate experimental procedures to test them. One suggestion is given here.

The woodlouse or slater is a common organism which tends to be found in moist, dark habitats such as under the surface of leaf litter in a forest.

Design an experiment to test the rate of movement of slaters (or a similar organism) in response to an environmental variable, such as temperature, moisture, light or shelter. Different dependent variables could be measured such as the number of turns per unit time, the speed at which a certain distance is covered or the percentage time at rest.

▲ Common shiny woodlice (*Oniscus asellus*) are small terrestrial crustaceans of the order Isopoda. They have a segmented, oval, somewhat flattened body. They live in moist environments, under stones and bark and in decaying vegetation. Some species in this order are able to roll themselves into a ball when threatened.

How are organisms adapted to air and water movement?

We live on a restless planet. Energy from the Sun creates variations in temperature and pressure that drive movement of air in the atmosphere and water in the oceans. Hurricanes, cyclones and tornadoes cause wind speeds of over 100 metres per second. Flow rates in oceans are slower, with the Florida Current among the fastest at 2 metres per second, but the mass of water being moved is more, so the overall power is much greater. Tidal flows and the pounding action of waves have major effects on coastlines. Rainfall and snowfall provide life-sustaining water supplies but also cause flooding; the descent of water from uplands to the sea down waterfalls and in rapids can have major impacts.

These natural abiotic movements pose clear risks for living organisms and for humans, but also opportunities. Consider the examples given here and then research examples of your own choice, both of the harm caused by severe weather events and of the adaptations that species have developed to live in a world of movement.

▲ Coconuts (*Cocos nucifera*) are large buoyant seeds that are naturally dispersed by the sea, so they can germinate and grow into coconut palms at the top of sandy beaches. Coconuts and other tree seeds sometimes travel thousands of kilometres across the ocean.

▲ The torrent duck (*Merganetta armata*) is native to the high Andes of South America. It lives on fast-flowing mountain rivers and is able to swim and dive in white water. It nests under ledges or on sheltered sites beside rivers where predators are unlikely to venture.

▲ Hazel (*Corylus avelana*) has male flowers grouped in hanging catkins. They are produced in early spring before the leaves open and shed huge quantities of light pollen grains when blown by the wind. Female flowers with projecting stigmas are in separate flowers.

▲ Wandering albatross (*Diomedea exulans*) use the techniques of dynamic soaring and slope soaring to fly using energy from winds and waves. They can travel nearly a thousand kilometres per day in this way in search of food, without flapping their wings.

Summative assessment

Statement of inquiry:

The changes in the weather patterns caused by current economic activity may not be fair to future generations.

Introduction

In this summative assessment you will consider how human activities influence the movement of water in the water cycle and on a continental basis. You will need to bear in mind whether it is fair that the benefits of the changes today come at a cost to future generations.

Water evaporation in forests

1. The data below shows the annual rate of water evaporation per square metre from forests of different ages and different types.

    a) State the rate of evaporation from a 60-year-old pine forest. [1]

    b) Calculate the mean evaporation rate for each age of forest, using the data from all forest types. Construct a graph to display these mean evaporation rates. [4]

    c) Outline the trends in the data displayed in the graph. [2]

    d) Suggest reasons for these trends. [3]

    e) Summarize the types and causes of water movement in the water cycle in a forest ecosystem. [5]

Age (years)	Evaporation rate (mm yr^{-1})						
	5	**10**	**20**	**40**	**60**	**100**	**140**
Pine	-	-	-	580	530	450	430
Spruce	-	-	-	540	570	490	440
Birch and aspen	310	350	445	550	590	470	430

Source of data: http://archive.unu.edu/unupress/unupbooks/80635e/80635E0d.htm

Factors affecting the rate of transpiration

You can make a simple apparatus for measuring the rate of transpiration by placing a cutting from a tree such as beech or sycamore in water. Cover the surface of the water with vegetable oil to prevent evaporation.

The rate of change in the mass of the system will be a measure of the rate of transpiration, so you will need to take careful measurements as the mass changes may be small (at the level of milligrams).

2. Describe a method for investigating the effect on transpiration of one environmental variable. Possible variables are: amount of light, speed of air flow from a fan and area of leaves attached to the stem. In your method, include details of how you propose to measure the rate of transpiration with accuracy and precision. [10]

3. Evaluate the apparatus you are using, which is known as a mass potometer. [5]

Transpiration and the Makarieva and Gorshkov hypothesis

▶ The yellow line approximately encloses the Atlantic Forest distribution

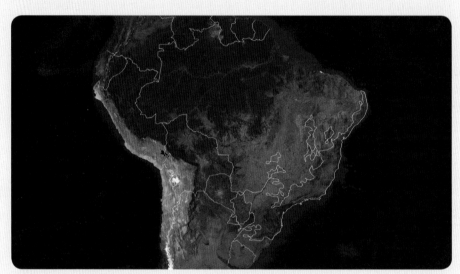

The Atlantic Forest follows the coast of Brazil and also covers a small part of Paraguay and Argentina.

Water evaporating from the Atlantic Forest in Brazil is carried by upward air currents to heights where it is cool enough for the water vapor to condense. Much of the condensed water falls to the ground as rain and can then evaporate again.

When water vapor condenses, there is a drop in atmospheric pressure, because the water occupies much less volume as a liquid than a gas. Low pressure in areas of high evaporation therefore creates winds that draw air in from areas of less evaporation.

4. Explain how clearance of forests could reduce rainfall in areas such as the Atlantic Forest of Brazil. [5]

In tropical forests such as the Atlantic Forest there is high rainfall and river flow rates. The "biotic pump" hypothesis has been developed by Makarieva and Gorshkov to explain how plants within these forests could increase rainfall and river flows. The diagrams shown on the next page illustrate the hypothesis. Diagram I shows forest adjacent to ocean and diagram II shows desert adjacent to ocean.

I

II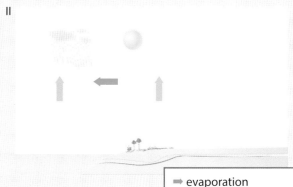

➡ evaporation
➡ movement of moist air

5. Using scientific reasoning, formulate a hypothesis for whether there will be more evaporation from the intact Atlantic Forest of Brazil, or from the surface of the Atlantic Ocean off the coast of Brazil. [5]

6. Using your scientific knowledge, explain how plants can increase rainfall and river flows according to the "biotic pump" hypothesis. [6]

According to the biotic pump hypothesis, clearance of the Atlantic Forest of Brazil will not only reduce rainfall in that forest, but also in the Amazonian rainforests to the west. Diagram III illustrates the effect of forest clearance on a coastal forest and diagram IV the effect of continuous forest cover across a continent.

III

IV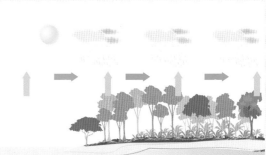

➡ evaporation
➡ movement of moist air

7. Explain what data you would want to collect in a scientific investigation aimed at testing the hypothesis that clearance of the Atlantic Forest of Brazil will reduce rainfall and so threaten the Amazonian rainforest. [8]

8. Discuss whether the further clearance of Atlantic Forest is justified for purposes of expansion of towns and cities, development of new industries, increased cattle farming or the growth of sugar-cane, coffee, tea, tobacco and biofuel crops. Try to reach scientifically supported judgments. Consider the global context of fairness and development in your discussion. [10]

6 Interaction

Interactions occur between all objects, even those as small as water molecules. One side of each molecule is slightly positively charged and the other slightly negatively charged so water molecules are attracted to each other. Because of these electrostatic interactions the surface of water behaves as though it is elastic—a property known as surface tension.

An interaction takes place when we sneeze with our mouth open. We force air out violently. Newton's third law of motion states that for every action there is an equal and opposite reaction. According to this law, there should be a reaction to the forward movement of air. What movement do you expect to occur as the reaction? See if you notice it next time you sneeze.

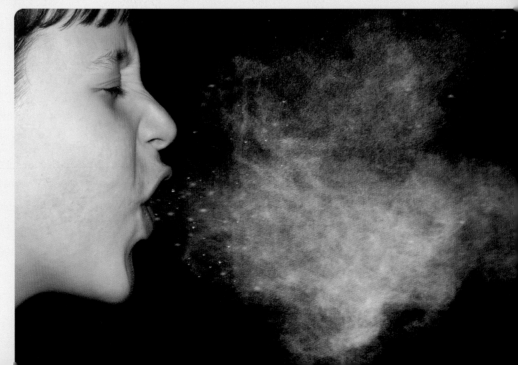

▲ By understanding interactions and being able to predict their outcomes, scientists have been able to send probes to distant parts of the solar system with amazing precision, for example, the rendezvous of the *Rosetta* probe with the comet 67P. In this example the main interactions were gravitational forces, which act between all objects with mass.

▲ A 305 meter radio telescope at Arecibo in Puerto Rico is part of a network of observatories that are attempting interaction with life elsewhere in our galaxy. The SETI program searches for transmissions from intelligent extra-terrestrial civilizations and the METI program transmits messages that distant civilizations might receive, though we would not receive any responses to these messages for thousands of years.

Key concept: Relationships

Related concept: Interaction

Global context: Identities and relationships

Introduction

Interactions are effects that things have on each other. The things could be living organisms, systems within organisms, non-living objects or chemical substances. Physics investigates fundamental interactions such as gravity and electromagnetism, interactions which have predictable results. In biology, interactions are much more complex and their outcomes are harder to predict, but they are nonetheless important.

Interactions with other animals, with other humans and especially with our colleagues, friends and family allow us to build relationships that shape our identity. The global context of this chapter is therefore identities and relationships.

▶ The Four Pests campaign was begun by Mao Zedong in 1958. The Eurasian tree sparrow was one of the targeted species because it was eating some of the rice grown for human consumption. The campaign was successful in almost eliminating tree sparrows from China in the years that followed, but because they also eat locusts and other insect pests of rice crops, the result was a substantial decrease in food availability, rather than an increase. This shows how important it is to understand interactions in biology

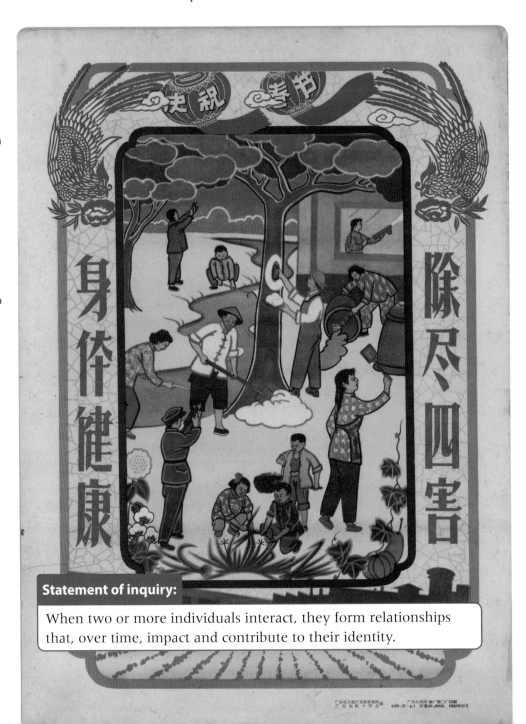

Statement of inquiry:

When two or more individuals interact, they form relationships that, over time, impact and contribute to their identity.

Interactions between animals are the main focus of this chapter. Some relationships between animals may seem one-sided, for example, the predator harms its prey by killing and eating it, but every species has effects on other species, and animals in a group all affect each other.

Interactions between animals involve responses. Most of these responses are mediated by the nervous system, so in this chapter we consider how sensory information is processed and how decisions are made that lead to a response.

Interactions between species can be analyzed to find whether they are beneficial or cause harm. For example, a mutualistic relationship between two species benefits them both. Parasitism is an example of a relationship that benefits one species and causes harm to the other. Relationships that harm both species are unlikely to persist. In this chapter, we look at a wide range of types of relationship and this is therefore the key concept.

▲ A cheetah stalks its prey, using sensory receptors and its nervous system to decide whether to begin a chase. This depends on how close the cheetah can get to the prey before it is detected

▼ Two types of mutually beneficial relationship are evident in this photo of a reef off Komodo in Indonesia. The fish are *Chromis viridis* (blue-green chromis), *Amblyglyphidodon aureus* (golden damselfish) and *Labroides dimidiatus* (bluestreak cleaner wrasse)

How are signals transmitted by the nervous system?

A basic function of the nervous system is to transmit signals from one part of the body to another. To understand how this is done we need some basic information. The following text box gives 10 important ideas about the nervous system.

▲ How does a message in a bottle differ from signals carried by the nervous system?

1. A nerve impulse is an electrical signal that is used to convey a signal in the nervous system.

2. Neurons are cells in the nervous system that can transmit impulses.

3. Neurons consist of two main parts: a cell body with a nucleus and cytoplasm, and long narrow nerve fibers extending out from the cell body.

4. Nerve fibers vary in length from relatively short to over a metre long, which is an enormous length for a structure that is part of a single cell.

5. Nerve impulses can travel at up to 120 metres per second along nerve fibers.

6. Nerve fibers are grouped in bundles, with a protective sheath around the outside. These structures are called nerves.

7. Nerves can contain anything from just a few up to millions of nerve fibers.

8. Every organ has one or more nerves connecting it to the brain or spinal cord.

9. A junction between two neurons is called a synapse.

10. Nerve impulses cannot pass across a synapse and instead a chemical signal is used. The chemical is called a neurotransmitter.

Transmitting signals

Use the information in the text box to write a summary of how signals are transmitted by the nervous system. Make your summary as clear and interesting as possible and include some illustrations if you can.

How does a nerve fiber transmit a signal?

Nerve fibers can vary in diameter from about 5 to 20 micrometres, but most are about 10 micrometres wide—a hundredth of a millimetre and about the same width as a blood capillary. Nerve impulses can move at up to 120 metres per second along nerve fibers, helping us to respond very rapidly to stimuli, especially those signifying danger or opportunity.

The structure of nerve fibers is simple. They are cylindrical in shape and consist of a cell membrane with cytoplasm inside. It is this membrane that is central to the movement of nerve impulses. There is always a voltage across the membrane due to an imbalance in positively and negatively charged ions between the cytoplasm inside and the fluid outside. This voltage remains at −70 millivolts (mV), except when an impulse is passing.

During a nerve impulse the voltage rises to +40 mV and then almost immediately returns to −70 mV. These voltage changes are due to channels in the membrane opening briefly and letting ions through, then closing. The first channels to open allow sodium ions to diffuse inwards, causing the voltage to rise to +40 mV. Other channels then open allowing potassium ions to diffuse out, causing a return to −70 mV. Pumps in the membrane then move the sodium and potassium ions back where they started, to prepare for another nerve impulse.

Nerve impulses have some distinctive properties:

- They are **"all or nothing"**—either there is a full nerve impulse with the voltage rising to +40mV or there is none at all.

- They are **"one-way"** because an impulse always starts at one end of the nerve fiber and travels to the other—it never goes in the opposite direction.

- They are a **"domino effect"**. An impulse at one point along a nerve fiber causes an impulse at the next point along the fiber and so on from one end to the other.

1 Can you think of any other examples of all-or-nothing, one-way, or domino effects?

2 Discuss whether the spread of a disease within a population has the same properties as transmission of a nerve impulse along a nerve fiber.

3 Discuss whether the movement of an impulse along a nerve fiber is an example of reaction or interaction.

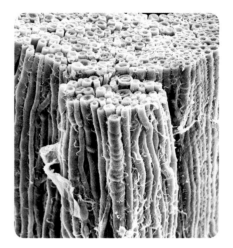

▲ Hundreds of nerve fibers are visible where a nerve has been cut. Rope-like collagen molecules hold the nerve fibers together in a bundle

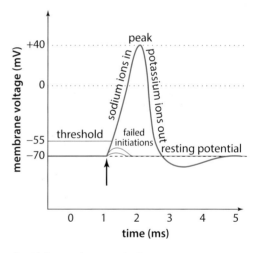

▲ Voltage changes during a nerve impulse. The start of the impulse is indicated with an arrow

PHYSIOLOGY ## What is a reflex action?

Imagine you are going to take a bath, but you forget to test the temperature of the water before you put a foot in and it is very hot. By the time you realize that you have done this, you will already have reacted by pulling your foot out. The hot water is an example of a **stimulus** and withdrawal of the foot is a **response**. The response occurs within a fraction of a second because it is carried out by neurons that transmit impulses very rapidly and only a small number of junctions between neurons (synapses) have to be crossed. It is probably the fastest type of response that the nervous system can make.

The endings of sensory neurons in the skin act as thermoreceptors and detect the heat stimulus. They then transmit impulses to the spinal cord. The sensory neurons have synapses with association neurons, which in turn have synapses with motor neurons. These motor neurons transmit impulses out of the spinal cord and on to muscles in the leg, which are stimulated to contract and pull the foot out of the hot water. The connections made between sensory and motor neurons by the association neurons ensure that an appropriate response is made to the stimulus.

Association neurons also transmit impulses up the spinal cord to the brain. This is how we become aware that we have put our foot into hot bathwater and have already responded. This type of simple response to a stimulus is a **reflex**. It is a useful way of responding very rapidly when the body is being harmed.

▶ Contraction of the psoas muscle withdraws the leg from hot water

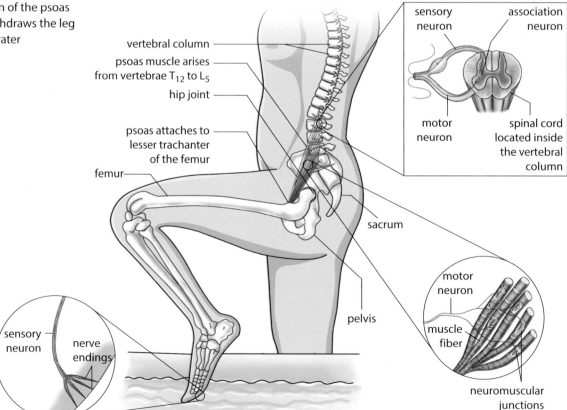

vertebral column

psoas muscle arises from vertebrae T_{12} to L_5

hip joint

psoas attaches to lesser trachanter of the femur

femur

sensory neuron

nerve endings

sensory neuron

association neuron

motor neuron

spinal cord located inside the vertebral column

sacrum

pelvis

motor neuron

muscle fiber

neuromuscular junctions

1. What does it mean when we say that the withdrawal reflex is
   a) unconscious   **b)** involuntary?

2. What is the advantage of carrying out the withdrawal reflex using the spinal cord rather than the brain?

3 Discuss whether the withdrawal reflex is a reaction or an interaction.

4 Can we be held responsible if we cause harm to others when we carry out a reflex action?

ⒶⒷⒸⒹ Experiment

The pupillary light reflex (PLR) is a mechanism by which the pupil at the center of the eye changes its size in response to light intensity. This response is carried out by muscle tissue in the iris and is involuntary, meaning that it is not controlled by the conscious activity of the brain.

There are two types of smooth muscle involved in changing the size of the pupil: circular and radial. These are antagonistic because they cause opposite movements of the iris. When one is fully contracted, the other is fully relaxed.

Hypothesis
The pupil becomes constricted in response to the stimulus of bright light entering the eye.

Materials
- Video camera
- Torch
- Video analysis software

Method
1. Dim the lighting and then shine a torch into the eye of a volunteer.

2. Take a video recording before, during and after the bright light stimulus, using a phone camera.

3. Import the recording into a video analysis software program and analyze the video frame by frame. If your software allows you to measure distances, you could plot a graph of pupil diameter over time.

▼ You should only use informed and willing volunteers in biology experiments

Results
1. Describe what happened.

2. **a)** What muscle action caused the pupils to become constricted?

   b) What muscle action would cause the pupils to become dilated?

3. **a)** What is the advantage of dilating the pupils?

   b) What is the advantage of constricting the pupils?

Extension to your experiment

Humans tend to have one dominant eye. Does the pupil constrict in the dominant eye if the stimulus of bright light is given only to the non-dominant eye, and vice versa?

PLR is a cranial reflex because it is mediated by neurons in the brain. The withdrawal reflex is spinal because the neurons that mediate it are in the spinal cord. Based on what you know already, are cranial or spinal reflexes faster? Why? You could investigate to see if you are right by timing how long these reflexes take.

What is the difference between voluntary and involuntary actions?

If we can choose consciously whether or not to respond to a stimulus, the response is voluntary. For example, an athlete preparing for a race has to decide when to start sprinting out of the block. She exerts voluntary control over her muscles and can decide whether to contract them or not, either to initiate an action or not. Voluntary control is a function of parts of the cerebral hemispheres in the brain. The network of neurons in this part of the brain is much more complex than that in the spinal cord, and the decision about whether to contract a muscle or not is made by the combined action of many synapses.

How are decisions made by the nervous system?

Signals can only pass in one direction across a synapse. This ensures that impulses pass along nerve fibers in the correct direction. The neuron that brings the signal to the synapse is the presynaptic neuron and the neuron that receives it is the post-synaptic neuron.

When an impulse reaches the end of a presynaptic neuron it triggers the release of a chemical. There are many different possible chemicals, which are known collectively as neurotransmitters, but only one type is released at each synapse. The neurotransmitter diffuses across the synaptic gap and binds to special receptor proteins in the membrane of the post-synaptic neuron. This is described in Chapter 4.

Neurotransmitters cause the voltage across the membrane of the post-synaptic neuron to change. They are classed as excitatory or inhibitory, depending on the direction of change. Excitatory neurotransmitters cause the post-synaptic neuron's membrane voltage to rise (become less negative), so they tend to cause an impulse. Inhibitory neurotransmitters do the opposite—they cause the voltage to become more negative, so an impulse will only be triggered with a larger amount of excitatory neurotransmitter. An impulse is triggered in the post-synaptic neuron whenever the voltage across its membrane reaches −50 mV. The impulse is transmitted away from the synapse and the membrane of the post-synaptic neuron returns to −70 mV. Each time the voltage rises to −50 mV an impulse is sent. This can happen hundreds of times per second.

One post-synaptic neuron may have synapses with many presynaptic neurons, some of which release neurotransmitters that stimulate

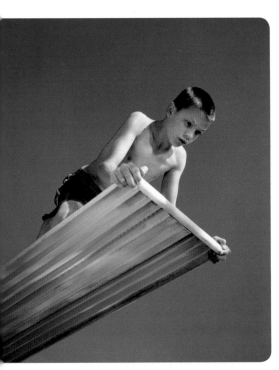

▲ Voluntary muscle action is used to jump off the high diving board, whereas dilating the pupils of the eye when we are scared is involuntary. Being cautious or a risk-taker is a part of our natural identity

impulses and others release neurotransmitters that inhibit them. The voltage across the membrane of the post-synaptic neuron rises and falls as the different types of neurotransmitter reach it. Every time it rises to −50 mV an impulse will be triggered. In the brain there can be hundreds of presynaptic neurons and all of them in combination decide whether an impulse is triggered in the post-synaptic neuron.

1. The presynaptic neurons labelled A, B and C in the diagram release neurotransmitters that stimulate impulses, but D releases an inhibitory neurotransmitter. The table shows some observations.

Presynaptic neuron in which an impulse arrives at the synapse	Is an impulse initiated in the post-synaptic neuron?
A	No
A and B together	Yes
B and D together	No
B, C and D together	Yes

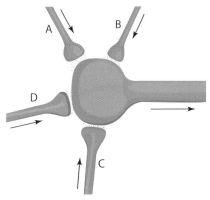

▲ The ends of nerve fibers from four presynaptic neurons are shown with the synapses between them and one post-synaptic neuron. The arrows indicate the direction of movement of the nerve impulses

Do you expect an impulse in the post-synaptic neuron if there are impulses in:

a) B   b) D   c) C   d) A, B and C?

e) Can you work out whether there would be an impulse with any other combinations?

2. When chasing its prey, there are multiple factors influencing a cheetah's decision to continue.
These factors either cause inhibitory or excitatory neurotransmitters to be released. What factors would cause release of:

a) inhibitory neurotransmitters?

b) excitatory neurotransmitters?

3. Discuss whether the chase is an example of reaction or interaction.

◄ In this life and death chase, both the cheetah and the impala make decisions every millisecond about which way to run. The cheetah has to decide whether it is worth continuing—most of its chases end in failure

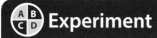 **Experiment**

How quickly do you expect your body to make a voluntary response to a stimulus? Do you expect voluntary responses to be faster or slower than involuntary reflexes? Propose your own hypothesis. What other factors do you need to take into account when designing an experiment to test this hypothesis?

Materials and method

A convenient method of measuring voluntary response time involves catching a dropping ruler. To carry out this investigation, you will need to pair up with another student. Student 1 will hold a 30 centimeter ruler at one end, so it hangs vertically. Student 2 puts their finger and thumb on either side of the 0 cm mark at the lower end of the ruler, without actually touching it. When Student 1 drops the ruler without warning, Student 2 has to catch it between finger and thumb. Once Student 2 has caught the ruler, make a note of the distance dropped (DD); the time taken from the moment the ruler starts dropping until it was caught can be deduced from this conversion table, where DD is distance dropped in centimeters and RT is response time in milliseconds:

DD	RT	DD	RT	DD	RT	DD	RT	DD	RT	DD	RT
1	45	6	111	11	150	16	181	21	207	26	230
2	64	7	120	12	156	17	186	22	212	27	235
3	78	8	128	13	163	18	192	23	217	28	239
4	90	9	136	14	169	19	197	24	221	29	243
5	101	10	143	15	175	20	202	25	226	30	247

1. **a)** Display your results graphically, with the response times for different people kept separate. Include the mean response time for each person with a range bar to show the variation from the person's fastest to slowest times.

   b) Using the data displayed in your graph, discuss whether the mean response times that you found in your trials are reliable and whether the differences between the people were significant.

2. The many different methods for measuring response time give different results, even for the same person. Can you explain how we respond faster in some tests than others?

3. Response times for tests such as catching a dropping ruler are usually longer than for reflexes such as withdrawing a foot from hot bathwater. Can you suggest a hypothesis to explain this?

Chain reaction

1. How fast can a long chain of people holding hands pass on a hand squeeze signal from the first to last person in the chain? The chain reaction challenge is best done with eyes closed so the signal cannot jump if someone sees a hand movement ahead of them in the chain. The first person in the chain should start an electronic timer as they send the hand squeeze signal and the last person should call out when the signal reaches them so the timer can be stopped.

2. What was the mean reaction time per person?

3. How many neurons did a signal pass through in each person from the stimulus to the response?

4. In chemistry, a chain reaction involves positive feedback, so the rate of the reaction becomes faster and faster until the reactants are used up. Discuss whether the analogy of a chain is appropriate.

ATL Creative thinking skills

Generating analogies

An analogy is a communication device that links something familiar to an idea or a concept that is meant to represent. As in the case of all communication strategies, it is important to think about the audience when making an analogy. What will they be familiar with? What will they be interested in?

In an analogy, the link between the familiar example and the concept it represents should be simple, obvious and clarifying. Analogies are commonly used in science. Can you think of some examples of analogies used in biology?

Hazard awareness tests

In many countries a hazard awareness assessment is part of tests that have to be passed before driving a vehicle on public roads. A video is played of the view that a driver might see while travelling through a busy area. The person being assessed has to press a key in response to each accident risk, such as a pedestrian suddenly crossing the road or another vehicle making an unexpected maneuver. The assessment is used to decide whether a learner driver is recognizing and responding to these hazards quickly enough.

▲ Becoming a driver involves learning to interact safely with all other road users, whether they are cautious or risk-takers

You can use the search term "hazard perception test" to find and download online tests and then use them to develop the neural pathways needed to respond quickly enough as a driver.

ATL Thinking in context

What is the relationship between video games and identity?

You can explore this issue by debating the answers to these questions.

1 a) There is some evidence that people who spend a lot of time playing video games develop faster response times. In what situations could this be an advantage?

b) Are there any counter-arguments that indicate that video games are not the best use of leisure time?

2 Some video games involve taking on a fictional identity. Who are we when we play these games, ourselves or the fictional identity?

▲ Video games require rapid responses and some people spend much of their free time playing them

3 If there are differences in identity between gamers and non-gamers, is this because people of particular identity types choose to play video games or because playing video games shapes identity in a particular way?

4. A higher percentage of boys than girls play video games. What are the reasons for this?

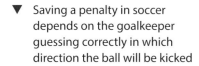

▼ Saving a penalty in soccer depends on the goalkeeper guessing correctly in which direction the ball will be kicked

Data-based question: Taking penalties

In soccer (football) a penalty kick is taken 11 meters from the goal line. The average velocity of the kicked ball is 112 km/hour. Only the goalkeeper defends the goal.

1. Calculate the time taken for the ball to reach the goal line.

2. The goal is 7.32 meters wide, so a goalkeeper standing in the middle may have to move 3.5 meters to reach the ball. Estimate the time taken for the goalkeeper to move far enough to intercept the ball if it is kicked to the extreme left or right of the goal.

3. There were 1,749 penalties in English Premier League football matches between 1992 and 2015. Of these, 1,480 resulted in a goal scored, 64 missed the goal and 205 were saved by the goalkeeper. Calculate the percentage of penalties that were scored and the percentage that were saved.

4. Discuss the reasons for such a small percentage of penalties being saved by the goalkeeper.

5. Suggest strategies that the goalkeeper could use to increase the chance of saving the penalty or that the penalty kicker could use to increase the chance of scoring a goal.

6. Data suggests that the best strategy for the goalkeeper is not to move either left or right. Suggest a reason for goalkeepers being reluctant to use this strategy.

Can past experiences influence reflexes?

PHYSIOLOGY

Biologists have shown that additional responses can develop during our life as a result of our experiences. The most famous early experiments into learning new responses were carried out by Ivan Pavlov, using dogs. Dogs salivate when they see or smell food. This cranial reflex is the result of pathways of neurons that link sensory receptors in the eye or nose to cells in the salivary glands that secrete saliva.

Pavlov fitted tubes through the dogs' cheeks so he could collect and measure the quantities of saliva secreted in response to stimuli. He showed that if another stimulus, such as the ticking of a metronome or the sound of a buzzer, was repeatedly given to dogs immediately before the dog saw or smelled food, it would eventually salivate even if no food was then presented. The dogs had learned to associate the new stimulus with the prospect of food. This type of learned behavior is called a conditioned reflex.

▲ Ivan Pavlov had tubes inserted into the side of dogs' cheeks so salivation could easily be observed

1. Discuss whether a conditioned reflex is an example of reaction or interaction.

2. Suggest a hypothesis for how new reflexes can be set up by the nervous system.

3. Find an example of a conditioned reflex that is not the result of an experiment. Domestic pets such as cats are possible sources of an example.

4. Explain the benefits to an animal of learning conditioned reflexes.

What types of relationship are there between species in a community?

Animals in an ecological community interact with each other using their senses, nervous system and muscles. The relationship between two species is based on the interactions that occur between them. There are a number of common types of interspecific relationship. The table lists four of these with an example of each. Can you find other examples or other types of relationship between animal species?

Type of relationship	Example
Predation: the predator catches, kills and eats its prey	North American brown bears (*Ursus arctos*) catch and consume salmon migrating upstream to their spawning grounds in the rivers of north-west America. Young bears learn how to catch the fish either by trial and error or by observing older, more experienced bears. Waterfalls on a salmon river are a favored site as the fish have to leap up the falls, so they are easier to catch. The salmon are rich in protein.
Competition: two species attempt to obtain and use the same limited resource	Pinyon pines (*Pinus edulis*) produce many large seeds in certain years and few in others. Birds such as the pinyon jay (*Gymnorhinus cyanocephalus*) come to harvest them by day, eating some immediately and burying the rest in soil. Mammals such as the pinyon mouse (*Peromyscus truei*) also feed on the seeds, mostly nocturnally. The more seeds that are taken by birds, the fewer are available to mammals (i.e. there is a negative correlation).
Parasitism: a parasite lives on or in its host, obtaining food from it and harming it	Varroa mites (*Varroa destructor*) are parasites of honey bees. They have no other host. Varroa lives on the outside of bee larvae and adults and feeds by sucking out their blood. Asiatic honey bees (*Apis cerana*) carefully groom each other to remove Varroa mites so infestations are limited. In recent decades, Varroa has spread to the western honey bee (*Apis mellifera*) and many colonies have been wiped out by it.
Mutualism: two species live in close association with both gaining benefit	Clownfish (*Amphiprion nigripes*) live among the tentacles of a species of sea anemone (*Heteractis magnifica*). They eat food not consumed by the sea anemone. The sea anemone's stinging tentacles do not cause harm because clownfish have a layer of mucus over the scales in their skin. There are two benefits for sea anemones: clownfish provide a cleaning service and also lure prey into the sea anemone's tentacles.

Data-based question: Red and grey squirrels

Red squirrels (*Sciurus vulgaris*) are native to northern Europe and northern Asia; eastern grey squirrels (*Sciurus carolinensis*) are native to North America, but are now also common in parts of Europe. In the United Kingdom the eastern grey squirrel was introduced at the end of the 19th century. It spread to East Anglia, an area in the east of the UK, during the 1970s, as shown by a long-term study of squirrel communities in the area.

▲ *Sciurus vulgaris*

▲ *Sciurus carolinensis*

In this study, biologists divided up a large area of East Anglia into 10 × 10 km grid squares and recorded the presence or absence of both species of squirrel in each grid square for 22 years, between 1960 and 1982. The graph shows the results.

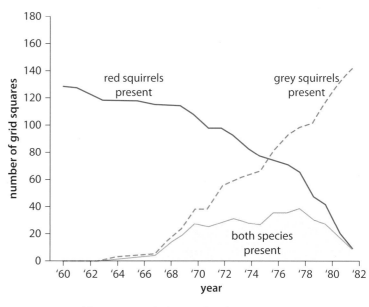

Source: Reynolds JC, *Journal of Animal Ecology* (1985), 54, 149–162

1. Using only the data in the graph, deduce which of these relationships could have caused the changes: predation, competition, parasitism or mutualism.

2. Red and grey squirrels are in the same genus (*Sciurus*), so they are closely related, making it unlikely that one of them is a parasite and the other is its host. Parasites and their hosts are usually from very different groups of animals. Can you think of any reasons for this? Can you find any examples of closely related species where one is a parasite and the other is its host?

3. The red squirrel disappeared from each grid square soon after grey squirrels arrived. Then in 1982, red squirrels disappeared completely from East Anglia. The spread of grey squirrels therefore had a devastating effect on red squirrels. Discuss whether competition or predation is more likely to cause the local extinction of a species.

4. What advice would you give about introduction of alien species, based on the data in this question?

Data-based question: Canada lynx and snowshoe hare

The Hudson's Bay Company bought furs from trappers in northern Canada for many years. The numbers of furs from the snowshoe hare (*Lepus americanus*) and its predator, the Canada lynx (*Lynx canadensis*), fluctuated, in response to changes in the size of the two populations. The data can therefore be used as an estimate of the relative numbers of hare and lynx in the wild.

▲ Snowshoe hares make up between 60 and 97% of the Canada lynx diet

1. The numbers of hares follow a cyclical pattern of rises and falls.

   a) How many cycles are there between 1845 and 1935?

   b) Calculate how long each cycle lasts on average.

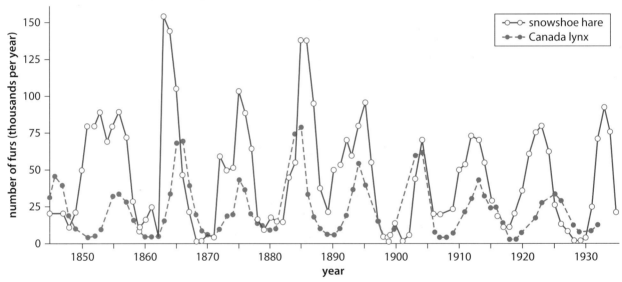

▲ The graph shows records from the Hudson's Bay Company from 1845 to 1935

2. The lynx also undergoes cyclical changes in numbers over similar time periods but changes occur after those in the hare numbers. Suggest an explanation for each of these changes:

   a) increases in the number of lynx

   b) decreases in the number of hares

   c) decreases in the number of lynx

   d) increases in the number of hares.

3. The lynx is one of group of species that are predators of the hare.

   a) What type of relationship does the lynx have with other predators of the hare?

   b) When there are few hares, some of the other predators may kill and consume lynx. Suggest three advantages to the other predators of doing this.

4. Snowshoe hare numbers fluctuate even in areas where they are not predated by lynx. Suggest another factor that could cause these fluctuations.

←

5 For there to be interaction between two species they must each be affected by the other.

　a) How is the population of hares affected by the lynx?

　b) Does the population of hares have effects on the population of lynx?

　c) Is the relationship between a predator and its prey an example of interaction?

What are the differences between predators and parasites?

ECOLOGY

The biological definition of "parasite" is an organism that lives on or in its host, obtaining food from it and causing it harm.

1. Give a definition of "predator".

2. a) Make a list of similarities in the relationships between predator with prey and parasite with host.

　b) Make a second list showing differences in these two types of relationship.

3. Even if parasites don't kill their host, they tend to reduce the numbers of the host in an area. Discuss how this happens.

4. With each of the animals shown in the photos, try to decide whether it is a predator or parasite of humans. You may need to research the lifestyle of some of the six animals if you are unfamiliar with them. How well do your definitions work in deciding which type of relationship each species has with humans?

▲　Tapeworm

▲　Mosquito

▲　Castor bean tick

▲　Cockroach

▲　Hookworm

▲　Vampire bat

5 A parasite has a clear effect on its host, but is it influenced in any way by the host?

Could parasites ever be good for us?

When a parasite invades the human body, our immune system should detect it and produce antibodies against it. Many parasites, however, have methods of evading the immune system. Before humans started applying principles of hygiene to their lives and before drugs to control parasites had been developed, it was common for humans to carry one or more types of parasite. This is no longer the case.

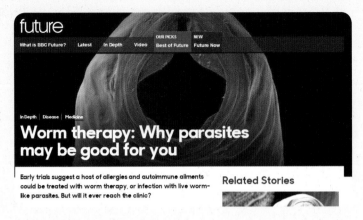

We might expect the consequences of this to be entirely positive, but recent studies suggest that intestinal parasites might have some benefits for their human hosts. Find a newspaper article about this and investigate the claims made in it.

ECOLOGY What types of relationship are possible between members of a species?

We might expect animals to be loyal to other members of their species and cooperate. When we look at animal behavior we see many different types of behavior, not all of them cooperative. This is not surprising, because members of a species all need the same resources so they are likely to be in competition with each other. The list below gives examples of relationships between members of the same species. Behavior patterns only observed in social animals such as honey bees have not been included.

Relationship	Example	
Territoriality	Rufous hummingbirds (*Selasphorus rufus*) establish and defend territories containing nectar secreting flowers such as the Indian Paintbrush. They even establish temporary territories during migration through western North America. The size of the territory can be adjusted so that enough food is available without excessive energy use in defending a large area.	
Group defence	Sea skaters (*Halobates robustus*) are flightless insects that live on the surface of coastal waters around the Galapagos islands. At times they form groups of 100 or more individuals called flotillas. Fish in the water below come up to the surface to predate sea skaters. The larger the flotilla, the lower the predation rate, due to better vigilance.	

Sexual conflict	Bighorn sheep (*Ovis candadensis*) live in mountains and deserts of western North America. During the breeding season in November, males frequently fight for females, with repeated head-butting and the clash of horns. After winning the fight against another male, a bighorn ram defends the females during the period when they are fertile, ensuring that no other males mate with them.	
Monogamy	Wilson's storm petrel (*Oceanites oceanicus*) is a seabird that feeds in southern oceans and only comes to land in the breeding season each year. Males and females form pairs and do not mate with any others, even though they breed in colonies. Males and females share incubation and the feeding of their single chick after hatching.	
Parental care	Emperor penguins mate in large colonies on Antarctica at the end of summer. A single egg is laid by the female. After this, she leaves the male to incubate the egg through the Antarctic winter. The female returns about 70 days later, finding her male partner and bringing food for their newly hatched chick. Both parents then forage at sea and bring food back for the chick.	
Predation	Northern pike (*Esox lucius*) are voracious predators of lakes and rivers in the northern hemisphere. They catch and eat invertebrates when they are young, and other fish, birds and mammals later on. Large pike, which can be over a meter long, eat smaller pike—they are cannibalistic. Smaller pike therefore have to hide from larger ones.	
Infanticide	The black-footed grey langur (*Semnopithecus hypoleucos*) lives in groups in both forests and urban areas in southern India. Most groups consist of one dominant male, many adult females and their infants. If a new dominant male gains control of a group, he usually kills all the infants. The male then mates with the females so the infants they then rear are his offspring.	

1 Can all of these relationships be classified as competitive or cooperative?

2 Considering your own identity, do you consider cooperation or competition to be more important?

ECOLOGY ## Can social animals prevent cheating?

Social animals gain benefits from living in groups. If a member of the group gains a benefit without helping to provide it, they are cheating. Consider these examples:

- Ostriches (*Struthio camelus*) sometimes feed singly and sometimes in small groups. They raise their heads periodically to look for predators that might attack them and then put their heads down again to feed. When they are in a group, looking out for predators (vigilance) is done cooperatively: this is beneficial because the larger the group, the less often each individual ostrich has to raise their head. An individual who fed continuously and never raised their head, relying on the others for vigilance, would be cheating. What are the disadvantages to an individual ostrich of being much more or much less vigilant than others in the group?

▶ Ostrich feeding on the Masai Mara in Kenya

- Ravens (*Corvus corax*) sometimes feed in groups, using cooperation to increase their success rate. An experiment was carried out using ravens kept in an aviary. To obtain a food reward, two ravens had to pull on opposite ends of a string at the same time. They learned how to do this but were more willing to cooperate with some members of the group than others and did not go on cooperating with individuals in the group who cheated by taking more than their share of the food reward. There were only seven ravens in the experimental group. Can you predict how the results might have been different with a very large experimental group?

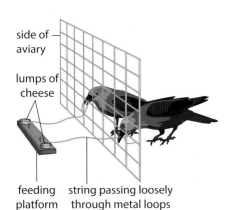
side of aviary

lumps of cheese

feeding platform

string passing loosely through metal loops

1. What will happen in a social group if there is initially no cheating, but then some individuals start to cheat and more and more follow their example until there is a high level of cheating?

2. What can prevent cheating in a group of animals?

3. a) Apart from in school tests or exams, can you suggest any human examples of cheating?

   b) What methods can human societies use to minimize cheating?

4. **a)** If ostriches in larger groups can spend more time feeding and less time looking for predators, what prevents enormous groups of ostriches from forming?

   b) Can you suggest examples of large groups of a species forming? In what circumstances does this happen?

5. Do you think ravens learn to cooperate or is it likelier that their genes dictate whether they are cheats or cooperators?

Do mutualistic species ever cheat on each other?

ECOLOGY

A typical mutualistic relationship has these features:

- Individuals of two species live together.

- They live in close proximity all the time or frequently come together.

- Both benefit from the relationship.

- Each individual performs a function that the other cannot.

- The two individuals are members of very different species, often from different kingdoms.

Corals are in the phylum Cnidaria and consist of polyps with a ring of stinging tentacles and a gut cavity with a single opening to the seawater outside. They feed by catching smaller organisms and detritus using their tentacles. The food is either digested in the gut cavity or is taken into the polyp's cells and digested there (a diagram of the endothelium used for digestion in Cnidaria is included in Chapter 4).

Some corals form a mutualistic relationship with a group of unicellular algae called zooxanthellae. These algae are taken in by cells of the coral polyp, but are not digested. Instead the algae stay alive and continue to photosynthesize. The algae gain a place to live where they cannot be consumed by other organisms and also a supply of carbon dioxide from respiration in the coral. Photosynthesis in the algae provides the coral with a supply of oxygen that it can use in respiration. It also provides a supply of food that gives the coral enough energy to construct a hard skeleton by secreting calcium carbonate. Coral reefs are therefore based on this mutualistic relationship.

As with other examples of mutualism, both species benefit from the health and success of the other, so cheating in a mutualistic relationship is rather unlikely. Coral cells continue to provide safety, oxygen and mineral nutrients to the algae inside them as long as they continue to benefit from foods and oxygen produced by the algae. If the algae stop photosynthesizing effectively or the coral is unable to use the food and oxygen from photosynthesis, then the algae are expelled. This is called bleaching of corals because the colour of the coral is paler without the algae. A variety of environmental stresses cause bleaching, including sea temperatures that are above the optimum for photosynthesis.

Does cheating ever occur in mutualistic relationships? Research other examples of mutualistic relationship before you answer this question.

▶ Bleached coral on the Great Barrier Reef in May 2016

ATL Organization skills

Preparing for eAssessment

At the end of MYP 5, students seeking an MYP certificate are required to undertake on screen assessments. The assessments are meant to measure the extent to which they have met the objectives of the MYP biology course as described in criteria A, B, C and D.

There are a number of strategies recommended to ensure that you are well prepared to demonstrate your skills:

- Complete the hardware compatibility checker to ensure the device that is going to be used during the assessment will work with the test files.

- Complete the familiarization task provided by the IB. This provides students with experience of the kinds of on screen tools that will be used such as calculators, videos, the resource library and on screen simulators to name a few.

- Review criteria A-D to ensure that the expectations of each criterion are understood.

- Within each of the criteria, there are command terms that require specific actions to be undertaken. Make a list of these terms and review the expectations with each of them.

- Complete at least one specimen exam and review the answers to gain familiarity with the style of the exam. Ask your teacher to provide sample answers.

For each assessment session, the IB chooses one global context. All of the assessments will have themes that are relevant to this global context. Review the definition of this global context and consider all of the units that you covered in your MYP career that were relevant to it. Imagine the possible links between biology and this global context that might be made in the eAssessment.

Summative assessment

Statement of inquiry:

When two or more individuals interact, they form relationships that, over time, impact and contribute to their identity.

Introduction

Whales are the theme of this summative assessment, with the focus on interactions in one species that have been thoroughly researched and in a second species where there is an urgent need for more investigation. The assessment includes opportunities to investigate a reflex in humans and also to consider interactions between whales and humans.

Sperm whales

- The sperm whale (*Physeter microcephalus*) has the largest brain of any animal on Earth.

- They can live for more than 70 years and grow to lengths of over 20 metres.

- Sperm whales mostly feed on squid, together with octopus and rays. They dive to feed at depths of 300–800 meters, but sometimes venture more than 2 kilometers deep (2,000 m).

- Sperm whales are only vulnerable to predation by orcas and pilot whales when young or weakened.

- Females and young males live in stable family groups that consist of several adult females together with their offspring.

- Calves are cared for cooperatively within family groups for about 10 years. Males are ejected from the group, usually when they are older than 10.

- Adult males live alone except during the mating season.

- Sperm whales are highly vocal, making a variety of sounds for echolocation of prey and communication within and between groups.

▲ Adult female sperm whale with a calf in the Indian Ocean. The calf has remora (suckerfish) attached to it

1. During the life of a sperm whale there will be many interactions between it and other animals inhabiting the oceans. What types of interaction could occur:

   a) between sperm whales and other species of animals? [3]

   b) between an individual sperm whale and others of its species? [3]

2. Explain possible advantages to sperm whales of living in groups. [3]

3. Females currently produce calves at intervals of between 4 and 20 years. In the past sperm whales were hunted and killed by humans, and the females gave birth to young more frequently. What is the explanation for a drop in the pregnancy rate since the end of whale hunting? [3]

4. What factors could explain the large brain size of sperm whales? [3]

Investigating the diving reflex

Sperm whales can dive in the oceans to depths of over 2 kilometers and spend over an hour underwater without taking a breath. Narwhals can dive to more than 1,500 meters. Diving is accompanied by major changes to the functioning of the circulatory system, which are known as the mammalian diving reflex. The first response is bradycardia (a slowing of the heart rate), followed by changes to the amount of blood flowing to different parts of the body.

5. Explain reasons for a slower heart rate during a long dive. [3]

6. Humans are mammals so we might have a diving reflex. One hypothesis that could be tested is: *"Heart rate slows down in humans when the face is immersed in cold water."*

Explain the reasons for expecting human heart rate to slow down if the face is immersed in cold water. [3]

7. Design an experiment to test the hypothesis. Include all the details of how variables will be controlled. Your method should exclude the possibility that a slowing of the heart rate is due to stopping breathing rather than contact with cold water. [6]

8. Explain how you can ensure that the investigation is safe and ethically acceptable. [3]

Estimating the ages of narwhals

The narwhal (*Monodon monoceros*) is the most northerly species of whale. Its most distinctive feature is a large tusk that develops from a canine tooth on the left side of the upper jaw. The tusk always has a left-handed spiral form and in males it can grow to a length of more than 3 meters.

Narwhals spend the winter in deep water where there is pack ice, feeding on halibut, cod, cuttlefish, squid and shrimp under the ice and sometimes diving to a depth of 1500 meters or more to catch them. The narwhal live in groups of between 3 and 10 individuals. These winter groups usually consist either of females with their young or of adult males, but mixed groups of males and females can also form, especially groups of juveniles.

At the end of winter the cracks in the pack ice that the narwhals have used as breathing holes open up into channels and they migrate to shallower coastal waters as they become ice-free. Much larger groups are formed during migration, sometimes with over 1,000 individuals, but having reached summering waters smaller groups reform. At the end of summer the narwhal must migrate back to deep water before the sea near the coast freezes over completely.

▲ Recent research suggests that the narwhal tusk acts as a sense organ

Narwhals emit a range of sounds. Clicks are used for navigation and echolocation of prey. Distinctive whistles and knocks are probably used for communication within groups. Mating takes place in April or May and gestation lasts 14 months, so calves are born in summer. Mothers feed their calves with milk for about 20 months during which time mother and calf always remain close together. Calves and young narwhal can be predated by polar bears, sharks and walruses but the only natural predators of adults are orca (killer whales).

The text below is from the introduction to a scientific paper entitled "Age-specific growth and remarkable longevity in narwhals (*Monodon monoceros*) from West Greenland as estimated by aspartic acid racemization" by Eva Garde, Mads Peter Heide-Jørgensen, Steen H Hansen, Gösta Nachman, Mads C Forchhammer. The paper was published on 27 February 2007 in the *Journal of Mammology*.

The narwhal (*Monodon monoceros*) is a toothed whale that reaches 4–5 m in length at physical maturity and is found year-round in Arctic waters mainly around Greenland and northern Canada. However, during the last 2 decades the West Greenland narwhal populations have experienced a population decline most likely attributable to increasingly intensive hunting. To ensure the best possible management and sustainable use of the narwhal populations, more biological knowledge of the species is needed. One key factor for studying a species' population dynamics is the availability of a reliable method for age determination of individuals.

Age determination of toothed whales has traditionally been performed by counting growth layer groups in the teeth. Validation has, in some cases, been done by reference to known-age animals in captivity. However, the use of dentinal growth layers has failed to provide reliable results for narwhals, especially in older individuals. No narwhals have been successfully kept in captivity and there are no animals available with known age and life history. Thus, there is an urgent need for developing reliable techniques for revealing growth increments in narwhal tissue and, hence, their age.

The aspartic acid racemization technique was originally developed to assess ages of fossils and marine sediments. However, since the 1980s several studies have used the technique for age estimation of mammals, including whales and humans. The method assumes that all amino acids, including aspartic acid, can exist in 2 different isomeric forms called L- and D-enantiomers. All of the amino acids normally incorporated into proteins in living organisms are of the L-form. In stable proteins, however, the L-form is slowly, and at a constant rate, converted to the D-form and the D/L ratio can thus potentially be used as a marker for age. Because aspartic acid has the fastest racemization rate of the amino acids in body tissues, it also is the most frequently used of the amino acids for age estimation of mammals.

In our study, eye lens nuclei were used for age estimation. The proteins in the nucleus of the eye lens are among the most stable in the mammalian body and subject to detectable racemization. Eyeballs from 75 narwhals were collected during the Inuit hunt of narwhals in Uummannaq and Qeqertarsuaq, West Greenland.

9. Explain the problems for the scientists in measuring the ages of narwhals. [3]

10. Discuss the validity of the scientists' methods for estimating the age of the narwhals. Can you suggest any improvements to the method? [3]

11. The bar chart below shows the age estimates produced by the research.

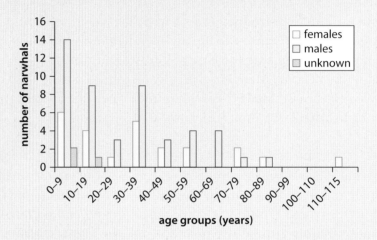

a) What was the age of the oldest narwhal? [1]

b) What was the most frequent age of the narwhals? [1]

c) Suggest a reason for the scientists not being able to determine the sex of some of the narwhals. [1]

12. The chart below is an age pyramid for the human population in Greenland in 2014.

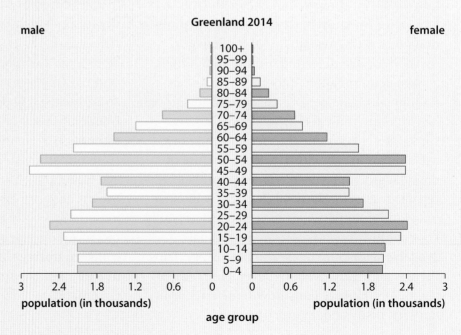

a) Draw an age pyramid chart for the narwhals investigated in West Greenland. [3]

b) Suggest reasons for the differences between the human and the narwhal age pyramids. [3]

 ## Hunting narwhals and Inuit identity

There are concerns about the continued hunting of narwhal. The research into survival rates in narwhal was done partly to investigate the effect of hunting.

13. Write a reference to the scientific paper on the ages of narwhal. The reference should be in a style suitable for a bibliography. [3]

14. Write a paragraph to explain how the narwhals' ages were estimated, using scientific language in a way that non-scientists should be able to understand. [3]

15. Narwhals have been hunted for at least a thousand years by the Inuit of Canada and Greenland, with an estimated annual catch of about 1,000. Similar numbers are reported to have been killed in recent years. The traditional method involved spearing the narwhals from boats, but high velocity rifles are now used. There are concerns that significant numbers of narwhals are fatally wounded by rifle shots but not recovered, so official catch figures underestimate losses due to hunting. Narwhals were a significant component of Inuit diets in the past, but the main products are now muktaaq (a food made from the skin and blubber) and the large ivory tusks which can be sold for $1,000 or more.

a) Predator–prey relationships can be sustained over very long periods with numbers of predator and prey remaining stable. Is the relationship between the Inuit and narwhals a predator–prey relationship? [3]

b) Should the Inuit be allowed to continue to hunt narwhals because it is an important part of Inuit identity even if it threatens the survival of the narwhals? [3]

c) Compared with other whale species there has been very little scientific research into narwhals, but it is known that they live in groups and communicate with each other in sophisticated ways. Should hunting of narwhals be allowed if we do not know what its effect is on these social animals? [3]

7 Balance

▼ A balanced diet consists of appropriate quantities of carbohydrates, lipids, proteins, minerals, vitamins, water and dietary fiber. It provides as much energy as the body uses, but not more. What are the four categories of foods in the pie chart and must they all be included in our diet? The photo shows different amounts of each food type. Does this mean that the diet is unbalanced?

▼ In some cities many people cycle to school or work and others use public transport, for example, a bus. Which mode of transport helps us more with the work–life balance?

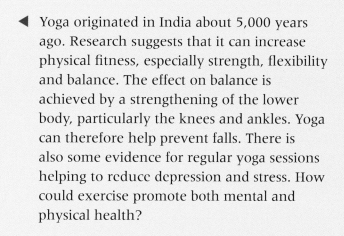

Yoga originated in India about 5,000 years ago. Research suggests that it can increase physical fitness, especially strength, flexibility and balance. The effect on balance is achieved by a strengthening of the lower body, particularly the knees and ankles. Yoga can therefore help prevent falls. There is also some evidence for regular yoga sessions helping to reduce depression and stress. How could exercise promote both mental and physical health?

Slacklining is an increasingly popular recreational sport that has developed since the 1970s. A length of flat webbing is tensioned between two anchors and slackliners balance on it or walk from end to end. The low tension of the line allows it to stretch and recoil, so slackliners can bounce as on a trampoline. Why is it easier to balance with outstretched arms?

In kayaking and white water rafting it is easy to flip the boat, with potentially dangerous consequences. Balance is achieved by even distribution of weight and by avoiding turbulent water. There have been tragic cases of boats in the Mediterranean capsizing because the refugees on board crowded over to one side when they saw a rescue boat. What can we learn about balance from such events?

Introduction

Systems are sets of interacting or interdependent components, which can be static or dynamic and simple or complex. They can be open (where necessary resources are renewed regularly), closed (where matter-based resources are not removed or replaced but energy flows in and out) or isolated (where neither matter nor energy flows in or out of the system). To maintain order in the human body and in natural or built environments, systems must be kept in balance.

A balance is a device used for weighing, consisting of a beam that is free to move on a central pivot and a scale pan at each end. The beam becomes level when equal weights are placed on the two pans. From this observation the concept of balance has developed.

The expanding human population has put great strain on natural ecosystems. Development has been, and will continue to be, necessary to provide for the human population. However, important questions remain to be answered: how can we combine development with peace, fairness and sustainability for all living organisms on Earth?

Key concept: Systems

Related concept: Balance

Global context: Fairness and development

▼ Balances have been used for thousands of years. This depiction on papyrus dates from 1300 B.C. and shows the Weighing of the Heart. In the mythology of ancient Egypt, the goddess Maat weighed the hearts of the dead to discover whether they had led a virtuous life

Statement of inquiry:

Development is only sustainable if systems remain in balance.

The concept of balance is useful in many contexts in biology. In this chapter the focus will be on two types of balance:

- homeostasis, which is regulation of the internal environment of an organism
- stability within ecosystems, which results from the relationships between the different organisms.

In both cases, balance allows complex systems to continue to function. If balance is lost, then entire systems are at risk.

Ecosystems and internal body systems are complex, dynamic and open. This makes balance more difficult to achieve. Natural ecosystems usually remain in balance but they can also be disrupted by natural events or by human actions. The internal environment of mammals is very precisely balanced using negative feedback mechanisms and much energy.

▲ Toco toucans (*Ramphastos toco*) prefer open habitats, so they may be one of the few species to benefit from unsustainable changes to forest ecosystems in South America, while other species of toucan are threatened. The toco toucan has the largest bill of any bird and uses it in homeostasis. Blood flow to the bill is increased in warm conditions and is restricted when it is colder. How could this help to keep the toucan's body temperature in balance at 38–39°C?

▶ Until the arrival of humans on Easter Island in the south-east Pacific, there was a subtropical broadleaved forest ecosystem. Unsustainable use, combined with the introduction of the Polynesian rat, led to the destruction of this ecosystem, with 21 tree species and all native bird species becoming extinct. The human population had risen to about 15,000 but without the resources provided by the forest, this dropped to only 2,000–3,000. Easter Island and other examples show how important it is for development to be sustainable

▶ Tropical rainforest in the far north of Queensland in Australia may be the oldest ecosystem on Earth. It could have existed for as long as 110 million years, demonstrating the amazing sustainability of ecosystems. In contrast, temperate forests of the northern hemisphere are only about 10,000 years old. What is the reason?

METABOLISM

How is blood glucose concentration kept in balance?

Glucose is supplied by blood to cells thoughout the body. The correct SI units for measuring the concentration are millimoles per liter (mmol/L). The scale shows a range of possible blood glucose concentrations.

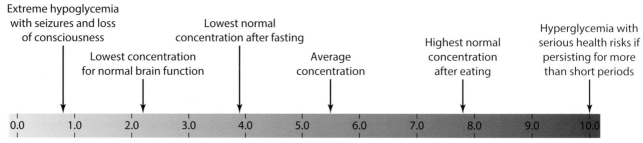

Extreme hypoglycemia with seizures and loss of consciousness

Lowest concentration for normal brain function

Lowest normal concentration after fasting

Average concentration

Highest normal concentration after eating

Hyperglycemia with serious health risks if persisting for more than short periods

0.0   1.0   2.0   3.0   4.0   5.0   6.0   7.0   8.0   9.0   10.0

Blood glucose concentration (mmol/L)

- The basic SI units for concentration are moles per liter. For example, one mole of glucose is 180 grams, so a glucose solution of one mole per liter has 180 grams of glucose dissolved in each liter of solution.

- Millimoles or even micromoles per liter may be used if the concentration is very small.

- Units can be shown in full or can be abbreviated. Unfortunately, scientists have not always used the same forms of abbreviation. For example, all of these mean the same thing:

    5 mmol/l
    5 mmol/dm^3
    5 mmol liter^{-1}
    5 mmol dm^{-3}

What does a forward slash mean? What do negative indices mean in SI units?

▲ Blood glucose concentration can be measured by pricking a finger with a sterile lancet and by placing the drop of blood on a test stick

Glucose concentration cannot be kept at a constant level because the entire volume of blood in the body contains only about 5 grams of glucose and body processes can add or remove it rapidly.

To keep blood glucose concentrations between narrow limits, the amount of glucose removed from the blood must be balanced with the amount that is added. This is achieved using hormones. A hormone is a chemical messenger secreted by a gland cell and transported in the blood. The two principal hormones used to control blood glucose concentration are insulin and glucagon. They are both secreted by cells in the pancreas. Insulin decreases blood glucose concentration whereas glucagon increases it.

1. Deduce which hormone causes these processes:

   a) conversion of glycogen to glucose

   b) use of glucose rather than fat by body cells to generate energy by respiration.

2. What hormone is secreted by the pancreas after a meal with a high sugar content?

3. Low blood sugar concentrations can cause feelings of hunger.

   a) Explain the reasons for hunger at the end of the night.

   b) Explain the reasons for hunger returning more rapidly after a breakfast with a high sugar content than a breakfast with a high protein or fat content.

4. Blood glucose concentration is sometimes very high at the end of vigorous exercise. Suggest an explanation for this.

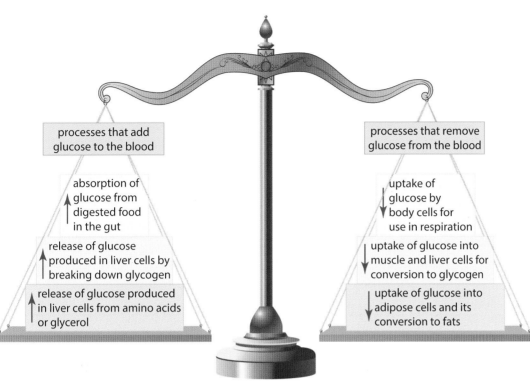

processes that add glucose to the blood	processes that remove glucose from the blood
absorption of glucose from digested food in the gut	uptake of glucose by body cells for use in respiration
release of glucose produced in liver cells by breaking down glycogen	uptake of glucose into muscle and liver cells for conversion to glycogen
release of glucose produced in liver cells from amino acids or glycerol	uptake of glucose into adipose cells and its conversion to fats

Present information in a variety of formats and platforms

The processes that add or remove blood glucose have been presented in this image as a set of scales. It is intended to illustrate the concept of balance. Can you think of a better way of presenting this information? On page 171 there is an opportunity to produce a poster explaining what we can do to avoid diabetes. What formats could you use to make the poster as effective as possible? This may depend on who the target audience is for the poster and where it will be displayed.

▲ There are approximately 40 grams of sugar in a 355 ml can of cola or other soda—eight times the amount that is normally being carried by the blood. What is the concentration of sugar in such a can of soft drink?

PHYSIOLOGY

What are the causes of the current epidemic of diabetes?

A person who has diabetes is unable to keep their blood glucose concentration in balance, either because their pancreas does not produce insulin (Type 1 diabetes) or because their body cells no longer respond to it effectively (Type 2 diabetes). As the role of insulin is to reduce blood glucose concentration, it therefore tends to rise too high, either recurrently or persistently.

The highest normal concentration of blood glucose in balance is 8 mmol/L. With untreated diabetes, the concentration can rise far higher. Concentrations over 30 mmol/L are likely to cause a diabetic coma and are life-threatening. Blood glucose concentrations over 100 mmol/L have sometimes been recorded. If there is glucose present in the urine, or blood glucose concentrations are still high two hours after drinking a test solution containing glucose, then it is likely that a person has developed diabetes.

Type 1 diabetes is the result of the body's own immune system destroying the insulin-producing cells in the pancreas. The reasons for this are at present unclear. It usually develops in children, so is sometimes called early onset diabetes. Type 1 diabetes is treated by monitoring blood glucose concentration and injecting insulin to prevent it from rising too high. Type 2 diabetes is much more common than Type 1 and usually develops later in life. It is treated by adjusting the diet to avoid a rapid intake of glucose.

Both types of diabetes are becoming more prevalent in almost all human populations, though the increases are greater in certain populations. This is illustrated by the two graphs.

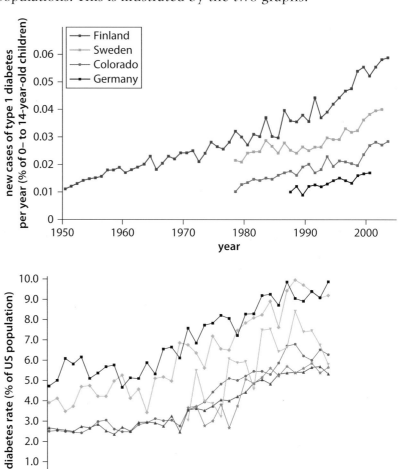

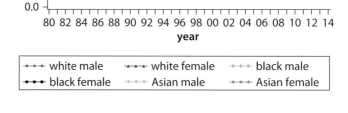

Use the data in the graphs and any other information that you can obtain to research the causes of diabetes. You could research one of the types of diabetes or both. You should consider these questions:

- Is the risk of developing diabetes influenced by our genes?

- Could factors in our environment—such as which infectious diseases we catch when our immune systems are developing—affect the chance of developing diabetes?

- What are the reasons for the increasing rates of diabetes?

When you have done your research, produce a poster to explain what we can do to try to avoid diabetes.

Osmosis in a model cell

METABOLISM

A solute is any chemical particle that is dissolved in a liquid to form a solution. In the cytoplasm of cells, the liquid is water so cells need to be able to take it in. Most cell membranes are therefore freely permeable to water. Water moves in and out of cells by osmosis. This type of movement is described in Chapter 5. The direction of water movement is determined by the difference in solute concentration between the cytoplasm of the cell and the fluid outside. Water moves from the area that has the lower solute concentration to the area with the higher solute concentration.

Model cells are useful for investigating osmosis. A model is a representation that allows a hypothesis to be tested. Models are particularly valuable in biology experiments when it would difficult to control all the variables in living organisms because their systems are so complex. The concept of models is explored more fully in Chapter 12.

Experiment

A model cell only needs to have a membrane and cytoplasm for osmosis to occur. The membrane can be made out of the PVC film that is used to seal food items (known as plastic wrap or cling film). It is about 10 μm thick, whereas a cell membrane is 10 nm thick.

1. What is the size ratio between the thickness of a cell membrane and that of the plastic film?

2. If you wanted to make a model of a 20 μm diameter cell, how wide would the model have to be, to give it the same size ratio as you calculated in Question 1?

3. What is the advantage of making the size ratio for the diameter and the membrane thickness the same?

Method

Follow these instructions to make a model cell:

- Cut out a piece of plastic film that is about 100 mm × 100 mm.

- Fold the film in half over the end of your finger.

- Bring the sides together to make a tubular shape around your finger.

- Remove the shape and pour in 0.5 mol/L sucrose solution. If you use 4.2 ml of sucrose solution you will get a model cell with a diameter of 20 mm, assuming it is spherical.

- Squeeze the ends of the tubular shape together to seal the tube, if possible with no air inside.

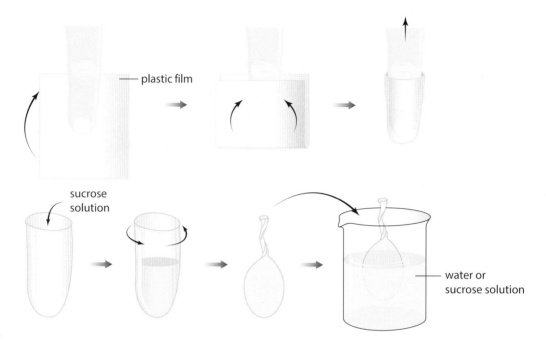

To investigate osmosis you could make two model cells and place one in pure water and the other in a 1.0 mol/L sucrose solution. You should leave them in for an hour or more, if possible. To find out whether the model cells gain or lose water by osmosis, find their mass before and after they have been in the solutions. When you take them out you will have to remove all the solution from the outside of the model cell or the mass will be incorrect.

METABOLISM

How is the solute concentration of the blood kept in balance?

The water permeability of the cell membrane carries with it a risk—if too much water enters our cells, they swell up and burst. If too much passes out, the cells become dehydrated. To prevent this, the solute concentration inside and outside of the cell must be kept the same. Maintaining this balance is one of the functions of the kidney, in the process of osmoregulation.

An adult of average size has about 4.7 liters of blood, of which 2.6 liters is blood plasma and the remainder blood cells. The plasma consists of proteins, glucose, mineral ions, hormones and carbon dioxide dissolved in 2.4 liters of water. All of these solutes cause water to move by osmosis, so biologists use an overall measure of the solute concentration. The concentration of one solute is measured in moles per liter. Each of these concentrations are added together to give the osmolarity (total solute concentration), which is measured in osmoles (osmol or Osm). The normal level for blood plasma is 290 milliosmoles per liter.

1. Is water added to the plasma or removed from it by each of these processes: **a)** sweating, **b)** exhaling, **c)** cell respiration, **d)** secretion of digestive juices such as saliva, **e)** absorption of water from food in the intestines, **f)** urination?

2. In Samuel Coleridge Taylor's poem *The Rime of the Ancient Mariner* there are these words:

   "

   # Water, water, everywhere,
   # Nor any drop to drink.

   "

   If someone on a boat is dying of thirst and they drink seawater, the osmolarity of their blood plasma becomes higher, not lower. Can you explain this using your understanding of osmosis?

3. Plasma proteins are a major component of the osmolarity of blood plasma. Children who are suffering from severe protein malnutrition develop swollen abdomens due to retention of excessive amounts of water in their tissues. Can you explain this?

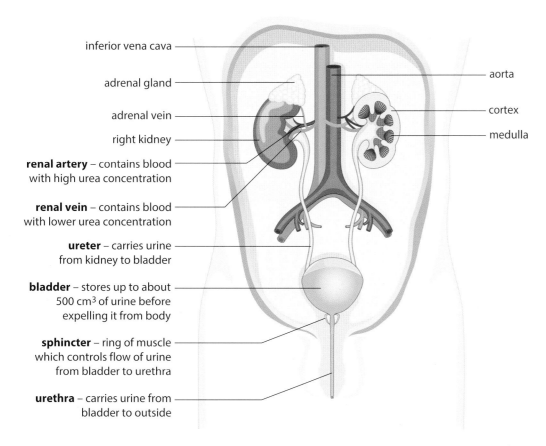

inferior vena cava

adrenal gland

adrenal vein

right kidney

renal artery – contains blood with high urea concentration

renal vein – contains blood with lower urea concentration

ureter – carries urine from kidney to bladder

bladder – stores up to about 500 cm³ of urine before expelling it from body

sphincter – ring of muscle which controls flow of urine from bladder to urethra

urethra – carries urine from bladder to outside

aorta

cortex

medulla

▲ The kidneys receive blood from the renal artery, remove urea and a variable amount of water from it and then return the blood to the circulation through the renal vein. The wastes removed from the blood are eventually expelled from the body through the urethra after being stored in the bladder

The osmolarity of blood plasma changes if water or salt is added or removed. To remain within a safe range (285–295 mosmol/L) there must be a balance between amounts gained and amounts removed. Thirst is a signal that we need to add water to the plasma by drinking fluids, to replace water losses.

The other method of balancing the amounts of water and solutes in the plasma is urine production, a three-step process that takes place in the kidneys.

- Blood is brought to the kidney by the renal artery, which divides up repeatedly to form about a million structures, each composed of a knot-like ball of capillaries called a glomerulus.

- Blood passes at high pressure through the capillaries in the glomerulus. These capillaries have very permeable walls that allow any particles to pass through apart from large molecules such as proteins, which are retained in the blood plasma. As there is a separation of particles according to size, this is a filtration process.

- The filtrate that has been forced out under pressure through the capillary walls is collected by the Bowman's capsule. This is a cup-shaped structure at the start of a narrow tube, called the renal tubule.

- As the filtrate flows along the renal tubule, all useful substances such as glucose are reabsorbed and returned to the blood. Waste products such as urea are not reabsorbed.

- Water is reabsorbed from the filtrate by osmosis. The amount of water reabsorbed can vary. If large amounts of water are reabsorbed, the kidney produces small volumes of concentrated urine which reduces the solute concentration of the blood. Reabsorption of small volumes of water increases the solute concentration of the blood because large volumes of dilute urine are excreted.

▶ Urine production

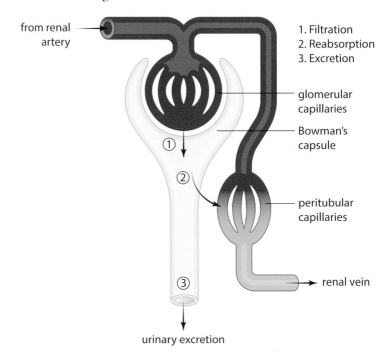

from renal artery

1. Filtration
2. Reabsorption
3. Excretion

glomerular capillaries

Bowman's capsule

①

②

peritubular capillaries

③

renal vein

urinary excretion

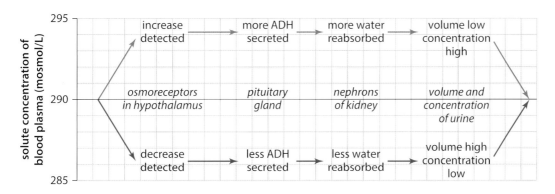

The solute concentration of blood plasma is monitored in a part of the brain called the hypothalamus. Adjacent to the hypothalamus is the pituitary gland. Whereas other glands secrete one or two hormones, the pituitary secretes at least nine. One of these is anti-diuretic hormone (ADH).

ADH increases the amount of water that is reabsorbed from the filtrate in the nephron. The flow chart shows responses to increases and decreases in blood solute concentration.

4. Approximately 20% of the blood pumped out by the left side of the heart passes to the kidneys. If the cardiac output is 5 liters per minute, what volume of blood is supplied to the kidneys per minute?

5. Appoximately 10% of the volume of the blood is filtered out as it passes through the glomerular capillaries.

   a) What volume of filtrate is produced per minute?

   b) What volume of filtrate is produced per day?

6. Assuming that a person produces 1.5 liters of urine in a day, what percentage of the volume of filtrate is reabsorbed as it flows through the nephrons?

7. Blood continues to be pumped to the kidneys at night in young children, but in older children and adults the flow is reduced. What is the advantage of this?

How does feedback control work?

METABOLISM

Within a system, feedback control uses information about the outcome of a process to make decisions about the future of that process. There are two types of feedback control: positive and negative. Positive feedback increases the gap between the original and the new level. Negative feedback decreases the gap, so the original level is restored. Negative feedback causes any change in level to be reversed, so it can be used to achieve balance.

Negative feedback mechanisms are used to keep internal conditions in the body within narrow limits. Biologists use the term **homeostasis** for the maintenance of a relatively constant internal environment in the bodies of humans and other animals. The

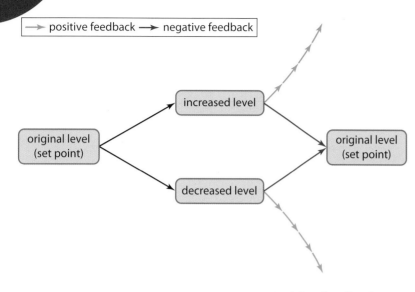

positive feedback → negative feedback

original level (set point)

increased level

decreased level

original level (set point)

advantage of homeostasis is that cells are kept in ideal and stable conditions, even if the outside environment is variable and sometimes hostile. The disadvantage is that large amounts of energy have to be used to maintain homeostasis. Blood glucose concentration, blood solute concentration, blood pH and core body temperature are examples of variables that are kept relatively constant as a part of homeostasis.

Positive feedback is much less common in the human body but it is sometimes used, for example, to increase progressively the force of muscle contractions during childbirth. Positive feedback sometimes also occurs when normal homeostatic processes have failed.

The benefits of negative feedback and the dangers of positive feedback are illustrated by considering what happens if blood glucose concentration rises. In non-diabetics, pancreas cells detect the rise and secrete insulin, which causes body cells to take up glucose from the blood, lowering the concentration. This is negative feedback. Insulin is also secreted in people with Type 2 diabetes, but the body cells are not sensitive to it, so glucose concentration can continue to rise. A positive feedback loop may then develop.

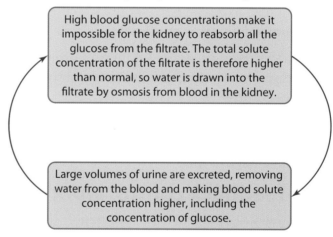

High blood glucose concentrations make it impossible for the kidney to reabsorb all the glucose from the filtrate. The total solute concentration of the filtrate is therefore higher than normal, so water is drawn into the filtrate by osmosis from blood in the kidney.

Large volumes of urine are excreted, removing water from the blood and making blood solute concentration higher, including the concentration of glucose.

This positive feedback loop causes blood glucose concentration and the overall solute concentration to rise higher and higher. Glucose can reach 50 mmol/L or higher and the overall solute concentration can rise above 320 mosmol/L, compared to a normal concentration of 290 mosmol/L. If balance is not re-established, this condition leads to coma and death in 10–50% of cases.

1. Explain which type of feedback occurs in these situations:

   a) cruise control in a vehicle

   b) an exothermic chemical reaction

c) a rock concert when a guitarist gets too close to a loudspeaker

d) the water tank of a toilet with a float valve.

2. Viral infections can result in fever, which is a higher than normal body temperature. Discuss whether fever is maintained by positive or negative feedback.

Data-based question: How can salmon adapt from fresh water to seawater?

Salmon start their life in streams and rivers and remain there for between one and three years, feeding and growing, before swimming downstream and out to sea. After some years in the oceans, mature adult salmon swim back up rivers to reproduce. Salmon therefore have to adjust from fresh water to seawater and then back again. This poses significant challenges for osmoregulation. The salmon that swim out to sea are called smolts, so the developmental changes that make salmon ready for this transition are called smoltification.

▲ The vertical bars of younger salmon are fading and a silvery sheen is developing, showing that this individual is undergoing smoltification in preparation for migration out into the ocean

1. In the gills, a large surface area of tissue is exposed to the surrounding water. Using the data in the table, deduce whether cells in the gills gain or lose water by osmosis when a salmon is

   a) in fresh water

   b) in seawater.

Fluid	Solute concentration (mosmol/l)
Fresh water	<15
Salmon blood plasma	285
Seawater	1000

2. a) Before smoltification, young salmon eat food, but drink little or no water. Despite this, they need to excrete large volumes of dilute urine to keep the solute concentration of their blood plasma in balance. Explain the reasons for this.

   b) Before smoltification Na^+ and Cl^- ions are pumped by active transport from the surrounding water into blood in the gills by protein pumps. Explain the reasons for doing this.

3. a) After smoltification and migration out to sea, salmon drink large quantities of seawater. Explain the reasons for doing this.

   b) Drinking large quantities of seawater makes it necessary for salmon to remove large amounts of Na^+ and Cl^- ions from their body every day. Suggest two methods of removal that the salmon could use.

4. Summarize the changes that occur in a salmon during the process of smoltification that allow it to adjust from a fresh-water habitat to seawater.

What factors can cause the exponential growth of a population?

In "An Essay on the Principle of Population" (published in 1798) Thomas Malthus stated:

> **"**
> **Population, when unchecked, increases in a geometrical ratio.**
> **"**

If many of the offspring in each generation survive and reproduce, the size of a population does increase at an ever faster rate. There are many natural examples of this.

One of the best documented examples is the spread of the the collared dove (*Streptopelia decaocto*). Originally an Asian species, it spread through Europe during the 20th century, reaching the UK in the 1950s. Collared doves have a clutch size of two eggs and can raise five broods per year. They sometimes breed when they are one year old and have a typical life span of three years. They therefore have the capacity to increase in numbers quickly. The table below shows the estimated population size during the decade after their arrival in Britain.

Year	Estimated UK population	Logarithm of UK population
1955	4	0.60
1956	16	1.20
1957	45	1.65
1958	100	2.00
1959	205	2.30
1960	675	2.83
1961	1900	3.28
1962	4650	3.67
1963	10,200	4. 01
1964	18,855	4.28

1. Plot a graph to show the population growth curve of collared doves in Britain from 1955 to 1964.

2. **a)** Geometrical increase is sometimes also called logarithmic or exponential increase. To test whether increase in the collared dove population was exponential, plot a second graph to show the logarithm of estimated population size for each year from 1955 to 1964.

b) If population increase was genuinely exponential, the points on the graph could be joined with a straight line. Discuss whether the increase in the collared dove population in Britain was exponential.

3. Calculate how many times the British population of collared doves doubled between 1955 and 1964.

With exponential growth the numbers in a population double in a set period of time. In bacteria, for example, the doubling time can be as short as half an hour. In plants and animals it is much longer. Writing about the human population, Thomas Malthus stated this in his essay: "In the United States of America, where the means of subsistence have been more ample, the manners of the people more pure, and consequently the checks to early marriages fewer than in any of the modern states of Europe, the population has been found to double itself in twenty-five years."

According to the United States Census Bureau, between 1910 and 2010 the population of the United States of America increased exponentially at an average rate of 1.5% per year. This means that the doubling time of the American population was approximately 50 years—not as fast as Malthus had observed in the 18th century, but still exponential. Even with a shorter doubling time, the US population is rising at an increasing rate—that is the nature of exponential increases.

4. If there is no immigration or emigration, reproduction and death are the two processes that can change the size of a population. Deduce which of these combinations will cause exponential growth in a population.

    a) Reproduction rate and death rate are equal.

    b) Very high reproduction rate and even higher death rate.

    c) Very low reproduction rate and even lower death rate.

Puffballs

Giant puffballs are produced when the fungus *Calvatia gigantea* reproduces. They contain as many as 7×10^{12} spores, making *Calvatia gigantea* possibly the most prolific parent. It has been claimed that the land surface of the Earth would be covered with puffballs if all 7×10^{12} spores grew and produced another puffball. Investigate this claim.

5. Explain the causes of exponential population growth in terms of relative rates of reproduction and death.

6. How can "ample means of subsistence" and "early marriages" make the growth rate of a population faster?

ECOLOGY

What factors can prevent the exponential growth of a population?

Many natural populations fluctuate from year to year, but never rise exponentially despite high reproduction rates. This is due to negative feedback mechanisms. Various factors become more or less intense, depending on the size of the population. They are known as density-dependent factors. Different factors affect plants and animals. The most important of these are shown in the table.

Animals	Plants
Food—the denser the population, the less food is available per animal and some individuals may not obtain enough 	Light—in dense populations some plants may be shaded by others and so not receive enough light 
Predation—if the population of a prey species rises, the numbers of predators rise and a higher percentage is predated 	Mineral nutrients—deficiencies of specific mineral elements may develop in dense populations 
Breeding sites—if animals need a special type of site for breeding, there may be not be enough for a dense population 	Water—there may not be enough water in the soil for the requirements of all plants in a dense population 

Disease and parasitism—pathogens and parasites spread more easily in denser populations so death rates are higher	Pests and diseases spread more easily in dense plant populations so death rates are higher

What is an ecosystem?

In nature, populations of different species live together and interact with each other. Some of these interactions are considered in Chapter 6. Ecologists call a group of populations living together in an area a community. A community includes all the species in the area—plants, animals, fungi, bacteria, and all other organisms. Typically there are very large numbers of species. Interactions within a community are biotic—they take place between living things.

Members of an ecological community also interact with their abiotic (non-living) environment. The abiotic environment includes soil, rock, water and air. Organisms take materials that they need from these various parts of the abiotic environment and release waste products into it. For example, plants absorb carbon dioxide from the air for use in photosynthesis and release oxygen into it. The idea that a community of organisms and its abiotic environment form one overall ecological system was put forward in 1935 by Arthur Tansley, who suggested calling it an ecosystem.

▼ Henri Rousseau painted *Fight Between a Tiger and a Buffalo* in 1908. What interactions between species, apart from predator–prey, could Rousseau have added to his depiction of a forest community?

◄ Mangrove is a type of forest ecosystem that develops along the coast in the tropics. What materials does a mangrove tree release into its abiotic environment and what materials does it absorb? What adaptations does a tree need for growing in soils that are inundated by seawater for part of each day?

How are supplies of mineral elements sustained in an ecosystem?

Rothamsted Research, north of London, UK, is the site of an extemely long-running agricultural experiment. Crops of wheat have been grown on a field called the Broadbalk every year since 1843. The field is divided into strips and each strip receives a different application of fertilizer. One strip is the control and has had no fertilizer for over 170 years. Yields on this strip are very low—about one tonne per hectare compared with yields of ten or more tonnes on fertilized strips. The results of this long-running experiment are shown in the graph below.

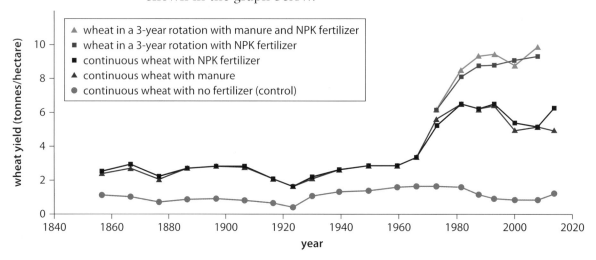

1. According to the Broadbalk results, which is better for crop yields:

    a) growing wheat every year or rotating it with other crops?

    b) manure or NPK (which is a chemical fertilizer containing those three elements)?

2. In the 1970s, the type of wheat used in the experiments was changed to a new short-stemmed variety. What were the effects of this on yields?

3. Yields on the control strip are very low but have not yet dropped to zero. What conclusions do you draw from this?

Plants such as wheat obtain carbon, hydrogen and oxygen from carbon dioxide and water. All the other elements that they need are obtained from the soil and are known as mineral elements. They are grouped according to the amounts that plants absorb.

● Nitrogen, phosphorus and potassium are required in large quantities (primary macronutrients).

● Sulphur, calcium and magnesium are required in moderate quantities (secondary macronutrients).

● Nine nutrients (Fe, Mo, B, Cu, Mn, Na, Zn, Ni and Cl) are required in small quantities (micronutrients).

In total, soil provides a source of 15 different chemical elements. In some ecosystems, plants have been absorbing these elements from the soil for millions of years and yet they have still not run out. Small amounts may come each year from underlying rock or be washed in from other ecosystems, but this would not be enough to sustain the vigorous growth of the plants that we see. The amounts that plants take out of the soil must be balanced by the amounts that are put back in. It is essential that all chemical elements are recycled within the ecosystem.

At Broadbalk, this balance is disrupted by removing the crop from the field. The mineral elements contained in the wheat grains are lost permanently from the soil. The Broadbalk experiment is therefore ultimately unsustainable. Natural ecosystems, where elements remain in the system, are sustainable for ever. The diagram here shows how one element can be recycled.

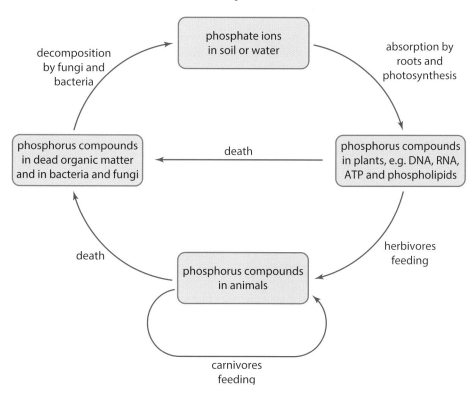

▲ The phosphorus cycle

What processes keep atmospheric CO_2 in balance?

Huge amounts of carbon dioxide are added to the atmosphere each year and are removed from it. The main process that removes CO_2 is photosynthesis, which happens in plants, algae and photosynthetic bacteria (cyanobacteria). CO_2 is also removed by animals that deposit calcium carbonate and other calcium salts in shells or skeletons. If these become part of limestone rock, the carbon may not be released for a long time.

Carbon dioxide is produced by cell respiration in all organisms and then excreted into the atmosphere or into water. Carbon dioxide is also released into the atmosphere from combustion in wildfires. Where limestone rock is exposed, weak acids in rainwater attack the calcium carbonate in it, releasing carbon dioxide into the atmosphere. The flow chart below shows these processes, with estimates of global fluxes in gigatonnes. A gigatonne is a thousand million tonnes, or a million million kilograms.

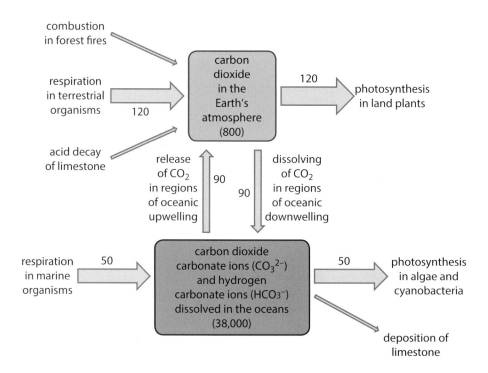

1. Using the data in the flow chart, explain how the concentration of carbon dioxide in the atmosphere can remain in balance.

2. Construct a diagram of the carbon cycle for terrestrial ecosystems such as forests, using the data in the flow chart and the phosphorus cycle diagram (on page 183).

3. Combustion of fossil fuels, production of cement, and land-use changes currently release approximately nine gigatonnes of carbon dioxide into the atmosphere each year, but the quantity of carbon dioxide in the atmosphere is increasing by only four gigatonnes per year. Explain this difference.

4. There is an estimated 10,000 gigatonnes of carbon in the Earth's coal, oil and natural gas reserves. Discuss the probable effects of burning all of the fossil fuel reserves and releasing the carbon dioxide into the atmosphere.

ⒶⒷⒸⒹ Experiment

Balancing photosynthesis and respiration

Carbon dioxide makes water slightly acidic when it dissolves. A narrow-range pH indicator can therefore be used to show whether carbon dioxide concentration has increased or decreased. The indicator usually used is called hydrogen carbonate indicator. The range of colours of this indicator are shown below. Yellow indicates the lowest pH and the highest carbon dioxide concentration. Purple indicates the highest pH and the lowest carbon dioxide concentration.

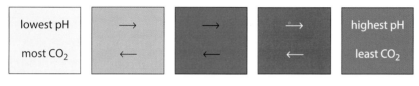

The diagrams below show some possible combinations of plant leaves and animals.

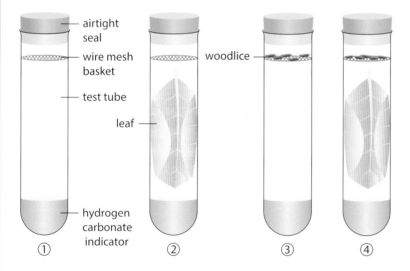

1. Explain the reason for all the tubes being the same size and containing the same volume of indicator.

2. The experiment should be ended as soon as the indicator has changed colour. Explain the reasons for not keeping animals inside the tubes for longer than this.

3. What is the purpose of the tube without a leaf or animals?

4. Assuming that the indicator starts red, indicating an intermediate pH and carbon dioxide concentration, what colour do you expect the indicator to be in each tube at the end of the experiment?

5 What combination of leaves and/or animals would be needed to keep the carbon dioxide concentration inside a tube in balance?

6. What colour would you expect the indicator to be in the tube with a leaf but no animals, if the tubes was covered with aluminium foil to exclude light?

ECOLOGY

What causes the rapid rise in carbon dioxide concentration at the end of a glaciation?

We live in an Ice Age in which a cycle of changes causes ice sheets to spread out from the poles (glaciations) and then rapidly retreat (interglacials). The glaciations occur as the climate becomes gradually colder over tens of thousands of years. Interglacials start very rapidly, with global average temperatures rising by as much as 6°C in a hundred years. These changes suggest that global climate can be altered by two positive feedback mechanisms, one increasing temperatures and the other decreasing them. A switch from one to the other causes glaciations to start and finish. These feedback mechanisms act by changing greenhouse gas concentrations and therefore the amount of heat retained in the Earth's atmosphere.

The Antarctic is covered by an ice sheet that is over four kilometers deep in places and has accumulated over millions of years. Samples of this ice have been obtained by drilling ice cores. If you hold a piece of this ancient ice next to your ear you can hear a popping sound which is the bursting of bubbles of trapped air.

▼ Antarctic ice cores are obtained using a special drilling rig

▼ Bubbles of ancient air are trapped in Antarctic ice

Scientists have carefully collected air from ice samples spanning the past 650,000 years and measured the carbon dioxide concentration in it. The graph below shows the results. The carbon dioxide concentration has varied from very low levels at the end of glaciations to much higher levels during interglacials. The graph also shows an estimate of temperatures based on the ratio between two isotopes of hydrogen (^{1}H and ^{2}H) in the ice. The higher the temperature, the more water molecules containing ^{2}H there are in snow falling on Antarctica.

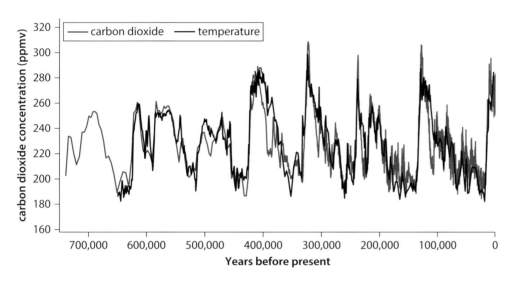

1. What were the highest and lowest carbon dioxide concentrations during the past 650,000 years?

2. What relationship between carbon dioxide concentration and temperature is shown by the data in the graph?

3. The difference between the highest and lowest temperatures according to the data on the graph is about 9°C. Calculate how much the temperature increases for each increase of 10 parts per million in carbon dioxide concentration.

4. **a)** State the current average carbon dioxide concentration of the atmosphere.

   b) Calculate how much higher the current concentration is than the highest concentration found in the ice cores.

   c) The carbon dioxide concentration of the atmosphere is currently rising at 2 ppm a year, which is 200 times faster than at the end of the last glaciation. What are the reasons for this?

   d) The concentration of carbon dioxide is now higher than at any time since the Oligocene epoch, 23 million years ago. Should scientists being doing anything about this and if so, what?

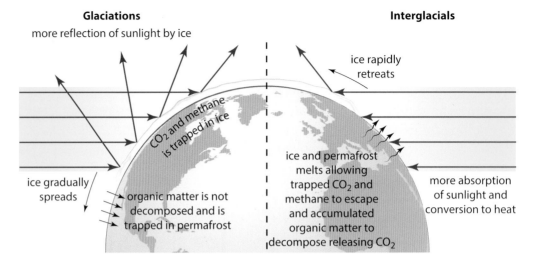

The positive feedback mechanisms that cause warming during interglacials and cooling during glaciations are quite well understood by scientists, but it is less clear what causes the switch from glaciation to interglacial. The Earth's path around the Sun changes between an almost circular orbit to an elliptical one (and then back to circular) over the course of 100,000 years. This change in orbit coincides closely with glacial and interglacial periods, so scientists believe it affects the Earth's climate.

1. How could a change in the Earth's orbit cause a switch from a glaciation with conditions becoming gradually colder on Earth to an interglacial in which there is rapid warming?

2. Can you find any other theories that might explain this switch?

3. At times during the Earth's history, ice sheets extended much further towards the equator than during recent glaciations. They may even have formed a complete cover—this is called Snowball Earth. What could have caused this and why has it not happened more recently?

El Niño—disruption to balance

In normal conditions, air above the warm water in tropical parts of the western Pacific is heated and rises. This draws more air across the Pacific from the east. The resulting winds that blow westwards across the surface of the Pacific are the Trade Winds. They cause westward water currents near the surface of the ocean. Sunlight warms this surface water as it moves across the Pacific, so by the time the water has crossed the Pacific from near Ecuador in South America to Indonesia its temperature has risen by about 8°C. This is the source of the warm water in the western Pacific that causes upward air currents and the Trade Winds to continue. The winds are so strong that the surface of the ocean is about half a meter higher on the west side than the east.

Westward movement of water across the Pacific causes water to move up towards the surface near the coast of South America. The water that is drawn up is cold, so it cools the air above it, which causes downward movement of air from the upper atmosphere. This completes a convective loop in which air rises in the western Pacific, moves eastwards at high altitude, sinks in the eastern Pacific then moves back westwards above the ocean surface. The cold water that moves upwards is nutrient-rich and therefore supports rapid growth rates in phytoplankton and results in the creation of diverse marine ecosystems and major fisheries.

Periodically this pattern of winds and water currents is thrown out of balance by a phenomenon called El Niño. If the Trade Winds blowing westwards become less strong for some reason, some of the warm water piled up on the western side of the Pacific moves back east and the westwards water current slows. The water in the western Pacific becomes cooler and because less cold water moves upwards on the eastern side of the ocean the surface water there becomes warmer. The convective loop of air currents that normally operates becomes weaker so there is a further reduction in the strength of the Trade Winds. This is positive feedback, so the effects become more and more pronounced during an El Niño event.

The area of warmest surface water moves eastwards during an El Niño event. Air rises above this warm water and divides in the upper atmosphere to move both east and west, with cold air sinking in both the western and eastern Pacific. The Trade Winds are therefore replaced in the western side of the Pacific by winds blowing from west to east, encouraging further movement east of the area of warmest water. Evntually it can reach the middle of the Pacific or beyond.

The heating and rising of air over warm areas of ocean results in condensation of water in the atmosphere and rainfall. As the area of warmest water and therefore the heaviest rainfall is further east than normal, Indonesia and other countries on the western side of the tropical Pacific that usually have heavy rainfall experience droughts. Countries on the west coast of South America which normally have very dry climates, such as Peru, experience heavy rainfall and floods. There are also consequences for weather patterns around the world because of the changes that happen in the tropical regions of the Pacific during El Niño. The concept of consequences is considered in Chapter 10.

El Niño conditions develop at irregular intervals of between two and seven years. They persist for anything from nine months to two years. The end of an El Niño period may be due to slow-moving but very extensive waves that displace the area of warmest surface water back towards Indonesia. This causes the Trade Winds to blow once again, with positive feedback mechanisms rapidly re-establishing normal conditions.

1. Use the information in the text to draw two annotated diagrams. One diagram should show the pattern of air and water circulation in the Pacific Ocean in normal conditions and the other when there is an El Niño event.

2. Draw a diagram or other form of infographic to represent the effects of El Niño on the part of the world where you live.

▲ Pelagic red crabs (*Pleuroncodes planipes*) are native to the eastern Pacific coast of Mexico, but during El Niño events they can are known to travel 1500 miles further north, to Oregon (US)

Summative assessment

Statement of inquiry:

Development is only sustainable if systems remain in balance.

Introduction

In this summative assessment you will consider how balance can be upset naturally and by human activity, taking El Niño and Chilean salmon farming industry as case studies. The question to bear in mind is whether it is possible to achieve sustainable development if global systems are not in balance.

 Toxic "red tides"

1. Fish farms along the coast of southern Chile produced nearly 600,000 tonnes of salmon for human consumption in 2015. Young salmon for stocking these farms are reared in tanks at land-based installations called hatcheries. Adult salmon are needed to produce fertilized eggs and a supply of fresh water is required for filling the tanks. The salmon are reared until they become smolts, which can then be transferred to the salmon farms in the sea. Explain the problems that would develop if salmon younger than smolts were transferred from fresh water to seawater. [4]

2. In late 2015 and early 2016 the largest ever "red tides" developed over huge areas off the coast of Chile. They consisted of vast numbers of algae and they spread rapidly. The appearance of large numbers of algae in fresh water or seawater is called an algal bloom. Explain how huge numbers of organisms such as algae can suddenly appear in an ecosystem. [4]

3. The algae produced a virulent neurotoxin that killed molluscs and fish and posed a threat to human health if seafood containing it was consumed. An estimated 27 million salmon in salmon farms were killed either by increased water temperatures or by the neurotoxin. Some of these dead salmon were dumped at sea. On one part of the Chilean coast, 40,000 tonnes of sardines were washed up dead and at another site, 337 sei whales (*Balaenoptera borealis*) were washed up in one of the biggest strandings in history. The red tides coincided with a powerful El Niño event, which warmed water off the Chilean coast by several degrees.

Populations of algae are always present in ocean water and for much of the time they stay in balance. Suggest reasons for the populations in the water off the coast of Chile becoming unbalanced. [4]

4. Suggest factors that could bring the populations of algae back into balance and, for a time at least, end the red tides. [3]

Modelling algal blooms

Find a pond, lake, river or aquarium in which the numbers of algae are in balance, so the water is clear rather than being bright green or red.

5. Formulate a hypothesis for what is preventing the numbers of algae from rising exponentially. Explain the reasons for your hypothesis. [3]

6. Design a scientific experiment to test your hypothesis, including how you will alter the independent variables in your investigation and how you will keep the control variables constant. [7]

7. Explain what your dependent variable is, how you will measure it and how you will analyse your results. [5]

Chilean salmon farming and the ISA virus

8. The maps below show the main area of Chilean salmon farms in two periods. Each red spot represents one salmon farm. The fish reared are Atlantic salmon, rather than the native Pacific species.

   a) Describe the distribution of salmon farms in 2006–2007. [3]

   b) Describe the changes in distribution that occurred between 2006–2007 and 2009–2010. [2]

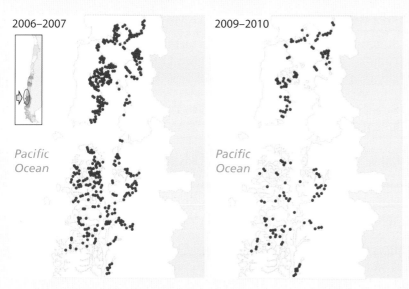

2006–2007

2009–2010

Pacific Ocean

Pacific Ocean

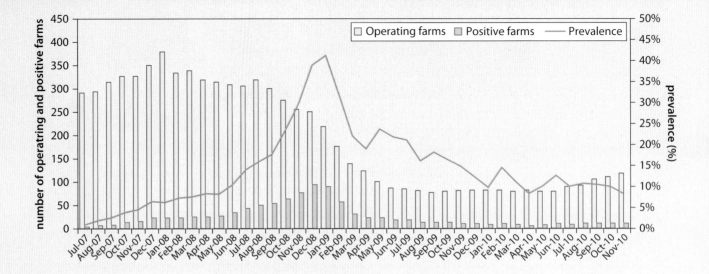

9. Infectious salmon anemia (ISA) is a viral disease of Atlantic salmon. The virus infects the red blood cells of the fish and destroys them. The chart above shows the prevalence of ISA on Chilean salmon farms (green line), the number of farms with the disease (blue bars) and the number of operating salmon farms (red bars) over a period from 2007 to 2010. Interpret the data to explain the changes in the number of operating salmon farms. [5]

10. Atlantic salmon and both rainbow and brown trout are non-native to Chile, but they have been introduced and there are now populations in the rivers and coastal water. Pacific salmon show strong resistance to the ISA virus. Both species of trout can become infected with the ISA virus but are not killed by it. However, an outbreak of ISA in a Chilean salmon farm often kills close to 100% of the fish.

   a) Suggest reasons for far higher mortality due to ISA virus in Chilean salmon farms than in populations of salmon and trout in rivers and the open sea. [3]

   b) Suggest how ISA could spread from one salmon farm to another. [2]

 Building a sustainable farming industry

11. Consider the statements below together with any other information that you can find on salmon farming in Chile and elsewhere.

   - Salmon farming developed at a rapid rate in southern Chile from the 1980s onwards. For example, exports to Japan were valued at $100 million in 1990. By 2000 they were $1 billion and by 2006 $2 billion.

- Many salmon farms have been constructed and in some cases they are in close proximity. Some farms are very large and stocking densities (fish per m²) are often very high.

- Salmon farming provides employment for more than 70,000 people in southern Chile. Only copper mining provides more jobs in Chile.

- Salmon is high in all these nutrients: protein, long chain unsaturated omega-3 fatty acids, vitamins A and D, and minerals including selenium and iodine.

- There is a need for increases in protein-rich foods to feed the growing human population, but there is a limit to the amount of wild salmon that can be caught without causing populations to collapse.

- Salmon are naturally carnivorous so pellets made from other fish species caught in the wild are usually used to feed them in farms. It can take as much as 3 kg of these wild-caught fish to produce 1 kg of farmed salmon.

- Salmon produce feces and the concentration near farms is far higher than with wild populations. Large deposits can accumulate, covering the sea bed. The feces gradually decomposes, releasing nitrogen, phosphorus and other minerals into the water.

- Pathogenic bacteria and viruses as well as parasites are a recurrent problem. Over 300 tonnes of antibiotics are released every year by Chilean salmon farms to control bacterial diseases, with increasing levels of antibiotic resistance.

- Crop plants that produce the omega-3 fatty acids needed in a salmon's diet have been bred using GM technology.

Now write an essay in answer to this question:

Can a sustainable salmon farming industry be developed in Chile or elsewhere in the world that can provide food for the growing human population without damage to the wider world? [15]

ATL Critical thinking skills

Addressing counterclaims

The final task in this assessment requires students to synthesize a range of information in support of an argument. Argumentative writing not only requires students to support their viewpoint, but also that they evaluate counterclaims. This involves anticipating alternative perspectives to your chosen viewpoint and addressing these alternative viewpoints.

8 Environment

Environment: all that surrounds us.

◀ This iconic photograph was taken by Apollo 8 crewmember Bill Anders on 24 December 1968, while in orbit around the Moon. It shows the Earth rising above the lunar horizon and has been called "the most influential environmental photograph ever taken". The impact of seeing the world from the vantage point of a lunar mission was best summed up by Anders: "We came all this way to explore the moon, and the most important thing is that we discovered the Earth." How has this and other "blue marble" photographs taken on the Apollo missions changed our view of the Earth so profoundly?

◀ In "Earth from Above", a United Nations-supported project, French photographer and environmental activist, Yann Arthus-Bertrand documents our planet using aerial photography. It is estimated that his photographs, printed on billboards and exhibited in more than 150 cities worldwide, have been seen by more than 200 million people. Does seeing the planet from a different point of view help us understand it better?

Environments change with time. Andy Goldsworthy is a British artist who creates short-lived works of art using materials found in the natural environment such as snow, ice, leaves, feathers, petals and twigs. They are constructed in such a way that they will disappear as they are changed by conditions in the environment.

The "Virtuoso Man" statue off the coast of New Providence in The Bahamas is about 2.5 meters tall and is made from a special type of cement, which has the same pH as the seawater, allowing marine life to colonize it. Why is it important for man-made structures to be as similar as possible to the environment that surrounds them?

Introduction

Every living organism has an environment. It comprises all the living (biotic) and non-living (abiotic) things that surround the organism. The environment of an individual organism is its habitat—the place where it lives. When we apply the concept of environment to an ecological community, the term becomes much broader and encompasses conditions in the ecosystem as a whole.

Environment is vitally important to living organisms because it influences development and health; it affects survival chances and is a major factor in driving natural selection and therefore evolution. Monitoring conditions in ecosystems is a fundamental task for environmental biologists. Both biotic and abiotic factors are measured to see if changes are occurring and action needs to be taken. Change is therefore a key concept for understanding environments.

▼ These blue gentian flowers (*Gentiana verna*) were photographed at 2,500 meters. The bright blue color is necessary to attract scarce pollinating insects. With climate change, snow cover in this alpine habitat might decrease. What consequence might this have for the blue gentian?

Statement of inquiry:

Environments provide aesthetic benefits and influence human cultural expression, but human-induced changes undermine these benefits.

Sudden environmental changes can be the result of volcanic eruptions, landslides, wildfires or earthquakes. Other changes, for example, shifts in climate, or development of new ecosystems as glaciers retreat, can take a long time. Some organisms play a significant role in structuring their environment and the loss of these organisms can lead to significant changes.

Abiotic factors are non-living features of the environment such as soil, water, temperature, light intensity and wind speed. Biotic factors are the other organisms that share a habitat and any effects that they have on the environment. Relationships between species in ecological communities are considered in Chapters 6 and 7; interactions between species and abiotic factors in ecosystems are referred to in Chapter 7.

In this chapter we look first at habitats and then at how abiotic factors affect organisms, and how organisms affect the environment. Later in the chapter we consider changes to the environment caused by humans and what effects they have had. Habitat destruction, pollution, climate change due to burning of fossil fuels and the introduction of alien species are some of the most widespread environmental changes caused by humans. There are often harmful effects for humans and other species, but occasionally there are unexpected benefits. The nuclear explosion at Chernobyl (Ukraine) is one example, with rare species now thriving in the surrounding area. Another example is the wild wetland of Văcărești, in the heart of Romania's capital city, Bucharest.

▲ Concrete dams were built to create a reservoir at Văcărești, but the scheme failed and a complex patchwork of grasslands, swamps and small lakes has now developed, with such valuable biodiversity that the whole area is protected

What can we learn about environments from Movile Cave?

Case studies are widely used in environmental research. A particular environment is studied to see what changes happen over time, allowing scientists to obtain evidence about the effects of biotic and abiotic factors. Often case studies look at environments that have been altered by humans, but the example that follows is the opposite—an environment that has remained undisturbed during the entire time that humans have been evolving.

Movile Cave, located close to the Black Sea coast in Romania was discovered in 1986. Until its discovery, the cave had been sealed off from the outside environment and life within evolved in isolation for 5.5 million years. The Movile cave system consists of a network of cracks and small chambers and is flooded by mineral-rich waters. This forms a unique ecosystem with an atmosphere that is unusually rich in carbon dioxide (3%) and methane (1%), but low in oxygen (8%). There are high concentrations of hydrogen sulfide and ammonia in the water and no light enters.

ECOLOGY

Food chains in the cave are different from those outside. The walls of the cave are covered with films of bacteria that gain energy from chemical reactions using sulfides and methane. Microscopic invertebrates feed on these films of bacteria, with other invertebrates feeding on them.

There are 33 types of organism in Movile Cave that occur nowhere else. These species are clearly related to organisms found outside the cave system. A species of woodlouse is similar enough to others outside the cave to be classified in the genus *Armadillidium*, but unlike them it has no eyes or skin coloring. The cave water scorpion, a species in the genus *Nepa*, is a predator of the woodlouse and is also eyeless. There are eyeless centipedes, pseudoscorpions and other highly specialized animals.

1. Suggest reasons for the high concentration of carbon dioxide and low concentration of oxygen in air in the cave.

2. Discuss whether the cave would provide a suitable environment for roosting bats.

3. Explain the advantages of being eyeless in Movile Cave.

4. An endemic species is one that is found nowhere else. Suggest reasons for such a high number of endemic species in Movile Cave.

5. What conclusion can we draw about evolution and environment from Movile Cave?

▲ Organisms have adaptations that aid their survival in their preferred habitat: here in Movile, a species of woodlouse, as yet unnamed, but in the genus *Armadillidium*, is being attacked by cave water scorpion, also unnamed but assigned to the genus *Nepa*

ECOLOGY

What is a habitat?

The environment in which an organism is normally found is its habitat. Organisms find the conditions required for their survival, such as food, shelter, protection, mates, water, territory and the absence of predators in this environment. Some organisms are tolerant of a very wide range of conditions; others can be very specific in their habitat requirements.

Habitats vary widely, from large areas of forest, grassland or desert to small sites such as a rotting log, or the body of a host organism that could be the habitat for a parasite. Habitats can be on land or in fresh water, as in streams and lakes. Marine habitats include kelp forests, coral reefs, the ocean floor and deep sea vents.

Organisms have adaptations that help them survive in their preferred habitat. For example, land plants often have rigid stems for support, while water plants have more flexible stems because the water around them is supportive.

Habitat case studies

1. For each of the following case studies of habitats, identify biotic and abiotic factors, using information from the text and the accompanying images.

The sea otter (*Enhydra lutris*) lives within a kilometer of the coast, in waters up to 20 metres deep. The California marine kelp forest is a favored habitat, along with sheltered beaches and barrier reefs that give protection from severe ocean winds and wave action during storms. The otters' territories are typically a few kilometers in length. The otters remain in the same territory all year, diving under the salt water to forage for prey (fish, sea urchins, molluscs and crustaceans). In the past, sea otters became a threatened species because they were hunted for their furs, but their numbers have recovered since.

The lagoon jellyfish (*Mastigias papua*) has a life span of about four months and is active in the summer and autumn. Its habitat consists of coastal waters such as bays and lagoons, where it feeds on animal plankton. Algae living in its tissues produce food for the jellyfish to use. During the day, the lagoon jelly travels upward, orienting its body to absorb maximum sunlight.

The number of lagoon jellies in some mangrove lakes declined dramatically in 1998, possibly because of an El Niño event. The temperature of the mangrove lakes rose, as did the saltiness, creating a less than ideal environment for the jellyfish. By the year 2000, numbers recovered.

Lagoon jellies are popular among aquarists because their algae symbionts make them colorful.

The spotted owl (*Strix occidentalis*) inhabits forests in the west of North America. It prefers old growth forest that has never been logged, because this provides mixed ages of tree and dense cover. Young are raised using natural holes in large trees as nest sites.

The spotted owl hunts at night and uses its hearing to locate prey. It usually feeds on small mammals such as squirrels and voles. It is itself preyed on by larger birds such as eagles.

The forests inhabited by the spotted owl vary, and there are several subspecies with slightly different features. The northern spotted owl inhabits old growth redwood forests that range from northern California to British Columbia. It has been at the centre of a conflict between conservationists and indigenous groups on the one hand, and loggers and farmers on the other. The US Fish and Wildlife Service has set aside 35,000 km^2 as critical habitat but this is still being challenged.

The elfcup fungus (*Chlorociboria aeruginascens*) grows on fallen logs and on trees with dead wood, in temperate deciduous forests in Europe and North America. It prefers poplar, aspen, oak and ash trees as hosts and it requires moisture to grow. The fungus stains the wood blue or green, making the timber very sought after by furniture makers and artists.

The fungus is inedible for humans.

2. Identify a habitat in your local area where a specific living organism can be found. Take a photo of the organism. Attempt to capture as many features of its habitat as you can in the photo. Annotate the image with descriptions of biotic and abiotic factors that have impacts on the organism.

ATL Thinking in context

Relate each of the case studies in the previous activity to the global context of personal and cultural expression, thinking about:

● the ways in which humans express ideas, beliefs and values

● the ways in which humans discover nature

● how humans appreciate artistry, craft, creation and beauty.

ECOLOGY

How much evidence is there that living organisms affect the environment?

Prairie dogs (*Cynomys sp.*) are plant-eating rodents that are native to the grasslands of North America. They dig extensive burrows that can subsequently provide nesting sites for birds such as burrowing owls and mountain plovers. The burrows consist of tunnel systems that prevent erosion and runoff by channeling rainwater, giving it time to infiltrate. The digging of tunnel systems also improves soil structure by increasing aeration and reverses soil compaction due to cattle grazing. The grazing patterns of prairie dogs change plant composition in the vicinity of their burrows. Plains bison, pronghorn antelope and mule deer preferentially graze where prairie dogs are active.

▲ Prairie dogs live in large social communities that are made up of several families

In most of its range, the sea otter, whose habitat was described earlier in this chapter, controls sea urchin populations by feeding on them. In the absence of this control, the sea urchins tend to overgraze kelp forests. Where sea otters have been reduced in number or lost completely, kelp forests often become degraded. Along with the catastrophic effects this has on species that use kelp forests as a habitat or food source, it also removes the shelter provided by the kelp fronds, reduces the protection of vulnerable coastlines from storms and increases the turbidity of seawater.

The acorn banksia (*Banksia prionotes*) is a flowering tree from Western Australia. Its habitat is on sandy soils, mostly on low lying areas and the lower slopes of dunes. Even if the water level is 15 meters below the ground, the acorn banksia can obtain water and mineral nutrients using its long tap roots. Some of this water is lost by lateral roots into the layers of soil near the surface, making it less dry. There is a period each year when the tree is the only flowering plant in its habitat, becoming a critically important food source for pollinators such as the brown honeyeater. Later in the season, honeyeaters are important pollinators of other species making the preservation of the banksia tree important for the overall function of the biological community.

▲ New Holland honeyeater perched on a banksia flower

As seen from these examples, living organisms can have a highly significant effect both on other species and on the abiotic environment.

1 What evidence do these examples provide for:

a) living organisms changing the abiotic environment?

b) biodiversity being affected by these changes to the abiotic environment?

2. The keystone of a bridge is a wedge-shaped stone at the summit of an arch that locks the whole structure together.

a) What is a keystone species in an ecosystem?

b) Which are keystone species in the examples described here?

c) What is the reason for trying to identify keystone species in natural ecosystems?

3. Can you find other examples of keystone species, without which the abiotic environment and ecological community of an ecosystem would collapse?

What is primary succession?

ECOLOGY

When a volcano erupts or a glacier retreats, areas of bare rock appear on which there is initially no life.

These areas become colonized by a biological community in a process known as primary succession. Pioneer species such as lichens, algae, mosses and fungi arrive as spores or seeds, which germinate and grow, with filaments or roots from them penetrating the rock and helping to break it down into smaller pieces; dead material and mineral particles collect around the pioneers, creating soil conditions that favor the growth of larger plants, such as grasses and shrubs. These plants

▲ Plants quickly colonize bare gravel left by the retreating Skaftafellsjökull glacier in Iceland

further improve the soil quality and may create the conditions needed for shrubs and then trees.

Throughout this process, the activities of living things induce changes in the amount of solar energy stored in the community, they increase water retention through greater infiltration and percolation, and they improve soil quality.

Sometimes a process similar to primary succession occurs in areas that used to have a biological community which has been disrupted by floods, fires or agriculture. This is known as secondary succession.

1 Imagine a world where life had not evolved.

    a) What would happen to newly formed areas of bare rock?

    b) What does this tell you about the effects of living organisms on natural environments?

2. Research an example of primary or secondary succession that happens in the area where you live. In a city you could choose gardens that are no longer cultivated or roofs.

    a) What are the first plants to colonize?

    b) What type of ecological community would eventually develop—grassland, forest or something else?

ECOLOGY

Do abiotic factors in the environment affect natural communities?

A group of organisms of the same species living in an area is known to ecologists as a population; all the populations living together in an area are an ecological community. In Chapter 6, we discuss the types of interaction that can take place between organisms in a community. Here we consider examples of the effects that abiotic factors in the environment can have on organisms in a community.

1. Deserts are areas that can have long periods of time without rain. Even a brief period of rain can cause a burst of activity from living things. For example, the normally bare desert in the Goegap Nature Reserve in South Africa has a burst of ephemeral plant growth with colorful flowers during the brief spring rain season.

2. In the San Rafael Mountains of California there is an area of serpentine rock and the soil that forms on it has a very high pH. The soil is also rich in nickel, chromium and magnesium and is poor in calcium. Few plants can tolerate these conditions and the vegetation is stunted. There are unusually high numbers of endemic plant species, such as the Santa Barbara jewelflower (*Caulanthus amplexicaulis*). Wherever the same rock type occurs in the world there are sparse ecosystems called serpentine barrens.

▲ An oryx between the spring flowers dominating the landscape in the Goegap Nature Reserve, Namaqualand, South Africa. The normally bare desert has been covered with quick-growing plants that have colorful flowers

3. In temperate regions, characterized by well-defined seasons, growing conditions for trees vary through the year. During spring and summer, when transpiration and photosynthesis are fastest, wide thin-walled xylem vessels are produced, while in autumn and winter, smaller thick-walled xylem cells appear. The result of this cycle is visible in tree trunks, where each year of growth is represented as a ring of xylem. The width of annual growth rings varies between years and can be correlated with differences in temperature, rainfall and other abiotic factors.

▲ Santa Barbara jewelflower, an endemic species of serpentine soils

▼ In this scanning electron micrograph of the annual rings from a larch tree (*Larix decidua*), the gray bands show large, open vessels, produced in spring and early summer. The yellow bands contain smaller vessels and are produced later each year. An annual ring consists of one fast and one slow growth region

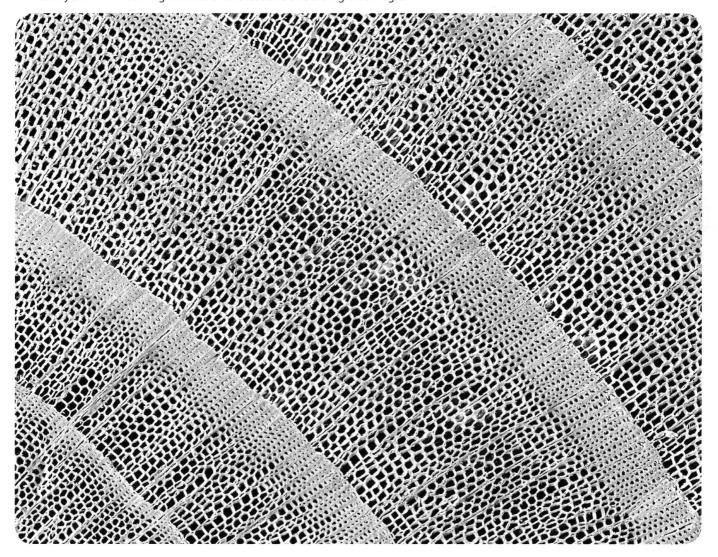

Data-based question: Tree growth

The photograph below shows a 40-year sequence of rings from a Douglas fir (*Pseudotsuga menziesii*). It grew in a plantation that was thinned periodically by felling some of the trees. The start of each annual ring is light and the end is dark. Four of the rings are dated.

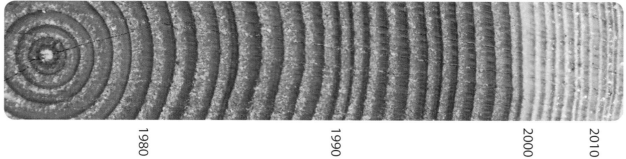

1980   1990   2000   2010

1. Starting with 1980, measure the width of the annual ring for each year and record the value in a table.

2. Explain how you standardized your procedure for measuring the rings.

3. Construct a graph of annual ring width, using whatever format you consider appropriate.

4. Suggest a reason for the narrow rings in the most recent years.

The Douglas fir tree grew in the Wyre Forest, in England. In this area, the rainfall during the main growing season (May to August) was above 200 mm in most years, but was below 160 mm in 1989, 1990, 1994, 1995 and 1996.

5. Using the data in the photograph and your graph, evaluate the hypothesis that low rainfall during the growing season reduces the growth of Douglas fir trees.

6. Discuss whether the data provides evidence that factors other than rainfall affect the growth of Douglas fir trees.

Pine trees are widely grown to produce timber. Young trees are raised by collecting seeds from mature trees and germinating them. A growth study was carried out on a site at a latitude of 57°, in the Highlands of Scotland. Trees were grown using local seeds collected from *Pinus sylvestris* trees near the trial site and from seeds collected from trees of the same species in others parts of Europe. The growth in height of the trees per year was measured. The scatter graph shows the latitude of each seed source and the growth, in height, of trees raised from it. The growth in height of trees grown from imported seeds is shown as a percentage of the growth in height of the trees raised from local seeds.

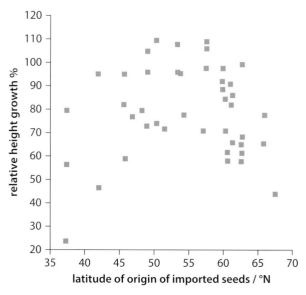

7. Identify the relationship between latitude of origin and growth:

   a) between 35° and 57°

   b) between 57° and 70°

8. Suggest reasons for the relationships between latitude of origin of imported seeds and the growth of the trees.

IB Organization

The two principle variables in climate are average annual temperature and average annual precipitation. The combination of these two variables determines the type of plant community that develops over time in an area.

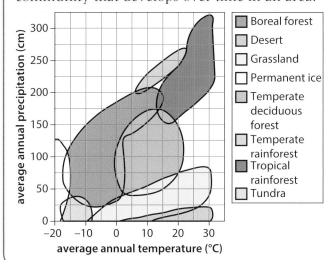

Using the graph, answer the following questions:

1. What type of plant community will develop at an average annual temperature of 15°C and average annual precipitation of 150 cm?

2. What range of rainfall permits forest development?

3. What is the range of temperatures over which desert can develop?

4. If you climb a high mountain, you will move through different plant communities: forest, herb-rich grassland, a community of scattered alpine plants and finally rock and snow. What will happen to these communities if global warming becomes more and more intense?

What is the greenhouse effect?

ECOLOGY

Electromagnetic radiation is a form of energy that can travel through space in the form of waves. These electromagnetic waves are characterized by wavelength and energy, and interact with molecules and materials around us in various different ways. For example, photosynthetic pigments such as chlorophyll absorb electromagnetic radiation in the range of 400–700 nm (visible light). Molecules of liquid water absorb microwaves, which have wavelengths between 1 and 1,000 mm. Molecules of gases in the Earth's atmosphere, such as carbon dioxide, methane, nitrous oxide and water vapor absorb infrared radiation which has wavelengths ranging between 700 nm and 1 mm.

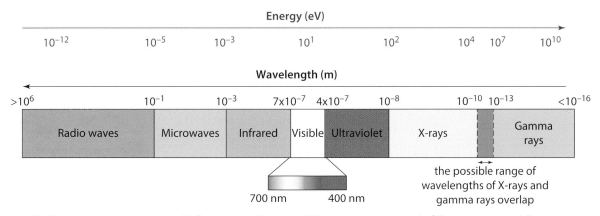

▲ Radio waves, microwaves and infrared radiation are at the lower energy end of the spectrum, while gamma rays, X-rays and ultraviolet light are at the higher end. Visible light is a mid-range energy radiation

Have you ever entered a room with a lot of windows on a sunny day and found it to be warmer than expected? Have you gotten into a car parked in a sunny area with all of its windows closed and found that it is uncomfortably warm inside? Why might this be?

The heating effect of sunlight passing through glass into an enclosed space was first observed in the greenhouses that are used in horticulture. Electromagnetic radiation in the form of sunlight enters through the glass and is absorbed by materials inside the greenhouse, warming them up. These warmed materials re-emit radiation, but in the form of infrared. Whereas the short wave lengths of visible light pass freely through glass, radiation with longer wave lengths, such as infrared, does not. Heat therefore builds up inside the greenhouse.

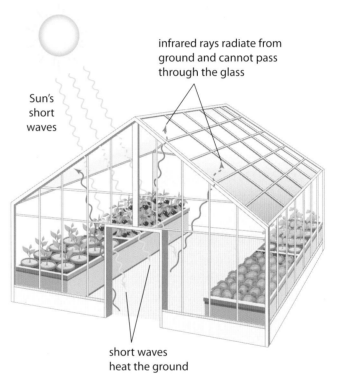

infrared rays radiate from ground and cannot pass through the glass

Sun's short waves

short waves heat the ground

▲ Photosynthesis rates in greenhouses can be faster than outside because the temperature is higher even though no artificial heating has been used

A similar process occurs in the Earth's atmosphere. Most of the electromagnetic radiation from the Sun has relatively short wavelengths (400–700 nm) and is not absorbed by any of the gases in the atmosphere, so it reaches the Earth's surface. Some of it is absorbed by plants and other organisms that use it in photosynthesis; some strikes ice or other reflective materials and passes back out through the atmosphere; much is absorbed by rock, soil or other materials on the Earth's surface, warming them. These materials then re-emit thermal infrared radiation with relatively long wavelengths (8–15 µm) and some of it is absorbed by gases in the atmosphere, preventing the energy from passing back out into space. This causes the Earth to be warmer than if all the infrared radiation was able to escape.

The gases in the atmosphere that absorb infrared radiation are known as greenhouse gases and the warming effect that they cause is the greenhouse effect. Carbon dioxide, water vapour, nitrogen oxides and methane are the principal greenhouse gases. Without any carbon dioxide or other greenhouse gases in the atmosphere, temperatures on Earth would be far too cold to support life. Thus the greenhouse effect is a natural phenomenon and in moderation it benefits living organisms.

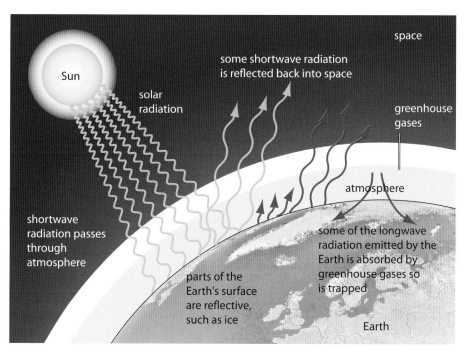

▲ The surface of the Earth absorbs, reflects and re-radiates some of the electromagnetic radiation from the Sun

If the concentration of greenhouse gases in the atmosphere rises, more thermal infrared radiation will be intercepted and the greenhouse effect will be greater. There have been rapid recent increases in most of the greenhouse gases. Carbon dioxide in particular is now at higher concentrations than at any time in the past 20 million years. The increase has taken place since the start of the Industrial Revolution and has led to what is called the enhanced greenhouse effect. The consequence is global warming and as average temperatures on Earth rise, the processes that generate wind, rain and other weather events increase, all of which are summed up as climate change.

What human activities cause emissions into the atmosphere of:

1. carbon dioxide?

2. methane?

3. nitrogen oxides?

Modelling the greenhouse effect

Fill a flask with water. Displace the water in the flask with carbon dioxide, either using bottled gas or by collecting the gas generated from a chemical reaction such as sodium bicarbonate and vinegar. The water can be displaced by inverting the flask in a pan and then displacing the water with the CO_2 gas.

Stopper the flask with a one-holed stopper. Insert either a data-logging thermometer or a standard laboratory grade thermometer through the hole. As a control, set up the same apparatus but with a flask that contains just air.

Position both flasks an equal distance from a 100 W light bulb and then record the changes in temperature over a 10-minute period. Compare how the temperature changes in the two flasks over time.

This experiment could be extended over one or more 24-hour cycles by using a timer to switch a light on and off to simulate night and day.

Data-based question: Greenhouse gases

The following graphs show the concentration of CO_2 in the Earth's atmosphere detected at Mauna Loa Observatory in Hawaii, from 1958 to 2015, and the monthly variation over a typical year.

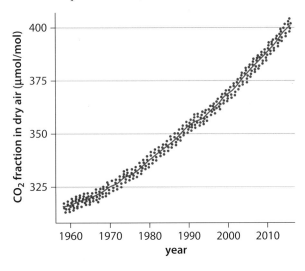

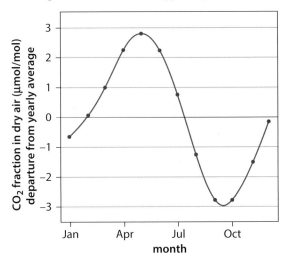

▲ An ongoing change in concentration of CO_2 levels, as observed by the continuous measurements taken on the Mauna Loa mountain top in Hawaii

▲ CO_2 variation (yearly average deviation)

1. **a)** Outline how the concentration of carbon dioxide has changed over the time period measured.

   b) What factors are contributing to this rise?

2. **a)** Identify the months when the concentration of atmospheric carbon dioxide is falling.

   b) Hawaii is in the northern hemisphere. Suggest a biological process that occurs during these months that could be responsible for removing carbon dioxide.

Changes in atmospheric concentrations of greenhouse gases have been investigated using some of the research methods described in Chapter 7, which allow scientists to gain an understanding of how the climate changed over the last 700,000 years.

The following graphs show the concentrations of three greenhouse gases since 1750, expressed either as parts per million (ppm) or part per billion (ppb).

(a)

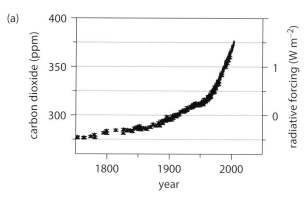

(b)

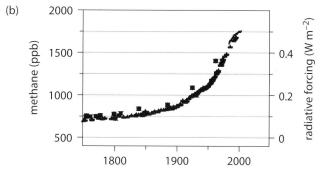

(c)

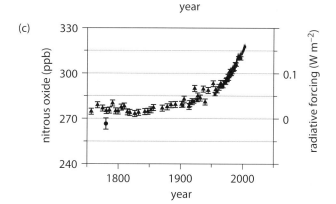

3. a) Using the three graphs, determine the concentrations of each of the gases in the year 2000.

b) Calculate the percentage increase of each gas since 1750.

4. Compare the concentration of carbon dioxide in the atmosphere in 2000 to the concentration of methane and nitrous oxide in the same year.

By what factor is the concentration of carbon dioxide greater than the concentration of:

a) methane? **b)** nitrous oxide?

5. The radiative forcing is a measure of the amount of heat energy trapped per unit area. Determine the current level of radiative forcing for each of the three gases.

6. Which gas contributes most to the greenhouse effect?

What are the sources of greenhouse gases?

Natural processes release greenhouse gases and also remove them from the atmosphere, but greenhouse gas concentrations are now rising due to human activity. Huge quantities of carbon dioxide are released by the burning of fossil fuels for electricity production, heating homes, and for transportation. Methane is released from the digestive systems of cattle and sheep reared on farms and also from decomposition of organic matter in landfill dumps, from rice paddies and from the thawing of Arctic permafrost. Nitrogen oxides are produced by engines in vehicles and are released by agricultural activities, including the use of fertilizers.

▲ At this landfill site, efforts are being taken to minimize the emission of greenhouse gases. Methane is released from household waste as it decomposes; at this site, it is captured and burned to produce electricity. The carbon dioxide released from the combustion of the waste is pumped into ponds to promote photosynthesis and therefore growth of algae. The algae are then used for biofuel production

Track your carbon footprint

A number of phone apps and websites allow individuals to analyze their lifestyle and identify personal contributions to greenhouse gases. The World Wildlife Fund (http://footprint.wwf.org.uk) and myclimate (http://www.myclimate.org) websites are only two examples. By answering a series of questions, anyone can become aware of ways in which they can take action to reduce their carbon footprint. Is there anything you could do?

Data-based question: Ozone depletion

Sunlight includes ultraviolet radiation (UV). As it passes through the atmosphere, ozone (O_3) absorbs about 98% of the UV radiation with wavelengths between 200 nm and 315 nm; 90% of atmospheric ozone is in a part of the upper atmosphere called the stratosphere.

1. What are the benefits to life on Earth of absorption of UV by ozone?

Chemicals released by humans, especially chlorofluorocarbons (CFCs) from aerosol cans and other devices, caused large decreases in ozone in the stratosphere, particularly over Antarctica. The Antarctic "ozone hole" increased in size from the late 1970s to the early 21st century, but throughout the stratosphere ozone concentrations decreased and more UV radiation penetrated to the Earth's surface.

2. Based on the data below, when did the ozone hole reach its maximum size?

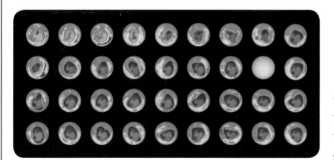

▲ The Antarctic ozone hole (purple and violet) from 1979-2014 (the sequence runs from left to right, from top left to bottom right)

The effects of UV on phytoplankton in the Antarctic Ocean have been investigated. UVA has wavelengths of 315 to 400 nm and UVB from 280 to 315 nm. Primary production due to phytoplankton photosynthesis was measured at different depths both in full sunlight and with either UVB, or UVA and UVB removed.

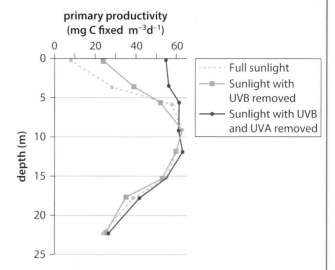

▲ Primary productivity as a function of depth and amount of UV exposure

3. a) Explain the evidence, provided by the data in the graph, for ultraviolet light harming phytoplankton.

   b) Using the data in the graph, discuss whether UVA or UVB causes more harm.

   c) Predict, with reasons, the effects of ultraviolet light on marine food chains in the Antarctic Ocean.

CFCs and other ozone-destroying chemicals were phased out as a result of an international treaty called the Montreal Protocol. By 2005 stratospheric ozone concentrations had stabilized. An article in the journal *Science* in 2016 reported that ozone abundance over Antarctic had begun to increase.

4. Discuss the conclusions that we should draw from the case of ozone depletion and how the world community responded to it.

ECOLOGY

What are the ecological consequences of global warming?

We can expect climate change due to global warming to have an impact on ecological communities. Some examples of impacts are summarized below.

Yellow cedars live in wetlands in cold climates like British Columbia. Analysis of weather station data indicates that there is a trend of warmer winters leading to reduced snow, but with persistent freezing weather in early spring. Yellow cedar has shallow roots that would normally be protected from the spring freeze by snow cover, but with declining snow cover, there is an increase in lethal root damage. Yellow cedar is still healthy where it is deeper-rooted on soils with better drainage.

Many biological events in temperate climates are driven by seasonal cues, especially in the spring and autumn. Research has repeatedly shown that the timing of spring events over the last 30 to 40 years is noticeably earlier. However, not all organisms have changed in the same way. For example, the European pied flycatcher arrives at the same time in its breeding grounds, but the caterpillars it feeds to its chicks are emerging earlier. This reduces the food supply, with the consequences of increasing chick mortality and declining flycatcher populations.

Walruses use ice floes as places to feed their young and as a base from which to dive to feed on bottom-dwelling prey such as clams. In 2007, the sea ice shrank, moving beyond the edge of the shallow water, to where it was too deep for the walruses to feed. Several thousand walruses sought an alternative place to rest between feeding trips by settling along the beaches of Alaska. Over time, such a dense assembly of animals in a single location will deplete bottom food resources along the coast. Furthermore, the mortality of young walruses is higher due to stampeding.

Coral reefs are among the most biologically diverse environments on earth. Corals live in close association with symbiotic algae called zooxanthellae. The renowned colour of corals is due to these algae. When corals are under stress, for example, when the ocean waters are too warm, the zooxanthellae can be expelled. At this point, the coral is said to be bleached. This picture shows bleached coral. Some of the coral appears brown as it still contains the zooxanthellae, which is needed to provide the coral with nutrients and thus maintain its color. This picture was taken in the Maldives, in the Indian Ocean. This situation threatens not only the coral itself, but the organisms that depend on the coral for their survival.

You can research more effects, but you must be careful only to use scientific sources and not political ones. We should remember that the cigarette industry continued to deny that tobacco causes cancer for decades after there was strong scientific evidence and similar campaigns of misinformation are likely over global warming.

Following the progress of forest FACE trials

Free Air Carbon Dioxide Enrichment (FACE) experiments are used by biologists to investigate the effect of raising the concentration of CO_2 in an open area. We might expect the rate of photosynthesis to increase, which would remove some of the excess carbon dioxide from the atmosphere. A series of large-scale FACE experiments are being set up in natural or semi-natural forests.

▲ The set-up used to raise the carbon dioxide concentration of an oak forest in Staffordshire (UK) from 400 to 550 ppm

Besides the FACE experiment in the oak forest in the UK (photo right), a similar experiment is taking place in a eucalyptus forest in Australia; four more forest FACE experiments are planned for the future.

Early results suggest that biomass in forests does increase initially due to increased photosynthesis, but that this is soon limited by a shortage of minerals in the soil, especially nitrogen or phosphorus.

You can follow the progress of these experiments online. They are being set up in a representative sample of the world's forests, so they should give a strong indication of whether natural forests can help to absorb the excess carbon dioxide that humans are releasing.

What evidence of climate change can be obtained from phenology?

Phenology is the study of the timing of natural events such as nesting in birds or flowering in plants. Evidence for climate change can be obtained from phenological studies.

Project BudBurst is a citizen science project that allows individuals to submit phenology data for any plant. The resulting database can be searched by species, date, flowering time, fruiting time, leaf color changes and many other variables.

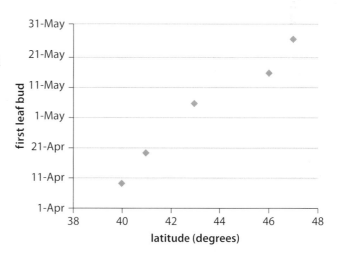

▲ The relationship between latitude and first leaf bud appearance for apple trees in the Eastern United States of America

1. Outline the relationship between latitude and first leaf bud.

2. Suggest the factors that affect when leaves first bud.

3. Discuss whether this is a cause and effect relationship or whether it is simply a correlation.

4. Discuss what might be the impacts on an ecosystem of earlier leaf budding.

5. Visit the National Geographic Project BudBurst website (http://budburst.fieldscope.org/map/24) and carry out further investigations such as the examples below.

   a) Are there similar trends in leaf budding for apple trees on the West Coast and the East Coast?

   b) Are the trends in other species similar?

ATL Communication skills

Collaborate with peers and experts using a variety of digital environments and media

Citizen science is the collection and analysis of data relating to the natural world by members of the public. There are an increasing number of citizen science opportunities where anyone, whether a scientist or not, can collect and enter data that they have collected. Some citizen science projects rely on collaboration between scientists in research institutes and the public, while others are entirely public-driven.

Data-based question: Is climate change causing any species to move their range?

The graph below shows the results of analysis of records of bird breeding (nesting) from a number of databases. Using the data available, scientists have identified a "half-way" location, whereby half of all records for a species are south of that geographical location and half are north of it. This type of analysis gives strong evidence for changes of range in many species.

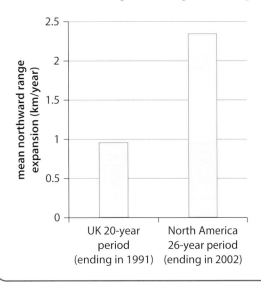

1. What is the mean rate of northward range expansion for bird species in the UK?

2. Calculate the total mean northward range expansion in North America during the study period.

3. a) Estimate how far the northward range has moved in North America since 2002.

   b) State one assumption you have made in your answer.

4. Predict the potential consequences of northward range movement of birds.

5. Discuss whether there is any doubt about the causes of the northward range expansion.

What are alien species?

Globalization has made it easy for species from one part of the world to be introduced into areas where they are not naturally found. Sometimes these alien species lack predators and competitors in their new environment, so they come to dominate ecosystems and threaten the survival of native species. An alien species has then become an invasive species.

Data-based question: Invasive alien species

Invasive alien species are a serious environmental issue in most parts of the world. Data from Nordic environments is shown here, with the numbers of invertebrate, vertebrate and plants or fungus species indicated in each bar.

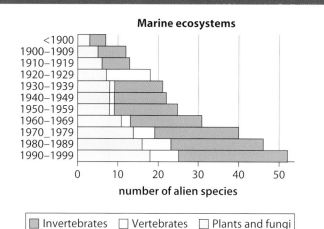

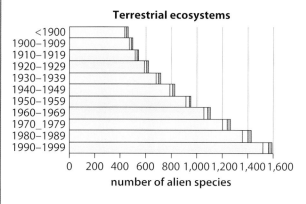

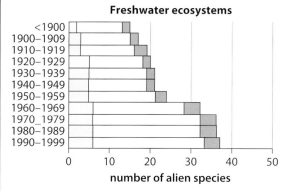

Invertebrates ☐ Vertebrates ☐ Plants and fungi

1. There are far more alien species in terrestrial habitats than in freshwater or marine habitats. Suggest reasons for this difference.

2. Analyze the data to find other differences between the three types of ecosystem and also similarities.

3. Choose an example of an invasive alien species in your area. Try to find answers to these questions:

   a) Where did the alien species come from?

   b) How did it travel to your area?

   c) What ecological problems is it causing?

   d) How could the alien species be controlled?

Action on deforestation

An intact forest landscape (IFL) is defined as an area of at least 500 km² in which remote sensing indicates that there are no signs of human activity. They are the most valuable areas for conservation of biodiversity, carbon storage, water cycles and other ecosystem functions. By 2000, the area of IFLs on Earth was already greatly reduced; a further loss of 7.2% was registered by 2013, with the rate of loss increasing.

The bar chart below shows IFL losses between 2000 and 2013 by region and according to cause.

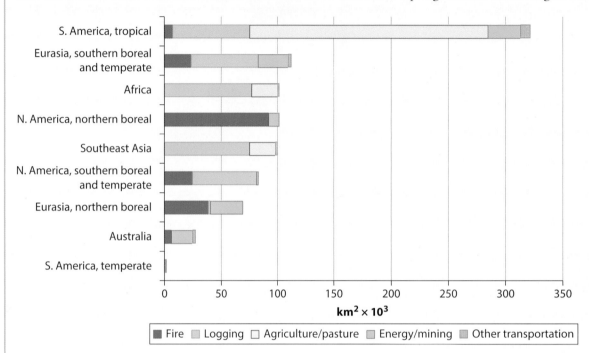

Source: Potapov et al. *Sci. Adv.* 2017;3:e1600821

1. Is deforestation an important enough issue for us to focus our efforts on reducing or eliminating it?

2. Is there anything that you together with your fellow students can do that will really make a difference?

3. Is the maxim "Think globally, act locally" relevant here? How does the data help us to decide what we should do?

Summative assessment

Statement of inquiry:

Environments provide aesthetic and health benefits and influence human cultural expression, but human-induced changes undermine these benefits.

Introduction

In this summative assessment we consider community structure in terms of the natural distribution of species. We investigate changes to community structure due to invasive species and air pollution. The question to be considered is the extent to which these changes in community structure interfere with the natural services provided by environments.

Community ecology

1. Distinguish between the greenhouse effect and climate change. [5]

2. Outline the following concepts:

   a) pioneer species [2]

   b) keystone species. [2]

Project ShoreZone aims to record habitats along coastlines throughout the world; the images it produces are truly beautiful as well as being scientifically useful. The photograph shown here is of the clear zonation that can be observed on the cliffs in Alaska's Prince of Wales Passage. From the waterline upwards, we can distinguish zones of red-brown colored barnacles (*Semibalanus cariosus*), then yellow-brown seaweeds (*Fucus distichus*), black lichen (*Verrucaria maura*) and above that spruces and other trees and shrubs.

▲ Sea cliff in Prince of Wales Passage, Alaska (United States of America)

3. Suggest reasons for:

    a) barnacles not growing higher up on the cliff [2]

    b) lichens or seaweeds growing only on the middle part of the cliff [2]

    c) trees and shrubs not growing lower down on the cliff. [2]

 ## Trees and air pollution

4. The air in urban areas contains a variety of pollutants, including particles of solids and gases. The table below shows the level of air pollution in urban areas of New York and rural areas nearby.

Area	Lead (μg m⁻³)	Nitrogen dioxide (ppb)	Nitrous oxide (ppb)	Sulfur dioxide (ppb)
Urban	0.09	37.7	39.3	18.7
Rural	0.04	6.2	0.5	2.3

Compare the levels of atmospheric pollution in urban and rural areas. [2]

5. Tree planting has been suggested as a way of improving air quality in urban areas. The growth of *Populus deltoides* in urban and rural areas near New York was investigated. Trees were grown in pots containing the same type of soil in all areas. High levels of mineral nutrients in the soil ensured that lack of nutrients was not the limiting factor on growth rates. The growth of the trees above ground (shoot biomass) and below ground (root biomass) was measured after one year. The bar chart below shows the results for two rural areas (green bars) and four urban areas (red bars).

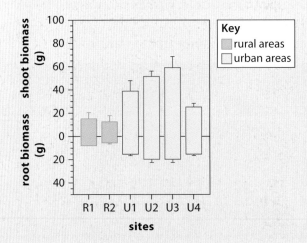

    a) Evaluate the methods used in the investigation, especially the manipulation and control of variables. [3]

    b) Evaluate the method of presentation of data in the bar chart. Can you suggest any improvements? [2]

c) Outline the conclusions that can be drawn about the growth of *Populus deltoides* from the data in the bar chart. [2]

d) Discuss whether the differences in growth rates of *Populus deltoides* between urban and rural areas could be due to differences in the concentration of air pollutants. [2]

6. a) The histograms below show the range of ozone exposure between May and September in urban and rural areas near New York. Compare the ozone exposures in urban, agricultural and forested areas. [2]

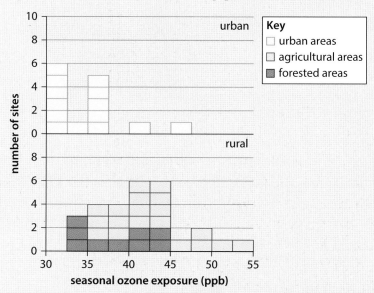

b) The concentrations of ozone and the shoot growth of *Populus deltoides* were measured at eight sites. The results are shown in the scatter graph below. Using the data in the scatter graph and in previous parts of this question, suggest a hypothesis for differences in the growth of *Populus deltoides* between urban and rural areas. Give reasons for your hypothesis. [2]

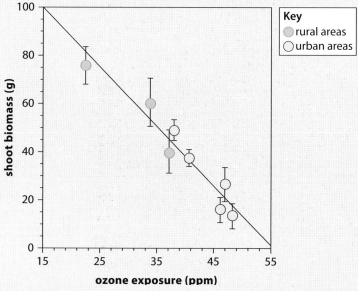

Source of data used in all graphs on pages 218-219: JW Greg, et al., (2003), *Nature*, **424**, pages 183–186

7. Trees are able to remove pollutants from the air and either store them in their biomass or trap them on their surfaces. This map shows the pollution removed by trees in counties across the US.

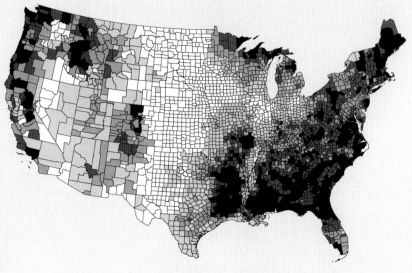

Pollution removal (tonnes per square kilometer

0.03 - 0.67   0.68 - 1.86   1.87 - 3.37   3.38 - 4.50   4.51 - 8.41

a) Generate two hypotheses to explain the trends observed. [2]

b) Choose one of these hypotheses and explain carefully a procedure that could be used to test it. [3]

The emerald ash borer invasion

The emerald ash borer (*Agrilus planipennis*) is an invasive alien insect in large parts of Canada and the United States, where it has killed over 100 million trees. Affected areas of the United States are shown in the map below.

▲ An adult emerald ash borer

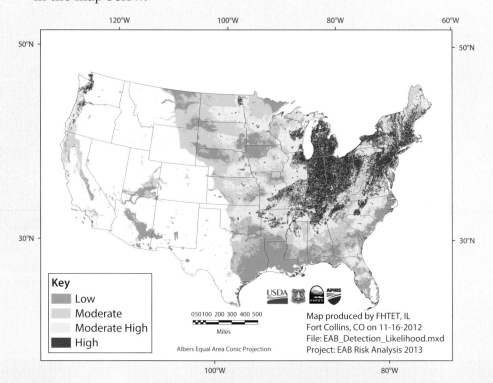

Key

Low
Moderate
Moderate High
High

050100 200 300 400 500
Miles

Albers Equal Area Conic Projection

USDA

Map produced by FHTET, IL
Fort Collins, CO on 11-16-2012
File: EAB_Detection_Likelihood.mxd
Project: EAB Risk Analysis 2013

Larvae of the insect reside inside the tree over winter and emerge the next season. Cold weather not only kills many larvae, but also limits the development of others, leading to a two-year life cycle, which slows down population growth. The table shows the results of an experiment in which percentage mortality of the larvae was tested over a range of sub-zero temperatures.

Coldest temperature experienced by the larvae (°C)	% mortality
−18	5
−23	34
−28	73
−29	79
−32	93
−34	98
−36	99

8. **a)** Identify the parts of the United States that are most significantly affected by the emerald ash borer. [2]

b) Display the data in the table using the type of chart or graph that you consider most suitable. [4]

c) Choose one of the heavily infested US states. Using an online database, find the coldest winter temperatures over a range of years and determine whether they have been cold enough to limit the reproduction of the emerald ash borer. Report your findings. [3]

d) Suggest a possible consequence if the average minimum winter temperature were to increase in the region of the infestation. [1]

e) Inquire into whether a warming trend has occurred in the regions of the United States most affected by the emerald ash borer. You could look at historical monthly minimum temperatures from meteorological databases. [2]

f) If you find evidence of a warming trend, outline the reasons for it. [3]

The impacts of the emerald ash borer

The Audubon Society of North America has been sponsoring an annual Christmas Bird Count (CBC) in the month of December for over 100 years. The results are stored in a public database that can be readily accessed online (http://netapp.audubon.org/cbcobservation/). In some years there may have been many people counting birds, but fewer participants in other years, and fluctuations in raw count numbers may be partly due to this. One way to standardize CBC data over time is to use the number of birds reported per party hour (a measure of the amount of time spent searching for birds or the amount of effort expended).

The emerald ash borer infestation is likely to have an impact on bird populations. Choose one of the hypotheses below and test it using the CBC database, filtering your search by location to focus on the Great Lakes region.

- The emerald ash borer infestation provides food for birds that eat insects inside trees so these birds increase in numbers.

- The death of ash trees will reduce the food supply of birds that feed on ash seeds so these birds decrease in numbers.

9. Write an account of what you have found in your investigation, using appropriate scientific language. [5]

▲ A trunk of a felled ash tree showing damage due to the emerald ash borer larvae

10. The Department of Environmental Conservation of New York State has posted an online article titled "Immerse Yourself in a Forest for Better Health", in which claims are made about the health benefits of forests. All the claims are backed up by references to published scientific research. For example, a reference is given to research indicating that the death of trees due to emerald ash borer is associated with over 20,000 extra deaths from heart and lung disease in 15 US states.

a) Explain the importance of references to published scientific research when making claims. [2]

b) One of the references is this: Donovan, G., Butry, D., Michael, Y., Prestemon, J., Liebhold, A., Gatziolis, D., Mao, M. (2013). The Relationship Between Trees and Human Health: Evidence from the Spread of the EAB. *American Journal of Preventive Medicine.* 44(2):139-45. Find the abstract of this research and summarize it, using language that non-scientists could understand. [3]

▲ The mark H-X on these three trees in Fort Erie, Ontario, Canada indicates that they are infested with the EAB and will be cut down

9 Patterns

Regularities are observable all around us.

Due to the Earth's tilt and its rotation around the Sun, we experience a pattern of repeating seasons. At Stonehenge, constructed 4000 to 5000 years ago, the central stone structures were aligned to the sunset of the winter solstice and the sunrise of the summer solstice, allowing celebrations of these natural phenomena each year. Why is the alignment of monuments such as Stonehenge now not quite perfect and when will it be perfect again?

Designs that contain a repeated motif are called patterns. Complex geometric and floral patterns are highly decorative and have been used for centuries in both art and architecture. What repeats can you see in this intricate tile mosaic?

In geometry, a transformation refers to the change in position of an object in the coordinate plane. Can you identify the transformations necessary to transform the dark blue leaf onto the red leaf? What about those necessary to transform the red leaf onto the light blue leaf? This pattern is known as a fractal because it is created by repeating a simple pattern over and over across different scales.

Symmetry in biology results from the balanced distribution of parts around an axis of symmetry. Though in nature symmetry is almost always approximate, a cut through an axis should result in two equal parts that are reflections of one another. In radial symmetry, there is a top and a bottom but no left or right. In pentaradial symmetry, a cut through any one of five arms gives two halves that are reflections of one another. This type of symmetry is characteristic of echinoderms, such as the sea star, but can also be found elsewhere, for example, in the cross-section of an apple.

Introduction

Patterns can occur in both time and space. When observing the natural world, scientists look for predictable things happening over time, or for predictable distributions of things in space. They then form testable hypotheses and theories based on these patterns. Generalization based on the observation of patterns is known as inductive reasoning. Once such generalizations are formed, predictions can be made and tested. Nobel prize-winning scientists James Watson and Francis Crick were able to recognize patterns in data that helped them make predictions about the structure of DNA.

Scientists often do experiments to investigate relationships between variables and plot their results on graphs. If there is a clear pattern in the results, for example the points on a graph form a straight line, it is evidence of a relationship between the variables. By looking for patterns in data, scientists find relationships.

With patterns over time, something might always happen at the same time of day or with predictable frequency. For example, an observer might notice that there is a certain time of day that a hummingbird comes to feed at a group of flowers. They might also note that this particular flower opens at a certain time during the day, so a reasonable conclusion might be that the feeding pattern and flower opening pattern are related.

Key concept: Relationships

Related concept: Patterns

Global context: Orientation in time and space

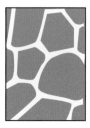 

▲ Reticulated   ▲ Rothschild

▼ Can you use the patterns on this giraffe's coat to identify whether it is a reticulated giraffe or a Rothschild's giraffe?

Statement of inquiry:

Observing patterns allows scientists to propose new theories that explain how the living world works.

Some of the most striking patterns in the natural world are the spots, stripes and vibrant colors of animal coats. These patterns in space may camouflage pray against predators as in giraffes, or allow a predator to stalk its prey undetected, or signal to predators that prey is distasteful or even toxic. Within a species they may act as a sign to potential mates of an individual's health or fitness.

Another type of pattern observed in living things is patterns of structure that are related to the role or niche of the organism. Unrelated organisms that have similar roles within an ecosystem often have similar forms. Can you see patterns in the adaptations of the butterfly and hummingbird shown here that might make it easier for them to extract nectar from flowers? Is anything truly random in nature, or are there always patterns?

In this chapter, we explore how patterns of similarities lead us to recognize universal features of living things. Patterns can often be described in terms of the spatial relationships between their repeating elements; they can be cyclical and recur over time, hence the global context here is orientation in time and space.

▲ Some hummingbirds such as the ruby-throated hummingbird (*Archilochus colubris*) migrate between seasonal feeding and nesting grounds.

ᴬᵀᴸ Creative and innovative thinking skills

Generate a testable hypothesis

Snail shells, plants that climb by twining (such as beans) and DNA could all exist in right or left handed versions.

- Generate a testable hypothesis for whether DNA, snails or twining plants are right or left handed versions, or both.

- Explain the basis of your hypothesis.

- Outline the steps you could perform to test your hypothesis.

Hypotheses should be tested one at a time. This requires keeping other variables constant or in other words "controlled".

▲ Pale clouded yellow butterfly (*Colias hyalae*) showing its proboscis in side view

METABOLISM

What properties are shared by all living organisms?

A pattern is created if something is repeated. When we look at the diversity of life, combinations of characteristics are often repeated in groups of species. Biologists study these patterns and from them try to discern the evolutionary origins of living organisms, and how they should be classified. There is strong evidence for all species on Earth evolving from a common ancestral species that existed billions of years ago. If this is true, then we might expect some of the properties of that ancestral life form to be shared by all organisms alive on Earth today. If we can discover these common properties, they could be used to distinguish between living and non-living things.

Living things share a number of characteristics, such as responding to the environment, growth, reproduction, being composed of cells, obtaining nutrients, expelling waste, and maintaining internal conditions that are distinct from their surroundings.

How do we determine that something is alive?

▲ In everyday terms, we recognize that the seedlings are living and that the flame is not

1. Examine the photograph and construct a Venn diagram to organize your answer to the following questions:

   a) What properties are found only in the flame?

   b) What properties do both the seedlings and the flame possess?

   c) What properties are found only in the seedling?

2. What properties do the seedlings possess that are missing from the flame, and that lead us to say that only the seedlings are alive?

Which organisms have a pattern of segmentation?

Some structures found in nature consist of repeated subunits. An example is the wax comb made by honeybees, which is a tessellation of hexagons. A tessellation is a geometric pattern formed by the arrangement of shapes that fit close together in a repeated pattern without overlapping and without gaps. Bees make honeycombs to store honey and pollen, and to rear offspring. What do you think the reason is for bees making the comb of hexagons and not triangles, squares or circles?

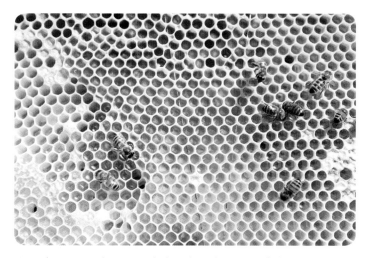

▲ A honey comb is two sided, with each corner of a hexagon on one side opposite the centre of a hexagon on the other side. What is the advantage of this pattern?

Symmetry in patterns

Symmetry generates obvious patterns. These are seen in the form of many organisms. The concept of form is explored in Chapter 2.

1. Can you find examples in that chapter of these types of symmetry:

    a) bilateral symmetry, where the left and right sides are mirror images of each other?

    b) radial symmetry, where rotation around a fixed point does not change the overall shape?

    c) helical symmetry, where rotation along a screw axis also causes translation?

The shell of the mollusc *Nautilus* consists of a series of whorl sections.

2. a) Is the structure of the shell helical or spiral?

    b) Does the shell have a symmetrical pattern?

The repeating subunits in the body of millipedes and centipedes are segments and this type of pattern is called segmentation. Millipedes and centipedes are in the class Myriapoda, which is part of the phylum Arthropoda. All arthropods, including all insects, have segmented bodies. What is the advantage of segmentation?

The segments show more variation in insects than in myriapods and groups of segments form distinctive sections of the body: the head (6 fused segments), the thorax (3 segments) and the abdomen (11 or 12 segments). What is the advantage of having different types of body segment?

Humans are in the phylum Chordata. Most members of this phylum have a vertebral column, which is another example of segmentation because it is a series of vertebrae rather than a single bone. What is the advantage of having a series of short bones rather than fewer, longer bones in the back?

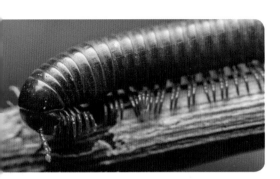

▲ Each segment in a millipede has two pairs of legs, whereas centipedes only have one pair per segment

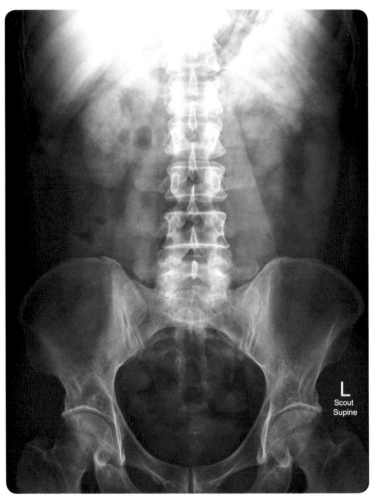

▲ This scan shows two of the twelve thoracic vertebrae (top) and five lumbar vertebrae. Humans also have seven cervical vertebrae in the neck, above the thoracic vertebrae. What could be the reasons for having different type of vertebrae?

How do segments develop in insects and other animals?

We now know that certain genes called homeotic genes are similar in function and sequence in all animals. These genes direct the development of embryos. One of the most commonly studied organisms in relation to homeotic genes is the fruit fly *Drosophila melanogaster*. The homeotic genes of this organism occur in two groups. Each group regulates the development of a different area of the fruit fly's body.

- The antennapedia group is composed of five genes and regulates the development of the head.

- The bithorax group is composed of three genes and is involved in the development of the abdomen and the thorax.

During development these genes are constantly expressed in order to give the different segments of the fly body specific structures and roles.

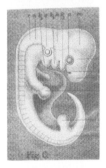

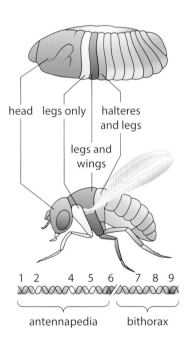

◀ The homeotic genes control the development of the same body regions in both the fly embryo and the adult fly

Although there are more homeotic genes in humans, they display the same patterns as the fly genes: their order on the DNA is the same and their action during the development of the embryo follows the same sequence as in the fruit fly. To test whether the human and *Drosophila* homeotic genes perform the same functions, scientists transferred a human homeotic gene to the embryo of a fruit fly and observed the correct development of the embryo.

▲ In the early 19th century, Ernst Haeckel observed the pattern that all vertebrates look similar in the early stages of their embryonic development. His diagram emphasizes similarities between tortoise (top), chick, dog, man (bottom) at early stages in their development. What similarities can be observed?

What patterns are there in the timing of life cycles?

Patterns do not only exist in the distribution of variables in space, but also over time. Consider the examples shown here and in each case discuss what the advantages of the pattern shown in the timing of the life cycle.

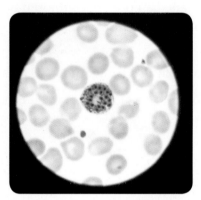

◀ The population of the insect *Magicicada tredecim* varies over time. Mature adults, known as cicadas, are consistently present in habitats in low numbers, however, every 13 or 17 years a population explosion occurs.

▲ The parasites that cause malaria have a very short life cycle. They invade red blood cells, reproduce inside them and then burst out and invade other red blood cells. This gives rise to a pattern in the symptoms of malaria with a cycle of coldness and shivering then fever and sweating that takes two days if the malaria is caused by *Plasmodium vivax* or three days if *Plasmodium malariae* is the cause.

▲ Red crabs (*Gecarcoidea natalis*) live in large numbers in the forests of Christmas Island. Males and females migrate to the coast and mate. All females release their fertilised eggs into the water at the turn of the high tide during the last quarter of the moon, in November or December.

Data based question: Phenology in butterflies

Phenology is the study of patterns in the timing of natural phenomena. The charts below show the times of when three butterflies are most likely to be seen flying in the UK (black circles). They also show when eggs (red circles), caterpillars (green circles) and chrysalises (purple circles) can found.

Brimstone (*Gonepteryx rhamni*)

	Jan	Feb	Mar	Apr	May	Jun	Jul	Aug	Sep	Oct	Nov	Dec
	1 2 3 4	1 2 3 4	1 2 3 4	1 2 3 4	1 2 3 4	1 2 3 4	1 2 3 4	1 2 3 4	1 2 3 4	1 2 3 4	1 2 3 4	1 2 3 4
Ovum					● ● ● ●	● ●						
Larva				● ●	● ● ● ●	● ●						
Pupa							● ● ●	● ● ●				
Imago	● ● ● ●	● ● ● ●	● ● ● ●	● ● ● ● ●	● ● ● ● ●	● ● ● ●		● ● ● ●	● ● ● ●	● ● ● ●	● ● ● ●	● ● ● ●

Adonis blue (*Polyommatus bellargus*)

	Jan	Feb	Mar	Apr	May	Jun	Jul	Aug	Sep	Oct	Nov	Dec
	1 2 3 4	1 2 3 4	1 2 3 4	1 2 3 4	1 2 3 4	1 2 3 4	1 2 3 4	1 2 3 4	1 2 3 4	1 2 3 4	1 2 3 4	1 2 3 4
Ovum					● ● ●	● ● ●		● ●	● ● ● ●			
Larva	● ● ● ●	● ● ● ●	● ● ● ●	● ●		● ● ●	● ●		● ● ● ●	● ● ● ●	● ● ● ●	● ● ● ●
Pupa			● ● ●	● ● ● ●				● ● ●	● ●			
Imago				● ● ●	● ● ●			● ● ●	● ● ●			

Painted lady (*Vanessa cardui*)

	Jan	Feb	Mar	Apr	May	Jun	Jul	Aug	Sep	Oct	Nov	Dec
	1 2 3 4	1 2 3 4	1 2 3 4	1 2 3 4	1 2 3 4	1 2 3 4	1 2 3 4	1 2 3 4	1 2 3 4	1 2 3 4	1 2 3 4	1 2 3 4
Ovum				● ● ● ●	● ● ● ●	● ● ● ●	● ● ● ●	● ● ● ●	● ● ● ●			
Larva				● ● ●	● ● ● ●	● ● ● ●	● ● ● ●	● ● ● ●	● ● ● ●	●		
Pupa					● ●	● ● ● ●	● ● ● ●	● ● ● ●	● ● ● ●	● ● ● ●		
Imago				● ● ●	● ● ● ●	● ● ● ●	● ● ● ●	● ● ● ●	● ● ● ●	● ● ●	● ● ●	●

Source of all data: http://www.ukbutterflies.co.uk/species_phenologies.php

1. Describe the life cycle of the Brimstone butterfly, including the timing of stages in the cycle.

2. Explain the differences between the data for the Brimstone and the Adonis blue.

3. Explain the differences between the data for the Brimstone and the Painted lady.

Data-based question: What patterns are observable in the structure of DNA?

Erwin Chargaff was aware that DNA contained four different types of nitrogen-containing base: adenine, thymine, cytosine and guanine. He analyzed the DNA of a great range of organisms to determine the percentage of each type of base. Some of his data is shown in the table. Analyze the data to identify any patterns.

Organism	% Adenine	% Guanine	% Cytosine	% Thymine
Corn	26.8	22.8	23.2	27.2
Octopus	33.2	17.6	17.6	31.6
Yeast	31.3	18.7	17.1	32.9
E. coli	24.7	26.0	25.7	23.6
Chicken	28.0	22.0	21.6	28.4
Wheat	?	22.7	22.8	27.1
Sea urchin	?	17.7	?	?

1. Determine the sum of the percentages for the four bases in corn.

2. Compare the relative amounts of guanine in the different organisms.

3. Determine the ratio of guanine to cytosine in:
   a) octopus
   b) chicken.

4. Deduce the approximate relationship between the amount of guanine and the amount of cytosine in all organisms.

5. Determine the ratio of adenine to thymine in:
   a) chicken
   b) corn.

6. Deduce the approximate relationship between the amount of adenine and the amount of thymine in all organisms.

7. Suggest why these ratios are not exact in all of the organisms.

8. Predict the expected percentage of adenine for wheat.

9. Predict the expected percentage of adenine, cytosine and thymine for the sea urchin.

How did patterns help Crick and Watson discover the structure of DNA?

A number of famous scientific experiments are associated with the study of DNA. Avery and Macleod established that the hereditary material was DNA and not protein. Hershey and Chase showed how new DNA was made. In the 1950s, significant effort was invested into uncovering the structure of DNA.

James Watson, Francis Crick and Maurice Wilkins shared the Nobel prize for determining the structure of DNA. Maurice Wilkins and Rosalind Franklin contributed data obtained by X-ray crystallography. A beam of X-rays is passed through a crystal of DNA and the pattern created by the diffraction of the rays was collected and analyzed. The X-shaped pattern of dots that Franklin obtained showed that DNA had a helical structure. The spacing of the dots indicated the dimensions of the helix, including its diameter (2 nm) and the length of one complete turn of the helix (3.4 nm).

The three types of subunit in DNA are nitrogenous bases, phosphate groups and five-carbon sugars called deoxyribose. Francis Crick and James Watson used Franklin's diffraction pattern to hypothesize that DNA might be a double helix, with two strands on opposite sides of the molecule. These strands would be made of alternating sugars and phosphates, with a base attached to each sugar. The strands would be linked by bonds between bases on opposite strands.

Watson and Crick knew that two of the bases (adenine and guanine) consisted of two rings of atoms and that the other bases (cytosine and thymine) had only one ring. From the diameter of the helix that the X-ray data had revealed, they deduced that adenine and guanine paired together would be too wide to fit between the strands of sugar and phosphate and that thymine and cytosine would be too narrow. This still left four possible pairings between bases. Chargaff's data showed the pairings that actually exist in DNA. What are they?

Crick and Watson tested their hypothesis for the structure of DNA by making models. This is described in Chapter 12. They published their discovery in 1953. It was the start of the branch of science now known as molecular biology, which continues to this day and has been immensely productive.

▲ Understanding what might generate the pattern visible in this image helped elucidate the structure of the DNA molecule

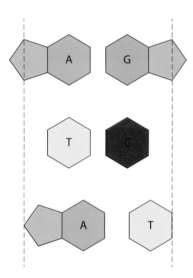

▲ Models used to test base pairing in a DNA molecule: the dashed lines mark the distance the base pair should occupy to match the X-ray diffraction pattern

Patterns in the structure of DNA

DNA is a nucleic acid because it is a long chain of nucleotides. An individual DNA molecule is composed of two strands of nucleotides held together to form a helical shape.

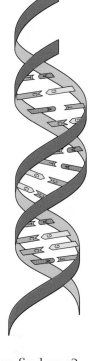

Looking at the picture of the DNA helix:

1. Describe the pattern of orientation of the two strands.

2. Describe the pattern of the major and minor grooves.

The words KAYAK, REDDER and ROTATOR are examples of palindromes because they read the same forwards as backwards. An example of a palindrome in DNA is:

```
5´    GAATTC    3´
3´    CTTAAG    5´
```

3. Why is this regarded as palindromic, even though neither of the strands have base sequences that read the same forwards as backwards?

4. Does a palindromic sequence have an extra type of symmetry?

5. Palindromic base sequences in DNA have some important roles. Can you find one?

How can DNA be repeatedly copied?

When the structure of DNA had been discovered, it was immediately obvious how copies of the molecule could be made. The bonds between bases on the two strands are weak. They are called hydrogen bonds and can quite easily be broken. The double helix can therefore be separated into two strands. New strands can then be made using each of the single strands as a mold or template. Many enzymes are needed to do this, but the principal ones are DNA polymerases. They make the new strands by linking nucleotides together. Each nucleotide consists of a deoxyribose sugar, a phosphate and a base. The nucleotides are added, one at time to make a longer and longer chain.

In the structure of DNA, adenine on one strand is only ever paired with thymine on the other strand and guanine with cytosine. This is called complementary base pairing. It is the key to copying DNA. The base on the template strand determines which base there should be on the new strand. If DNA polymerase tries to add a nucleotide with the wrong base, it will not form hydrogen bonds with the base on the template strand and it will be rejected. Because of this, the two DNA molecules produced when DNA is copied have exactly the same base sequences as each other and as the original molecule – they are replicas, so the process of copying DNA is called DNA replication.

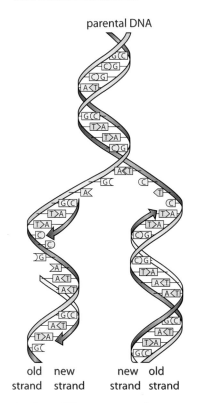

parental DNA

old strand new strand   new strand old strand

▲ Four different types of nucleotide are used to replicate DNA

When is DNA replicated?

The DNA inside a cell has to be replicated before the cell divides, so that both of the cells produced by division can have a full set of genes.

Looking at the internal organisation of a cell, cells are either:

- prokaryotic, meaning that their DNA is located in the cytoplasm and that they have no membrane-bound cell compartments (bacteria are an example of prokaryotes).

- eukaryotic, with DNA inside a nucleus and membrane-bound organelles in the cytoplasm such as mitochondria, Golgi apparatuses and endoplasmic reticulum (plants, animals and fungi have eukaryotic cells).

DNA replication and cell division happen in different ways in prokaryotes and eukaryotes.

- Prokaryote cells mostly have just one circular DNA molecule. This is replicated and the two molecules produced are pulled to opposite ends of the cell, which then divides. This whole process is called binary fission and in some bacteria it can be completed in less than thirty minutes.

- Eukaryotes have multiple DNA molecules, making cell division slower and more complicated. The DNA molecules are linear, rather than circular and have proteins associated with them. Before cell division each DNA molecule in the nucleus is replicated and the two molecules produced are then packaged up and carefully moved so that both of the cells produced in the division gets one copy of every DNA molecule. The usual method for doing this is **mitosis**, but there is a second method called **meiosis**, which is described in Chapter 2.

Why do cell division and cell enlargement alternate?

The diagram below shows a pattern followed by multicellular eukaryotes during growth and when lost or damaged cells are replaced. It is a cycle in which cell division and cell enlargement alternate.

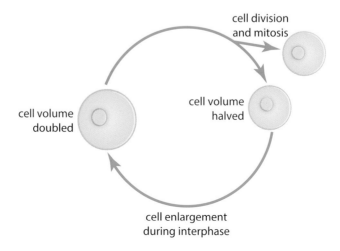

cell division and mitosis

cell volume doubled

cell volume halved

cell enlargement during interphase

Before cell division can happen there must be two nuclei in the cell. The process used to divide one nucleus into two genetically identical nuclei is mitosis. It requires the DNA to be tightly packaged up into condensed chromosomes.

Cell enlargement happens during a phase in the life of a cell called interphase. During this phase the cell is very active, producing proteins and other substances needed for growth. The DNA is all replicated and some structures within the cell such as mitochondria increase in number. Many of these activities require access to the DNA and for this the DNA must be unpackaged and spread out through the nucleus.

So, cell division involves mitosis which requires the DNA to be tightly packaged up, and cell enlargement requires the DNA to be unpacked. These processes therefore cannot happen at the same time, which explains the pattern of alternating division and enlargement.

1. What would happen if a cell divided before it had replicated its DNA?

2. What would happen if a cell divided repeatedly without enlarging?

3. Zygotes perform a series of cell divisions without any cell enlargement between the divisions. How can this happen?

What pattern of events occurs during mitosis?   CELLS

Mitosis is the process that divides one nucleus into two genetically identical nuclei. It is easier to observe in plants cells than animal cells.

① Early prophase

Microtubules are growing

Chromosomes are becoming shorter and fatter by supercoiling

② Late prophase

Each chromosome contains two identical DNA molecules formed by replication in interphase

Microtubules extend from each pole to the equator

The nuclear membrane has broken down and chromosomes have moved to the equator

③ Metaphase

Microtubules from the two poles are attached to different DNA molecules in each chromosome.

④ Anaphase

Each chromosome has split into two genetically identical chromosomes.

Microtubules pull the genetically identical chromosomes to opposite poles

⑤ Early telophase

All chromosomes have reached the poles and nuclear membranes form around them

Microtubules break down

Chromosomes uncoil and are no longer individually visible

⑥ Late telophase

The cell divides (cytokinesis) to form two cells with genetically identical nuclei

One of the most convenient places to observe mitosis is in the tip of a growing plant root. A photograph of cells from the root tip of an onion is shown in the questions at the end of this section. Most of the cells have a rounded nucleus with the DNA spread out, because the cell is enlarging rather than dividing—it is in interphase. The other cells in a root tip are in mitosis and have visible chromosomes. By studying the cells in mitosis, a series of changes can be observed. The stages in this series of events have been given names: prophase, metaphase, anaphase and telophase.

Interphase

The DNA of the chromosomes is spread out through the nucleus and the cell is able to use it to provide the information needed for all cell activities. During this phase, the DNA is replicated so that each chromosome contains two identical DNA molecules.

Prophase

The chromosomes are condensing (shortening and thickening) by a coiling process. At this stage the chromosomes are still inside a nuclear membrane. Though difficult to see, each chromosome is a double structure because the DNA has been replicated.

Metaphase

The nuclear membrane disappears and the chromosomes are pulled by microtubules into a line at the centre of the cell (the equator). These microtubules link the chromosomes to the poles of the cell. Each chromosome still contains two identical DNA molecules.

Anaphase

The microtubules pull each chromosome apart, separating the identical DNA molecules and pulling them to opposite poles of the cell. Each chromosome now contains just one DNA molecule.

Telophase

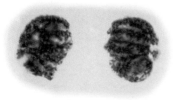

The chromosomes reach the poles and nuclear membranes reform around them. The DNA of the chromosomes uncoils and spreads out. The cell can now divide into two identical cells

Interphase

The two cells are now in the phase where many cell activities are happening and the cells start to enlarge.

1. Four onion root tip cells in the micrograph are in metaphase. Which cells are they?

2. How many cells are in anaphase?

3. Cells in telophase are in pairs, they have relatively small nuclei and the chromosomes are not fully spread out so the nucleus still appears lumpy. How many pairs of cells in telophase can you identify?

4. Cells in prophase have strands or lumps visible in the nucleus because DNA molecules are being coiled up to form condensed chromosomes. How many cells in prophase can you see? Which of these is closest to the start of prophase and which is closest to the end?

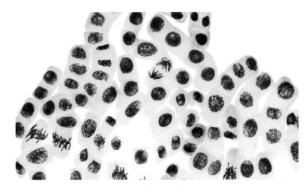

▲ Cells from the root tip of an onion showing cytoplasm (pink) and nuclei (purple)

5. The relative lengths of time of the four phases of mitosis can be deduced from the numbers of cells in each phase. Which phase takes the shortest and which takes the longest time?

Why do cells divide before they have grown to a very large size?

CELLS

Unicellular organisms, such as Amoeba, never grow to a very large size. Cells in multicellular organisms divide before they reach a large size. There are various possible explanations for this.

- Cells need to absorb some substances from their surroundings and release other substances. The surface area of the cell membrane affects how quickly the cell can do this, while the volume of a cell affects how quickly it uses and produces materials, and therefore how quickly it needs to transport materials in and out. As a cell gets larger, the ratio between the surface area and the volume makes transport more and more of a problem.

- Animal cells consist mainly of water. The cell membrane that holds in the cell contents is very thin and has little strength. As cell size increases there is more and more risk of the cell suffering a structural failure. A tissue made of many cells will therefore be stronger than a single cell of the same volume.

- A typical cell has one nucleus, which contains all the organism's genes. These genes contain essential information that is actively used during the life of a cell. One nucleus could not provide access to the information rapidly enough for a very large cell.

▲ Small organisms consist of a single cell—they are unicellular. These different types of bacteria on the surface of a human tooth are about one micrometre (0.001 μm) in diameter and are unicellular

Almost all organisms that are larger than a millimetre in diameter consist of more than one cell—they are multicellular. This ant and the plant that it is on both consist of many cells, so they are multicellular

Evaluating evidence and arguments

1. Are the explanations written in the text on page 239 all valid?

2. Which of the explanations do you think is most important as a reason for larger organisms being multicellular? Debate this with other students and try to achieve consensus.

3. Can you think of any other explanations?

4. Are there any consequences of being unicellular that are an advantage?

5. Calculate surface area to volume ratios for 1, 10 and 100 mm diameter cubes. What happens to the ratio as cubes get larger? What are the implications for limits to cell size given the functions that cell membranes perform?

CELLS

What patterns are there in tissues?

A tissue is a group of cells with the same structure and function. Tissues are only found in multicellular organisms, all of which are eukaryotic. Mitosis is used to produce many genetically identical cells and if a group of these develop in the same way, the result is a tissue. Cell to cell adhesion holds the tissue together and the cells must have a suitable shape to avoid unwanted gaps.

Some tissues have a regular appearance, but we cannot expect them to have the geometrical precision of a tessellation. The pattern can be one, two or three dimensional, as the examples here show.

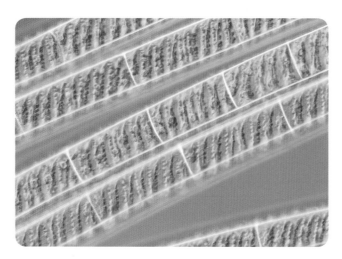

The alga *Spirogyra* is multicellular but unless it is reproducing sexually, each individual is a just a filament of cylindrical cells. Its tissue therefore has a unidimensional pattern

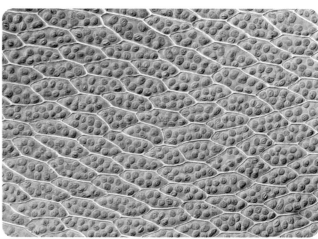

Leaf cells in the moss *Bryum capillare* are arranged in a single flat layer, so the pattern is two dimensional

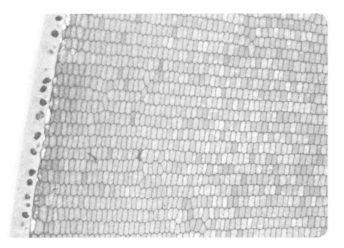

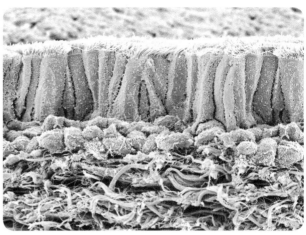

△ The lens of the eye has cuboidal epithelium on the outside and inside a very regular array of transparent fiber cells that are 4-7μm wide and 10-12μm long. They have no nucleus or organelles. Here they are seen in transverse section

△ Ciliated columnar epithelium: the lining of the trachea (yellow) is an epithelium consisting of column-shaped cells with cilia on the exposed end. These cells waft mucus up out of the airways, to help keep the lungs clean

What are the advantages and disadvantages of asexual reproduction?

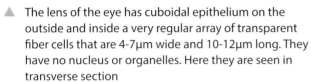

In asexual reproduction there is only one parent. All offspring are genetically identical. DNA replication is the first stage in asexual reproduction. What happens next depends on the type of organism.

- In bacteria and unicellular eukaryotes such as Amoeba, the parent cell divides in two (binary fission). The parent can only reproduce asexually once, because it no longer exists after producing its two offspring. The offspring each consist of a single cell and can go on to become single parents themselves.

- In multicellular organisms, a parent can reproduce asexually repeatedly. There are many different methods. In some cases the offspring only consists of a single cell but in other cases it is a group of genetically identical cells produced by the parent.

Asexual reproduction is sometimes called cloning. Artificial methods of cloning are described in Chapter 10.

1. What is the advantage of asexual reproduction for organisms that are successful because they are well adapted to their environment?

2. What is the disadvantage of asexual reproduction to a species during a period of environmental change?

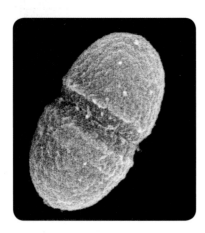

The bacterium *Enterococcus faecalis* lives in the human intestine. Here it is reproducing asexually by binary fission. To remain in the intestine its reproduction rate must be equal or higher than the rate of its removal in feces

3. Choose one of these hypotheses and investigate it:

a) Asexual reproduction is more prevalent in small populations with a low population density.

b) Asexual reproduction is more prevalent in species with a short generation time.

c) Asexual reproduction has evolved many times.

Plantlets are produced asexually along the edges of the leaves of *Bryophyllum diagremontianum*. They already have roots when they drop off the plant and start their independent existence

Summative assessment

Statement of inquiry:

Observing patterns allows scientists to propose new theories that explain how the living world works.

Introduction

In this summative assessment we first consider the cyclical pattern associated with metamorphosis in cicadas. We then examine spatial patterns as they relate both to the human body and to plants. We finally investigate the geographic pattern associated with the distribution of traits on a geographic scale. The question to keep in mind while completing the assessment is how observation of orientation in place, space and time helps us to better understand the natural world.

Cyclical patterns in the cicada life cycle

1. **a)** Outline the properties that are shared by all living things. [6]

    b) Design a test that could be performed to determine if the yellow objects in the image below are insect eggs or candy. [3]

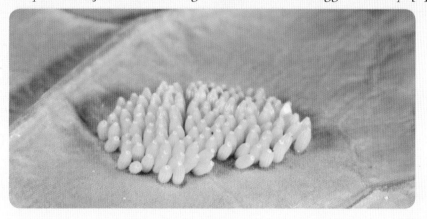

▼ Adult cicada emerging from the final nymph stage

2. The periodical cicada *Magicicada septemdecim* has a life cycle where the insect spends a prolonged period of time underground developing. While underground, it goes through five periods of life known as instars. At the end of each instar period, it sheds its outer skin. The fifth instar emerges from underground and sheds its skin to become the short lived adult. At the point of the emergence, a burst in the adult population above ground occurs.

    The graph shows the percentage of underground nymphs that are in each stage. Using the information in the graph, answer the following questions.

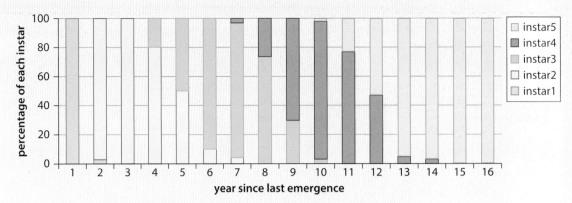

Changes in percentage of larvae in each instar stage over a 16-year period

a) In year 5, determine the percentage of nymphs that are in the instar 3 stage. [2]

b) Predict what events will occur in the life cycle of *Magicicada septemdecin* in year 17. [2]

c) Deduce how many years a complete life cycle takes in this species, from one emergence of adults to the next. [2]

d) Predict what the graph of the population of adult cicadas would look like over time. If an emergence occurred in 2011, in what year would the next emergence occur? Determine when the previous emergence occurred. [3]

e) Predict these patterns in relation to this periodical cicada,

   i) In the area where the periodical cicada are found there is a caterpillar that eats oak leaves. During an emergence year, birds preferentially eat cicadas rather than caterpillars. Predict the effect on oak leaves. [3]

   ii) Mature trees have fungus associated with their roots that can infect and kill the cicadas. Explain why cicada nymphs might be found in higher numbers on the roots of immature trees. [3]

   iii) The mole is an animal that lives underground and eats invertebrates including fifth instar cicada nymphs. Predict the pattern of the mole population in the area where the periodical cicadas are. [3]

   iv) The cicada nymphs attach themselves to plant roots and suck on the root tissue. Predict the pattern of tree damage over the life cycle of the cicada. [3]

Investigating proportions of the human forearm

3. The golden ratio is an irrational number approximately equal to 1.62. It is argued to appear many times in human knowledge systems like geometry, art and architecture. The Ancient Greek mathematician Euclid wrote about it 2,300 years ago, though he

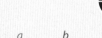

$a + b$ is to a as a is to b

did not use the "golden ratio" name. Some erroneously claim that the ratio applies in some situations where it doesn't, such as in the Nautilis shell, and others state that it doesn't apply when it does.

a) Show that the golden ratio applies to every pair of adjacent bones in the finger. [3]

a	b	$a + b$	$\dfrac{a + b}{a}$
8	5	13	$\dfrac{8 + 5}{8} = 1.62$
5	3	?	?

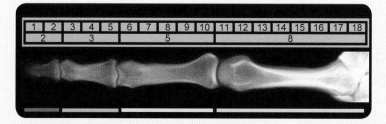

b) Design a data table to record measurements of the elbow to wrist (*a*) and wrist to longest finger (*b*) of you and your classmates to determine if the golden ratio applies. [7]

 ## Investigating patterns in the leaf distribution in plants

In a photosynthetic plant, an arrangement of leaves as far apart as possible in a given space would allow for the maximum amount of sunlight to be captured.

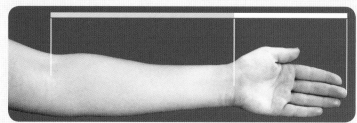

The following patterns were developed from the website Mathisfun. Each orange object represents a cell. Within the simulation, when the cell divides it can take a turn. In the simulation, a turn of 1 represents a 360° turn, a turn of 0.5 represents a 180° degree turn, a turn of 0.25 represents a 90° turn.

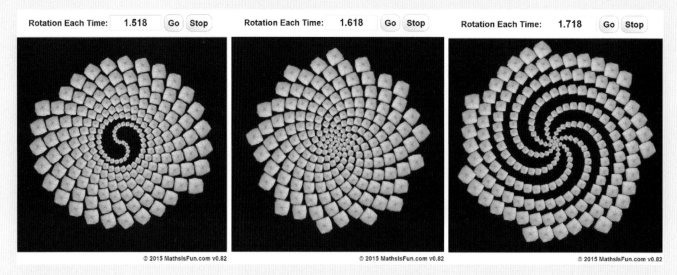

Rotation Each Time: 1.518 | Go Stop
Rotation Each Time: 1.618 | Go Stop
Rotation Each Time: 1.718 | Go Stop

© 2015 MathsIsFun.com v0.82 © 2015 MathsIsFun.com v0.82 © 2015 MathsIsFun.com v0.82

4. Use the three images generated from the simulator to explain the leaf pattern in the *Aloe* plant. [5]

 ## Using genetic patterns to protect against poaching

This article is abridged from http://sciencenetlinks.com/science-news/science-updates/genes-and-geography/.

Read the passage and answer the questions that follow.

DNA and geography

We tend to see large differences between human populations. Scientific evidence, on the other hand, tells us that whether we divide ourselves up by nationality, ethnicity, or skin color, genetically we're all pretty similar. Take two people from anywhere on Earth and you will find that more than 99.9% of the coding sequences in their DNA are the same. In other words, everything that makes us unique is concentrated in less than one one-thousandth of the genome.

Even within that tiny fraction of DNA that varies between people, the differences between populations aren't as dramatic as once thought. In fact, the overwhelming majority of genetic differences between individuals are just as variable within small populations as they are across the entire world. Comparatively speaking, only a small handful of genetic signatures are more common in some human populations than in others. The process of mutation is responsible for these small differences.

Microsatellites are non-coding sequences, consisting of short sequences of bases that are repeated. The repeats are adjacent to each other. So far no function has been found for these base sequences, so natural selection does not favor one version of a microsatellite over another. In particular, it seems to be of no consequence how many times the base sequence is repeated. Microsatellites are passed from parent to offspring, with the number of repeats usually remaining unchanged. However, compared with base changes in the coding sequences of our genomes, changes to the number of repeats in microsatellites occur far more frequently. Differences between populations therefore develop relatively rapidly and can be used to provide evidence of the separateness of populations.

Researchers can use these tiny slivers of our genetic code to predict where people come from. They accomplish this by using a computer program that analyzes hundreds of genetic sequences at once. By looking for patterns of microsatellites the researchers are able to make accurate statistical guesses about people's ancestries.

Microsatellites occur in other species and are increasingly being used to obtain evidence of origins. This can be extremely important, for example in the fight against elephant poaching in Africa. Illegal killing had fallen to very low levels in the 1990s due to a ban on trade in elephant ivory. Since then a weakening of resolve and failures by both national governments and the international community have allowed poaching to resume. The survival of one of our few remaining species of megafauna is once again threatened.

To try to combat poaching, a data base of microsatellite profiles of elephant populations across the whole of Africa has been built up. Researchers obtained samples of feces from as many individuals in each population as possible. They extracted DNA from it and studied the lengths of its microsatellites. The data obtained allows microsatellite profiles of DNA extracted from ivory to be compared, so the elephant population from which tusks came can be identified.

5. State how similar human beings are genetically. [3]

6. Distinguish between genes and microsatellites. [3]

7. a) Explain why microsatellites are useful in tracing geographic origin. [3]

   b) Once the origin of the ivory is determined, suggest what specific actions might be taken to limit elephant poaching. [3]

   c) Suggest specific situations in which microsatellite sequences may be used. [3]

10 Consequences

A consequence is the result of something that happened before.

Consequences can be unexpected, predictable, avoidable, unavoidable, positive and negative. Consider these examples of events in history. What types of consequence do they each illustrate?

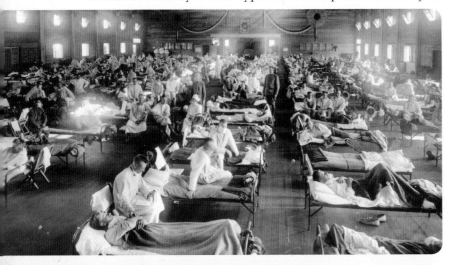

This makeshift hospital ward was at Camp Funston in Kansas, where the first case of "Spanish flu" was recorded in 1918. Spanish flu was the consequence of random mutations in an avian influenza virus that produced a new strain, which could infect humans. The disease spread rapidly to almost all parts of the world, infected a third of the world's population and killed over 50 million people. Can you think of any other consequences that this epidemic might have had?

Catherine of Aragon was Henry VIII of England's first wife. Her pregnancies repeatedly resulted in miscarriage, stillbirth or the early death of a son. Only one daughter survived. Henry wanted a male heir and was determined to remarry. He needed the Pope in Rome to annul his marriage. In the 16th century, annulments were usually granted with some discreet diplomatic pressure, but Rome had just been invaded and sacked by the troops of Holy Roman Emperor Charles V. The Pope was in effect a prisoner. By coincidence, Charles was the nephew of Catherine of Aragon and not surprisingly the Pope refused to annul her marriage to Henry. As a consequence, Henry rejected the power of the Pope and set in motion the changes that led to England becoming protestant. Can you find other examples of unlikely coincidences having major historical consequences?

About 66 million years ago an asteroid that was more than 10 km across collided with the Earth, forming a crater over 180 km wide and 20 km deep. The immediate consequences of the impact were megatsunamis, acid rain and six months of darkness. A mass extinction event followed, in which all remaining ammonites, non-avian dinosaurs and many other species died out. Although impossible to prove, it seems very likely that the asteroid impact was a "first cause" that set off complex interrelated changes on Earth.

We can trace our individual origins through chains of causes and consequences that extend beyond our parents and grandparents, through millions of generations of mammalian evolution and beyond our non-mammalian ancestors to the start of life. Biologists have debated whether the pathways of evolution would be the same if we ran the tape of life again on Earth or on another planet, or whether the consequences of chance events such as asteroid strikes or volcanic eruptions can be so profound that evolution would follow different paths. We do not yet and may never know the answer to this question.

Key concept: Change

Related concept: Consequences

Global context: Scientific and technical innovation

> ❝
> Science is the knowledge of consequences and dependence of one fact upon another.
> ❞

Introduction

Philosopher Thomas Hobbes wrote this in 1651. Consequences are effects or results or outcomes of earlier events. Understanding the potential consequences of a chain of events means being better prepared to react to the changes that events can trigger. Hence, consequences are closely linked to the key concept of change.

Genetics is one of the clearest examples of consequences. Differences of just one base in our DNA can have major life consequences. Knowledge of this has come from 150 or more years of scientific research, using carefully controlled experiments to discover the causes of inherited characteristics and how they change. This research has allowed technical innovation, such as the genetic modification of crop plants or animals to make them more useful to us. It is even now possible to edit the genes of humans. These innovations raise important questions over the impact that we have on the natural world and whether it is ethically right for us to use innovations in genetics in all possible ways.

▶ Gene editing can be used to improve the lives of people suffering from genetic conditions, such as Duchenne muscular dystropy

Statement of inquiry:

Scientific and technical innovations can change the impacts that we have on the world.

Experimental science allows consequences to be investigated objectively. In a typical scientific investigation, one independent variable is deliberately varied, with all other variables kept constant. Another variable is measured to see if it changes with the independent variable. If it does, we can conclude that the independent variable causes the changes. We call the variable that responds, the dependent variable.

In biology, it is sometimes impossible to do the obvious experiment for ethical or other reasons. An approach that is then often used is to look for correlations. For example, research in the 1990s revealed a correlation between myopia (short-sightedness) and sleeping with lights on as a young child. It would be easy to conclude that myopia is a consequence of night-time lighting, but probably the explanation is that parents with myopia are more likely to leave a light on in their children's bedroom than parents with normal vision, and genetic factors passed from parent to child increase the chance of myopia. This example reminds us that we have to be careful not to assume that a correlation shows that there is a causal link—it does not.

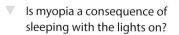
Is myopia a consequence of sleeping with the lights on?

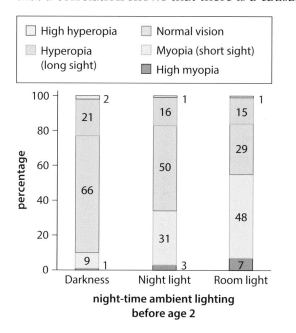

The research into myopia illustrates one of the big questions in biology—whether our characteristics are a consequence of the DNA that we inherit from our parents or our experiences, especially the environment created for us by our parents in the early formative years. This is known as the nature–nurture debate and we shall consider it in this chapter. Scientific and technical innovation is helping to provide some answers. Knockout mice are an example. Several thousand different strains have been developed. In each strain one gene has been removed, replaced or inactivated, allowing all the consequences of having this gene active to be investigated.

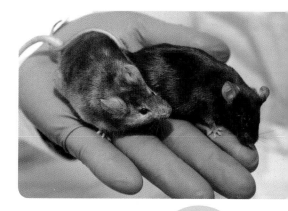
In the mouse on the left, a gene that affects hair growth has been knocked out

What do we inherit from our parents?

All our genes are inherited from our parents. Since the 1950s it has been known that genes are composed of DNA, so essentially we are inheriting sequences of bases. These sequences of bases mostly determine sequences of amino acids in proteins, but more widely they influence almost all of our characteristics very profoundly.

During sexual reproduction, genes are passed from parent to offspring in gametes. In humans, genes from the father (in the sperm) fuse with genes from the mother (in the egg). Mostly the base sequences of genes in a gamete are precisely the same as in the parent's cells, but occasionally there is a mutation and a sequence change occurs. Usually just one base in one gene changes, but even changes as small as this can have major consequences. A mutation produces a new form or version of a gene. The various versions of a gene usually only differ by one or two bases. They are known as the alleles of the gene.

Gene mutations are rare events. They can be caused by radiation or by mutagenic chemicals, but it is a matter of chance where in the sequence a mutation occurs and what the new base will be. Mutations do not occur because a new allele of a gene is needed. This would happen if living organisms were designed rather than evolved and we would then only see changes to base sequences that are beneficial. Many mutations are harmful (deleterious) and cause genetic disease.

This leads to an important principle in biology: acquired characteristics are not inherited. For example, a tennis player develops stronger muscles and bones in the arm used to hold the racquet. If the tennis player has children, the stronger muscles and bones in the playing arm are not inherited. That would only happen if playing tennis caused specific mutations in genes that influence these characteristics; there is no genetic mechanism for this. Of course, a tennis-playing parent may encourage their child to play tennis, but that is different. The child is acquiring the characteristics during their lifetime rather than inheriting them from their parents.

Parents pass on just half of their genes in each sperm or egg. It is a matter of chance which combination of genes comes together in a gamete and is therefore inherited by a child

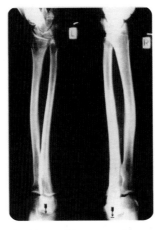

X-ray of the arms of a right-handed professional tennis player

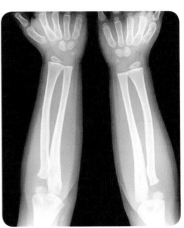

X-ray of the forearms of a newborn baby

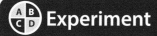

Experiment

By comparing and contrasting the X-rays of the forearms of the right-handed tennis player and of the newborn baby, what can you deduce about:

a) bone development in newborn babies?

b) the effect of physical activity on bone development after birth?

It might not only be tennis that causes one arm to have stronger bones and muscles than the other. Consider this hypothesis: right-handed people have stronger right arms and left-handed people have stronger left arms.

Design a scientific investigation to test this hypothesis. A simple method would be to measure the circumference of both arms of left- and right-handed people.

Is this a valid method for assessing arm strength? Can you suggest a better method? What variables would need to be controlled? How would you analyze the results?

ATL Critical thinking skills

Draw supported conclusions

When drawing conclusions from scientific experiments, it is important that sufficient relevant data is collected. When comparing the tennis player's X-ray with the infant's X-ray, a cautious approach might be to develop a testable prediction while at the same time recognizing that one pair of images is insufficient to support a conclusion. In general, a sample size less than five is too small, and the more data that can be collected, the better.

Nature–nurture debate

Some human characteristics are entirely the consequence of our genes, such as our eye colour. Others are entirely the consequence of our environment, for example, the languages that we speak. A third group of characteristics are partly due to genetic factors (nature) and are partly acquired from our experiences (nurture); intelligence is an example of this. There have been many debates about the relative importance of nature and nurture. Consider the examples below. Is each one due entirely to nature or nurture, or are any due to a combination. How could the relative importance of nature and nurture be investigated?

▲ Skin colour, hair colour and freckles

▲ Sickle cell anemia

▲ Tattoos, ear piercing and hair length

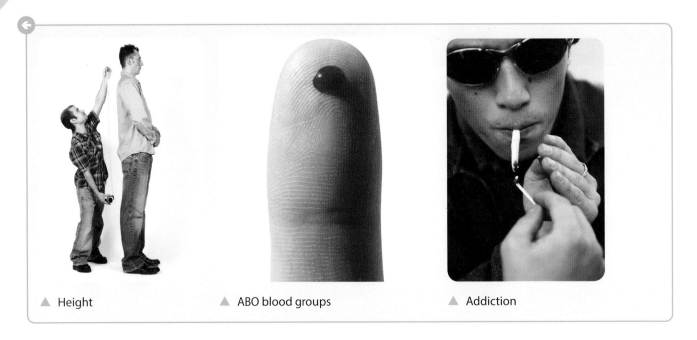

▲ Height   ▲ ABO blood groups   ▲ Addiction

GENETICS

How did Mendel discover genes?

Gregor Mendel is the father of genetics because his experiments were the first to show how genes are inherited. Mendel was working at a time when DNA hadn't been discovered and it was generally believed that we show a mixture of the characteristics of our parents. This theory is called blending inheritance. If blending inheritance happens, over the course of many generations it will lead to less and less variation in a population. For example, a human population starting with blue and brown eye colours and a mixture of heights would change to one where everyone had an intermediate eye colour and the same height.

Mendel did his experiments between 1856 and 1863 using purebred varieties of pea plant. In a purebred variety, all the plants and their progeny (offspring) have the same characteristics. Purebred varieties can be developed quite easily by growing many plants of one variety together so pollen is unlikely to be spread to them from other varieties and by saving seed only from plants with the desired characteristics. In peas it is particularly easy because the flowers tend to self-pollinate.

Mendel chose varieties of pea that differed in distinctive ways, for example, the colour of the flowers (purple or white) and the height of the plant (tall or dwarf). He performed simple hybridization experiments by transferring pollen from the anthers of one variety to the stigmas in flowers of another variety. We call these experiments crosses and the progeny are called first filial or F1 hybrids. The results of all of Mendel's crosses were the same—all of the F1 hybrid plants were like one of the parental types. The other type had apparently

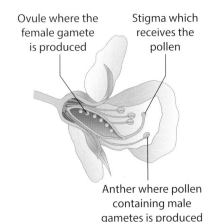

Ovule where the female gamete is produced

Stigma which receives the pollen

Anther where pollen containing male gametes is produced

disappeared. For example, in a cross between purple-flowered and white-flowered peas, all the F1 hybrids were purple-flowered and they were just as purple as their purple parent. This is not blending inheritance.

Mendel allowed the F1 hybrid plants to self-pollinate, to find what type of progeny they produced. Again, the results were always the same. Both of the original parental types appeared in this F2 generation, in a 3:1 ratio. Using the purple/white example again, 75% were purple-flowered and 25% were white. Despite apparently disappearing in the F1 generation, white-flowered peas had reappeared and they were just as white as the original parents. Neither the purple flower coloration nor the white had been changed by the hybridization process. Again, this showed that the theory of blending inheritance was false. Mendel had revealed that discrete factors which determine our characteristics are passed unchanged from parent to offspring. Different factors could come together in a hybrid but then separate again when the hybrid produces offspring. This is Mendel's law of segregation. We now call these factors genes.

What makes Mendel's hybrids all the same?

Mendel investigated seven different characteristics in peas and in every case found that the F1 plants were all of one of the parental types rather than the other. He called this constancy and used italics to emphasize this statement: *"Transitional forms were not observed in any experiment"*. For example, all the F1 plants were purple-flowered if one parent was purple and the other was white. Mendel realized that there must be a factor that makes pea plants purple-flowered and another factor that makes them white. These factors are alternative versions of a gene: alleles.

Pure-breeding purple- or white-flowered pea plants only have the allele for their own flower colour, so always pass it on to their progeny. Hybrid plants have one allele for purple flowers and one for white flowers, but have purple rather than intermediate-coloured flowers. This is because the allele for purple flowers is dominant and the allele for white flowers is recessive. A recessive allele is hidden if a dominant allele is present. Mendel used letters to denote alleles. In this case, the purple pigment in the flowers is an anthocyanin, so *A* is used for the dominant allele and *a* for the recessive one.

To understand dominance, we must remember that most genes code for a protein. Using the base sequence of a dominant allele, an active version of a protein is produced, resulting in a characteristic such as purple flowers. Recessive alleles either code for a modified protein that lacks normal activity, or they do not result in the production of any protein. If both dominant and recessive alleles are present

A cross between yellow-seeded and green-seeded peas gives all yellow-seeded F1 hybrids and, if these are grown and allowed to self-pollinate, a 3:1 ratio of F2 peas

GENETICS

▼ Flower colour in peas can be purple or white

then some of the active form of the protein is made, so we see the dominant characteristic. If recessive alleles are the only ones present then none of the active protein is made and a different characteristic is seen, for example, white flowers.

Recent research has shown that the gene affecting flower colour in Mendel's peas codes for a transcription factor. This protein binds to a pea plant's DNA at specific places and switches on the genes needed for anthocyanin production. With allele **A**, these transcription factors are produced during flower development, so cells in the petals synthesize anthocyanin. No transcription factors are produced if only allele **a** is present, so the genes for anthocyanin remain switched off and the flowers are white.

GENETICS

What causes Mendel's 3:1 ratio?

Mendel knew that his F1 hybrids had inherited two different factors from their parents, one dominant and one recessive. For example, an F1 hybrid of a cross between purple-flowered and white-flowered pea plants has one dominant **A** for purple flowers and one recessive **a** for white flowers. He deduced that the F2 plants had an equal chance of inheriting these two factors and that they could inherit two of the same factor or one of each. He used algebra to explain the 3:1 ratio in the F2 generation.

$$(A + a)(A + a) = AA + 2Aa + aa$$

AA and **Aa** are purple-flowered and **aa** are white-flowered, so the overall ratio is 3 purple to 1 white.

We can now explain the events that are occurring in the pea flowers much more fully. Inside the anthers, pollen grains containing male gametes are being made. Inside the ovule, a female gamete is being made. The cells of the pea plant are diploid—they contain two sets of chromosomes. The gametes are haploid with only one set of chromosomes. The number of chromosomes is halved by meiosis. This special type of nuclear division is described in Chapter 2.

Meiosis happens both in the anthers and in the ovule of the pea plant. In the diploid cells, there are two copies of each chromosome type and therefore two copies of each gene. Cells produced by meiosis only receive one of each type of chromosome and therefore one copy of each gene. If the two different alleles are present, it is a matter of chance which of them is passed to a gamete. Of the pollen grains and egg cells produced by a pea plant that has both **A** and **a** alleles, half will contain **A** and half **a**. It is also a matter of chance which gametes fuse together during fertilization. The chance of two dominant **A** alleles coming together is ½ × ½ = ¼. Similarly, the chance of **a** and **a** coming together is ¼. There are two different ways of **A** and **a** coming together as the pollen grain could contain **A** and the egg cell **a** or vice versa. The chance of **Aa** is therefore 2 × (½ × ½) = ½.

The possible outcomes of genetic crosses can be shown using a diagram called a Punnett square.

	Male gametes	
	A	**a**
A	**AA**	**Aa**
a	**aA**	**aa**

Female gametes

Wild pea plants use tendrils for support as they climb high in other plants, but some cultivated varieties grow much shorter stem sections, so are dwarf

Data-based question: Tall peas and dwarf peas

1. Some varieties of pea plant grow to about two metres tall and others, called dwarf varieties, grow to less than half a metre. Mendel crossed pure-breeding tall and dwarf varieties together to produce F1 hybrids, which were all tall. What can you conclude from this?

2. The F1 hybrids were allowed to self-pollinate to produce an F2 generation. Use a Punnett square diagram to explain the reasons for expecting a 3:1 ratio in the F2.

3. There were actually 1064 F2 plants in total, of which 787 were tall and 277 were dwarf.

   a) Calculate the ratio of tall to dwarf plants.

   b) Explain why the ratio wasn't precisely 3:1.

4. Mendel allowed the F2 generation to self-pollinate. He found that seed collected from self-pollinated dwarf plants produced only dwarf progeny. He collected seeds separately from each of 100 tall F2 plants. He grew the progeny from each of the 100 plants separately. Progeny from 28 of the F2 plants were all tall and from the other 72 included both tall and dwarf plants.

   a) Explain these results using the word *homozygous* if two of the same allele are present and *heterozygous* if there are two different alleles.

   b) Calculate the expected percentage of homozygous and heterozygous tall pea plants in the F2 generation.

GENETICS

Does inheritance work in the same way in other species as in peas?

Mendel published his research in the 1860s, but it was largely ignored for more than 30 years, partly because it was thought to apply only to peas. At the end of the 19th century, several biologists were questioning the theory of blending inheritance and when they rediscovered Mendel's work they realized its significance. Examples of Mendelian inheritance were soon discovered in many other plants and in animals.

One of the examples of Mendelian inheritance discovered in animals is rose comb. If pure-breeding chickens with single comb and rose comb are crossed together, all the F1 birds have the normal single comb, so the allele for single comb is dominant. If these F1 chickens are mated with each other, three-quarters have single combs and one-quarter have rose combs.

Some examples of inheritance were discovered that were slightly different from Mendel's peas. For example, a cross between pure-breeding black and white breeds of chicken produced F1 hybrids that were grey (often called "Andalusian blue"). When the grey F1 birds were crossed with each other there was a 1:2:1 ratio of black, grey and white chickens in the F2 generation. This fits with Mendel's findings apart from the dominance of the alleles—neither allele is dominant over the other, so a chicken with one allele for black feathers and one for white feathers has grey plumage.

▲ Single comb

▲ Rose comb

Other examples of inheritance were discovered that did not fit Mendelian ratios at all, but they could be explained by the processes that occur during sexual reproduction. The fusion of male and female gametes was discovered in the 1870s and meiosis in the 1880s, both between the time of Mendel's research and its rediscovery. It was therefore known that homologous chromosomes separate during meiosis, halving the number of chromosomes, then two sets of chromosomes are united during the fusion of male and female gametes in fertilization. In some cases, non-Mendelian ratios were due to pairs of genes being located close together on the same chromosome and in others to genes being located on sex chromosomes.

1. In humans the allele for brown eyes is dominant over the allele for blue eyes.

   a) Can two blue-eyed parents have brown-eyed children?

   b) Can two brown-eyed parents produce a blue-eyed child?

2. The Holstein breed of cattle is widely used for milk production. In order to produce milk, each cow must have a calf every year. Holsteins have a black head and black coat with white patches. Hereford cattle are reared for beef. They have an all-white head and a red coat with no white patches. Many Holstein cattle are artificially inseminated with semen from Hereford bulls. The progeny all have a white head, a black coat and no white patches. Discuss the possible outcome if these Holstein-Hereford crosses were bred together.

▲ Holstein cow

▲ Hereford bull

▲ Holstein–Hereford cross

3. Welsh Mountain sheep can have black or white coats. If pure-breeding black and white sheep are mated together, the F1 progeny all have black coats while they are lambs, but the coat gradually lightens to a grey-black colour when the sheep are older. What is the expected outcome if two F1 sheep are bred together?

Note that there is also a dominant gene for white coats in sheep, for example, in Bluefaced Leicesters.

▲ Black female sheep   ▲ White male sheep

GENETICS

What are the consequences of having parents who are closely related?

In most countries it is illegal to marry a brother or sister and in some countries it is also illegal to marry a first cousin. Such laws protect us against the high risk of disease in offspring of closely related parents. The harmful consequences of mating between close relatives were known long before the genetic reasons were understood. Using the principles that Mendel discovered we can now explain them, using one disease as an example.

Archibald Garrod was a pioneer of research into genetic diseases. He investigated alkaptonuria, which causes a person to produce deep brown urine that turns black on exposure to air. Garrod made these observations:

▲ Normal urine and urine from a person with alkaptonuria

- Although alkaptonuria is extremely rare (1 case in 250,000 people), he found families in which several individuals had the disease.

- If one parent had the disease, their offspring very rarely did, but an unusually high proportion people with alkaptonuria had parents who were first cousins.

- In five large families that he found, where there were five or more children and at least one of them had alkaptonuria, there were a total of 57 children who were normal and 19 who had alkaptonuria.

These observations suggest that the disease is caused by a rare recessive allele. We can use the symbol **H** for the normal dominant allele and **h** for the recessive allele that causes alkaptonuria. A person with alkaptonuria has two **h** alleles and no **H**. The child of a person with alkaptonuria rarely has the disease because their other parent is very likely to have two **H** alleles, one of which they are certain to inherit. Two parents who do not have the disease can produce a child with alkaptonuria if they each have one **H** allele and one **h**. The chance of one of their children having the disease is 25%. Having two parents that carry an **h** allele is very uncommon unless the parents are related. The pedigree diagram shows how a man can have a child with alkaptonuria if he marries his first cousin, because he and his wife have both inherited the **h** allele from a shared grandparent.

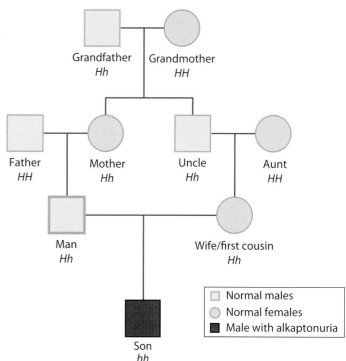

It is now known that alkaptonuria is a consequence of mutations in a gene which codes for the enzyme HGD. This enzyme is involved in a metabolic pathway that breaks down the amino acid phenylalanine if it is present in excess. The HGD enzyme converts homogentisic acid, which is a dark colour, into a colourless compound. If the dominant **H** allele is not present, the enzyme cannot be produced, so homogentisic acid accumulates in the blood and is excreted in urine, making it dark brown or black.

1. What is the chance of a child with alkaptonuria if a man with the disease has children with a woman who has these combinations of alleles:

   a) *Hh*   **b)** *hh*   **c)** *HH*

2. Calculate whether the chance of genetic disease is higher from a mating between a brother and sister or from a mating between two first cousins.

3. Self–pollination in plants is an even closer mating than between siblings, yet genetic diseases are rarely observed when progeny are the result of self-pollination in a pure-breeding variety. Explain the reasons for this.

How much genetic variation is there in humans?

This is a big question, without a simple answer. We can break it down into smaller questions for you to research.

1. Genes are made of DNA and are grouped together on long DNA molecules called chromosomes. DNA molecules are very narrow, so chromosomes are only clearly visible when they coil up during mitosis. This is the process that divides a nucleus into two genetically identical nuclei shortly before the cell splits in two. Chromosomes can be spread out and be counted if a cell in mitosis is placed on a microscope slide and pressure is applied to burst it.

● **Do all humans have the same number of chromosomes or is there variation?**

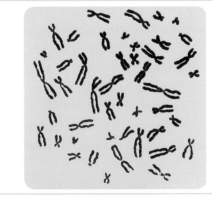

2. Every chromosome has a linear sequence of genes on it, usually with sections of non-coding DNA between one gene and the next. Chromosomes that have the same sequence of genes (and therefore the same structure) can pair up during meiosis. Special stains can be used to show differences in structure between chromosomes. These reveal that body cells normally have two of each type of chromosome, with the same sequence of genes.

● **Do all humans have the same sequence of genes on their chromosomes?**

3. The pairs of chromosomes that form during meiosis are oriented randomly, so each gamete can receive either one of each pair of chromosomes. A horse roundworm, *Parascaris equorum*, has two pairs of chromosomes which gives four possible combinations of chromosomes. The yellow fever mosquito, *Aedes aegypti*, has three pairs and so eight combinations of its chromosomes are possible.

● **How many combinations of chromosomes could there be in one human's gametes?**

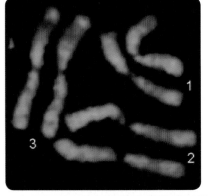

4. A gene is a length of DNA with a specific sequence of bases. Alleles of a gene differ in their base sequence. The commonest differences are single nucleotide polymorphisms (SNPs), which affect just one base. SNPs can have major consequences. For example, one base change from adenine to thymine in the hemoglobin gene causes sickle-cell anemia.

● **How many different single nucleotide polymorphisms have been discovered in humans?**

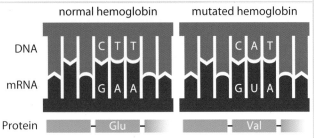

normal hemoglobin   mutated hemoglobin

DNA

mRNA

Protein   Glu   Val

Is genetic variation increasing in humans?

Mutations are continually adding to genetic variation. Even identical twins have some genetic differences because of mutations during their development. Research into mutation rates suggest that we pass on 60–70 mutations that we did not receive from our parents, to our children. Unless mutations are eliminated at the same rate, genetic variation must be increasing in humans.

Mutations can occur at any position along the DNA of any chromosome, but when human genomes were compared, it was seen that specific regions of human chromosomes have precisely the same base sequence; these sequences are called highly conserved sequences. If a highly conserved sequence is found unchanged in the genomes of other species (mouse, rat and dog, for example), it is known as an ultra-conserved element. Mutations certainly occur in highly conserved and ultra-conserved sequences, but they do not persist in the population.

Some of these conserved sequences code for the active site of an enzyme. If a mutation changes the amino acid sequence at the active site, the enzyme will almost certainly fail to catalyse its reaction. If the chemical reaction catalysed by the enzyme is vital to survival, individuals with the mutation will die. This could happen at a very early stage in development—even in the egg, sperm or zygote. The mutation is of course eliminated when an individual with it dies.

In a similar way, mutations are eliminated from genes that code for vital proteins such as hormone receptors, or from promoters that regulate gene expression. Here too, mutations to the base sequence have very harmful consequences, so individuals with the mutation die. Individuals that do not have the mutation can survive and pass on the normal gene sequence to their offspring. This is an example of a process called natural selection.

Natural selection eliminates deleterious mutations but research has shown that of the 60–70 new mutations per generation only about two are deleterious. Nearly all the other mutations are neutral—they neither increase nor decrease the chances of survival. This could be because the mutation is in DNA that does not function as a gene, or is in a gene but does not change the amino acid sequence. The fate of neutral mutations is a matter of chance, because we only pass on one of our two copies of a gene to our children. A few neutral mutations spread through the human population but most disappear. Genetic variation in the human population is therefore probably at an equilibrium level and is not increasing.

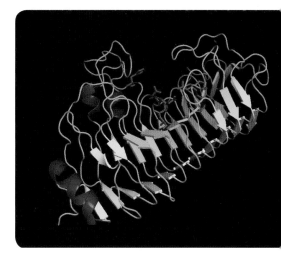

▲ Computer-generated model of a pectinase, showing in pink the six amino acids at the active site that digest pectin. Pectinases from different fungi vary considerably, but the amino acids in specific parts of the enzyme, such as the active site, are identical, indicating that mutations there would be deleterious

Genetic drift

1. Put nine blue balls and one red ball into a bag. The blue balls are a normal allele and the red is a mutant. The bag represents a parental generation.

2. Shake up the balls in the bag and take one out randomly; if it is blue add one blue ball to another bag, if it is red do likewise; these are the offspring. Replace the ball that you took out of the parental bag so there are still nine blues and one red.

3. Repeat stage 2 until you have 10 balls in the offspring bag.

4. The offspring bag now becomes the parental bag. Repeat stages 2 and 3 to produce another generation.

5. Continue until all the balls are blue or red.

If you end up with 10 red balls you have simulated a natural process in populations called genetic drift.

a) Is it more likely that the red mutant allele will spread through the population or be eliminated?

b) The chance of the red mutant allele replacing the blue one can be calculated mathematically. Is the chance greater in small or large populations?

c) How could this activity be modified to simulate beneficial or deleterious mutations?

Data-based question: Comparing amino acid sequences

The image shows the amino acid sequence of a structural protein called histone H1. Each letter in these sequences stands for a specific amino acid; all 20 amino acids found in proteins can be represented using just one letter: for example, A stands for alanine and K for lysine.

Histone H1 (residues 120-180)

HUMAN KKASKPKKAASKAPTKKPKATPVKKAKKK LAATPKKAKKPK TVKAKPVKASKPKKAKPVK
MOUSE KKAAKPKKAASKAPSKKPKATPVKKAKKK PAATPKKAKKPK VVKVKPVKASKPKKAKTVK
RAT   KKAAKPKKAASKAPSKKPKATPVKKAKKK PAATPKKAKKPK IVKVKPVKASKPKKAKPVK
COW   KKAAKPKKAASKAPSKKPKATPVKKAKKK PAATPKKTKKPK TVKAKPVKASKPKKTKPVK
CHIMP KKASKPKKAASKAPTKKPKATPVKKAKKK LAATPKKAKKPK TVKAKPVKASKPKKAKPVK

1. Count how many differences there are between each pair of organisms and use the chart to record the numbers.

2. Which two species show:

   a) the smallest amount of genetic variation?

   b) the second smallest amount of genetic variation?

3. Suggest an explanation for the differences in genetic variation between these five species.

	Mouse	Rat	Cow	Chimp
Human				
Mouse				
Rat				
Cow				

How does natural selection work?

Natural selection is the "big idea" that links together the whole of biology. It is a process that began when life first appeared on Earth and has continued ever since over billions of years. It has resulted in all the diverse forms of life that now exist. Charles Darwin developed the theory of evolution by natural selection in the 1830s, but delayed publication of his ideas until 1859. Natural selection is the inevitable consequence of three things:

1. **There is variation in populations.**

   This variation is due to mutation and sexual reproduction.

   How does sexual reproduction cause variation in a population?

2. **Chances of survival and reproduction are affected by an individual's characteristics.**

   There are many factors that have an impact on chances of survival and reproduction:

   - Some individuals are more successful at competing for food, so they are likely to grow more rapidly and have more resources for reproduction and they are less likely to die during periods of food shortage.

   - Some individuals are better at evading predators, for example, by escaping when chased or by effective camouflage.

   - Some individuals are more resistant to disease, so they survive during epidemics that kill others.

   - Some individuals are more successful at attracting a mate, for example, by their physical appearance, their courtship displays or by fighting their rivals.

   Can you find real examples of these or other factors?

3. **Offspring inherit characteristics from their parents.**

   Some characteristics are acquired as a result of our environment, but most are due to our genes and can therefore be passed on to offspring.

   Does evolution by natural selection happen with characteristics that were acquired as a result of our environment?

▲ The peppered moth (*Biston betularia*) is vulnerable to predators when it roosts during daylight hours on the branches of birch trees. There are two forms of the moth, one having black wings and the other white wings with black peppering. Which form has the better chance of survival in areas with unpolluted air where birch branches are pale and covered in lichens? Which form is favoured by natural selection in polluted industrial areas here birch branches are covered in black soot with no lichens?

Two or more seed types, large and small, are spread over an area, such as a laboratory bench. Students are given a wide variety of gripping tools such as test tube holders, blunt forceps, laundry tongs, barbecue tongs, tweezers. Each student or group of students uses one tool, for a short time, at the same time as the other students. The students that have caught fewest seeds, either by their number or mass, are eliminated and the seeds are re-spread for more rounds of feeding and elimination of the students with the least-adapted tool for picking up seeds. Is one tool best for all of the seeds?

EVOLUTION

What caused variation in human skin color?

Differences in human skin color are very visible, despite being due only to small variations in the amounts of melanin, the black pigment synthesized by skin cells. Exposure to ultraviolet light causes synthesis of more melanin, but most of the variation between people is due to genes, so it can be inherited.

Fossil evidence shows that the first modern humans (*Homo sapiens*) lived in sub-Saharan Africa. Their pre-human ancestors in Africa had developed dark skin over a million years ago. Between 100,000 and 70,000 years ago groups of humans migrated out of Africa and spread through Europe, North and South America and Asia. As they migrated north there were changes in skin color, resulting in the current pattern of lighter skin colors in long-established populations living further north.

Read the information given here and then write an explanation based on natural selection for the variation in human skin color.

- Sunlight contains ultraviolet radiation.

- Sunlight is more intense near the equator than the poles.

- Melanin absorbs ultraviolet radiation.

- Ultraviolet radiation converts cholesterol in the skin into pre-vitamin D3 which is then converted into vitamin D.

- Ultraviolet radiation causes mutations in skin cells that can result in malignant cancers.

- Vitamin D deficiency reduces calcium absorption in the intestine and causes rickets.

- Few foods naturally contain vitamin D.

- Ultraviolet radiation causes degradation of folate (vitamin B_{12}).

- Folate deficiency in pregnant women increases the risk of developmental abnormalities in babies.

▲ Inuit living in the far north have darker skins than expected. This may be related to their traditional diet which includes much oily fish and marine mammals that are rich in vitamin D

What is the difference between natural selection and evolution?

One of each of these pairs of statements refers to evolution and the other to natural selection. In each pair, which is which?

DEFINITIONS

Progressive change in the characteristics of a population or species over the generations	Non-random transmission of genes from one generation to the next because better-adapted individuals have a greater chance of survival and reproduction

EARLY DESCRIPTIONS

… daily and hourly scrutinizing, throughout the world, every variation, even the slightest; rejecting that which is bad, preserving and adding up all that is good; silently and insensibly working, whenever and wherever opportunity offers, at the improvement of each organic being in relation to its organic and inorganic conditions of life. (Charles Darwin, *The Origin of Species*, 1859)	… would it be too bold to imagine, that in the great length of time, since the earth began to exist, perhaps millions of ages before the commencement of the history of mankind, would it be too bold to imagine, that all warm-blooded animals have arisen from one living filament, which the GREAT FIRST CAUSE endued with animality, with the power of acquiring new parts… and of delivering down those improvements by generation to its posterity, world without end! (Erasmus Darwin, *Zoonomia*, 1794)

EXAMPLES OF EVIDENCE

Differences between fossils in rocks of different ages	Differences in rates of survival and reproduction between varieties of a species that differ in heritable characteristics

CAUSE OR CONSEQUENCE

Causes evolution	Consequence of natural selection

Data-based question: The evolution of penguins

The evolution of penguins has been investigated by comparing the morphology of living species and the base sequences of genes. Fossil evidence has also proved useful.

Using all the data available to them, biologists have constructed a tree diagram to show how closely related the different species are to each other. This is called a cladogram and allows us to deduce the most likely evolutionary origins of penguins.

▲ Emperor penguins swimming

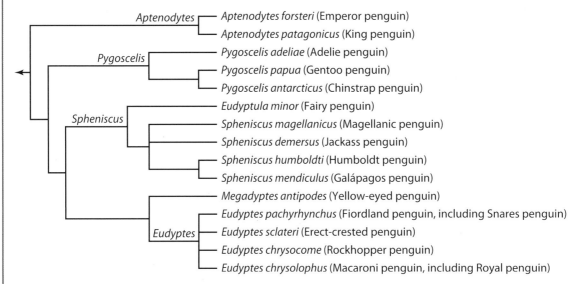

1. To which species is the *Aptenodytes forsteri* (Emperor penguin) most closely related?

2. How can we explain the presence of wings even though penguins do not fly?

3. Fossil evidence suggests that the common ancestor of penguins lived about 70 million years ago. Roughly how often have splits occurred between penguin species since that time?

4. Penguins vary considerably in size with the largest species in the far south and the smallest species close to the equator. Suggest reasons for penguins evolving to become

   a) larger if they migrate southwards

   b) smaller if they migrate northwards.

5. In several cases, biologists do not all agree whether populations of penguin are separate species or are just varieties of one species. This is quite a common problem when animals and plants are being classified. Darwin used it as evidence in his great book *Origin of Species*. Explain how the problem of populations that might or might not be separate species can be seen as evidence for evolution by natural selection.

What causes new species to evolve on islands?

The text below was adapted from an article on the website of the Convention on Biological Diversity. This convention was signed by 150 government leaders at the 1992 Rio Earth Summit.

Islands boast a truly unique assemblage of life. Species become island dwellers either by drifting on islands as they break off from larger landmasses or by dispersing across the ocean to islands newly emerged from the ocean floor. Once on these islands, populations become confined to small, isolated areas located some distance from other large land masses. Over time, this isolation exerts unique evolutionary forces that result in the development of a distinct genetic reservoir and the emergence of highly specialized species with new characteristics and unusual adaptations. These can include gigantism or dwarfism and loss of the ability to fly, disperse or defend against predation. Genetic diversity and population sizes tend to be low and species often become concentrated in small confined areas.

Many island species are endemic, meaning that they are found nowhere else on Earth. Islands harbour higher concentrations of endemic species than continents do. The number and proportion of endemics rises with increasing isolation, island size and topographic variety. For example, over 90% of Hawaiian island species are endemic. In Mauritius, some 50% of all plants, mammals, birds, reptiles and amphibians are endemic. The island of Cuba is home to 18 endemic mammals, while mainland Guatemala and Honduras, both nearby, have only three each. There are more than 8,000 endemic species on Madagascar, making it the nation with the highest number of endemic species in sub-Saharan Africa.

It has often been remarked that islands make a contribution to global biodiversity that is out of proportion to their land area. In this sense, they can be thought of collectively as biodiversity "hot spots", containing some of the richest reservoirs of plants and animals on Earth.

▲ Lopevi is one of over 80 small volcanic islands that make up the archipelago of Vanuatu. New islands can also be formed from coral reefs

1. There is no evidence for new species being created from non-living matter on Earth. There is abundant evidence for existing species splitting to produce new species. This process is called **speciation**. What are the most important factors causing speciation to happen frequently on islands?

2. The dodo is a famous example of a species that has been completely annihilated. It inhabited the island of Mauritius. Many island species have died out. This process is called **extinction**. What are the most important factors causing extinction to be happening frequently on islands at the moment?

What is genetic modification?

There are two types of gene transfer: vertical and horizontal.

- Vertical transfer of genes is from parent to offspring. It is a one-way flow of genes down the generations. It only happens during sexual or asexual reproduction and a full set of genes is transferred.

- Horizontal transfer could happen in either direction between two individuals. Genes from a donor are added to the existing genome of a recipient. Usually the number of genes transferred is small.

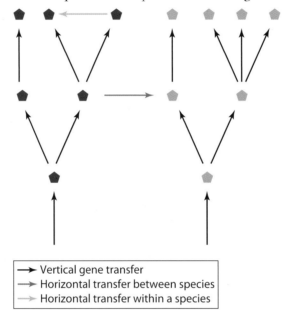

→ Vertical gene transfer
→ Horizontal transfer between species
→ Horizontal transfer within a species

Vertical transfer of genes happens in all species, but horizontal transfer is much more common in some species than others. It often happens in bacteria, where small extra loops of DNA called plasmids can pass from a donor cell to a recipient. This can take place between bacteria of different species and explains how genes for antibiotic resistance can move from one species to another. A consequence of horizontal gene transfer is that the evolution of bacteria cannot be represented by branching tree diagrams—there are cross-links between the branches!

Because mechanisms for horizontal gene transfer naturally exist in bacteria, it is relatively easy for biologists to insert extra genes artificially. The first example of this was in 1973 when an antibiotic resistance gene was inserted into the bacterium *Escherichia coli*. Later in the 1970s, the gene for human insulin was put into the same type of bacteria. As a consequence, abundant supplies of human insulin soon became available for treating diabetes. Many useful proteins are now produced using bacteria that have been genetically modified.

Horizontal gene transfer has until recently been extremely uncommon in plants and animals. Some examples are known, typically where two organisms live together as a parasite and host or in a mutualistic relationship, but as a general rule gene transfer in plants and animals is only vertical. However, since the 1970s it has been possible to transfer genes to plants and animals artificially. Examples are given below.

Crop plants that:

- make a toxin which kills insect pests feeding on them

- are resistant to a herbicide so weeds can be controlled in a growing crop

- produce vaccines and antibodies for use as treatments against infectious diseases in humans

- contain nutrients that promote health such as omega-3 fatty acids

Farm livestock that:

- make useful proteins and secrete them in their milk so they can be easily harvested

- produce hormones that increase growth rates

- release less polluting phosphate in feces by digesting plant foods more effectively

- produce allergy-free milk for human consumption or high protein milk for cheese production

The process of transferring genes artificially to an organism is genetic modification or genetic engineering. The organisms produced are genetically modified organisms (GMOs).

1. What is the latest example of genetic modification in either a crop plant or a farm animal that you can find?

2. Can GM crops be legally grown in your area or are they banned?

3. Using what you know about gene transfer, evaluate the importance of keeping "natural" and GM organisms separate.

4. Would a GMO be favoured by natural selection over a non-genetically modified one? What would this depend on?

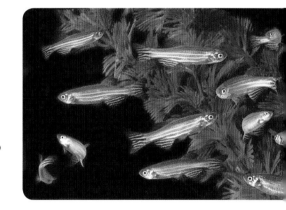

▲ GloFish are zebra danios (*Danio rerio*) that have been genetically modified to produce a red, green or orange fluorescent pigment

What tools are in a genetic engineer's tool kit?

Genetic modification is possible because a molecular toolkit, consisting of naturally occurring enzymes, DNA and RNA molecules and micro-organisms, has been assembled. Some of these are shown in the table. How could each one be useful in gene transfer?

Restriction endonucleases: DNA cutting enzymes	The enzyme *Eco*R1 cuts DNA here: G AATTC CTTAA G	These enzymes act like molecular scissors by cutting DNA at specific base sequences. Thousands of different restriction endonucleases have been discovered that can cut at over 200 different base sequences.
DNA ligase: DNA joining enzymes	GAATTC CTTAAG ↓ GAATTC CTTAAG	This type of enzyme makes sugar-phosphate bonds to seal nicks and so link together chains of DNA nucleotides. This is necessary when a gene is inserted into a plasmid or larger DNA molecule.
Plasmids: vectors for gene transfer		These are small extra loops of DNA that are found in bacteria and a few other micro-organisms. The main chromosome in a typical bacterium is also circular but is about 50 times larger. In the lab, plasmids are used for gene transfer.
***Taq* DNA polymerase:** a DNA copying enzyme		This enzyme can work at high temperatures without being denatured since it evolved in the bacterium *Thermus aquaticus*, which lives in hot springs. In the lab, this enzyme is used to make multiple copies of a DNA fragment.

Is genetic modification ethical?

Scientists must always consider the ethical implications of their work. Ethical questions are often very complex, but scientists have an obligation to consider both the beneficial and the harmful consequences of their research before starting. Consequences of scientific research may be hard to predict and there could be disagreement about whether they are good or bad.

There has been considerable controversy over the ethics of genetic modification. Debate one or more of these questions, or frame an ethical question of your own for debate.

Is it ethical to transfer genes to animals from other species?

Is it ethical to cure disease in humans using genetic modification?

Is it ethical to use genetically modified crops to increase the food supply for humans if they cause harm to wildlife?

Is it ethical to produce and sell GM foods if the long-term consequences are not known with certainty?

Is genetic modification of humans ethical if it allows research that could result in new therapies for disease?

▲ *Hydra viridissima* is a pond animal that can reproduce asexually by budding. A small outgrowth forms on the side, which develops into a new polyp and then detaches

What is cloning?

Cloning in its broadest sense is asexual reproduction. Many plants can reproduce asexually and gardeners have developed methods of doing this artificially, by taking cuttings, for example.

Some animals can reproduce asexually, including aphids and *Hydra*, but most types cannot. It is relatively easy to clone an animal artificially by splitting an early-stage embryo into small groups of cells. Often each group of embryonic cells develops into a separate individual. It is much more difficult to clone an older animal that has differentiated cells, but techniques for this have now been developed.

The first successful cloning of an animal older than an embryo was carried out in the 1960s by John Gurdon. He used the frog *Xenopus*, which lays unfertilized eggs in water. Gurdon removed the nucleus from an egg cell and replaced it with a nucleus taken from an intestine cell of a *Xenopus* tadpole. Some of the eggs that he treated in this way developed successfully into new tadpoles and very likely could have gone on to become adult *Xenopus* frogs. John Gurdon was awarded a Nobel prize in 2012.

It was not until 1996 that a mammal was cloned using differentiated cells from an adult. The cloned animal was a sheep. As with *Xenopus*, egg cells were obtained and their nuclei were removed. Cells were removed from the mammary gland of an adult sheep and were cultured. These cells were starved to make them inactive. One of the small inactive mammary gland cells was placed next to each of the large egg cells missing its nucleus. A pulse of electricity was used to make the two cells join together. In just one case out of several hundred, the fused cell developed like a zygote. The lamb that was subsequently born was named Dolly, and is probably the most famous sheep ever to have existed.

Each potato tuber planted grows and then reproduces asexually to form 10 or more new tubers. This is a natural method of cloning and explains how vast numbers of genetically identical potatoes can be produced

Cattle, horses, goats and other mammal species have since been cloned and improvements in technique have greatly raised the success rate. It might now be possible to clone humans using differentiated cells from an adult, but this has not been done because of serious ethical concerns.

1. What is the advantage of cloning an adult animal rather than an embryo?

2. Is the natural process of human embryos splitting to produce identical twins a form of cloning?

3. What are the ethical objections to cloning humans?

Dolly meets the media

Summative assessment

Potato tubers (variety Desiree) that are ready to harvest

Introduction

Potato (*Solanum tuberosum*) is the world's most important non-grain food crop and is central to global food security. More than 300 million tons of potato tubers are produced each year. Potatoes have about 40,000 protein-coding genes—many more than humans.

 ## Late blight disease

1. In the 1840s, many people in Ireland had become dependent on potatoes for food. When crops of potatoes failed year after year because of the disease "late blight", the consequences were immense—one in eight Irish people died of starvation and many more emigrated to America. The destruction of entire potato crops was the consequence of a lack of genetic diversity. Explain how there was so little genetic diversity in potato crops grown in Ireland at that time. [3]

2. Cultivated varieties of potatoes have been developed from wild species in South America. The process took hundreds or maybe even thousands of years. Explain how a cultivated variety of plant can be developed from a wild species and reasons for it taking such a long time. [3]

3. Late blight is caused by the micro-organism *Phytophthora infestans*. In wild potato species, many plants are resistant to this micro-organism and do not suffer from late blight. Explain how resistance to *Phytophthora infestans* could develop in populations of wild potato. [3]

Some leaves on this potato plant are already dying due to late blight and soon the disease will spread to other leaves and stems and also to the growing tubers

4. Some cultivated varieties of potato have been produced that are resistant to *Phytophthora infestans*, but this resistance often only works for a few years and then the variety starts to suffer from late blight. Suggest reasons for a cultivated potato variety that was resistant becoming susceptible to late blight. [3]

5. In the past, resistant potato varieties were produced by cross-breeding cultivated varieties with wild species that contained a resistance gene. Scientific and technological innovations have made it possible to transfer

individual genes for resistance from wild species such as *Solanum venturii* to cultivated varieties of potato. Suggest advantages of this new method for developing resistant potato varieties. [3]

Cloning potatoes

6. When an improved new variety of potato has been produced, millions of tubers of this variety are needed for farmers to plant. If one tuber is planted and allowed to clone naturally, up to 20 tubers may be produced by the end of the growing season. Explain the need for a more rapid method of cloning a new variety of potato. [3]

7. Choose an artificial method of cloning potatoes—you could use cuttings, portions of a tuber with a bud, or small pieces of tissue from inside a bud (micropropagation). Think of an innovation that might improve this method of cloning; for example, rooting hormone might encourage buds to develop roots more rapidly.

   a) Formulate a testable hypothesis, based on your innovation. [3]

   b) Explain the scientific reasoning for your innovation. [3]

   c) Design an experiment to test your hypothesis. [9]

Analyzing potato cloning methods

8. a) Present the data that you have collected in your experiment, using suitable tables and charts. [5]

   b) Interpret the data and explain your results using scientific reasoning. [5]

   c) Evaluate the validity of your method and your hypothesis [3]

   d) Suggest improvements or extensions to your experiment. [2]

Genetically modified potatoes

Late blight is a troublesome disease of potatoes. The disease spreads from July onward and in some years farmers have to spray potato crops with fungicide as many as 15 times to prevent the disease. In 2014, it was announced that a new blight-resistant GM potato variety had been produced by biologists at the Sainsbury Laboratory in England. The gene Rpi-vnt1.1 from the wild species *Solanum venturii* had been transferred to the potato variety Desiree. See http://rstb.royalsocietypublishing.org/content/369/1639/20130087

Field trials over three years showed a high level of resistance to late blight in the genetically modified Desiree plants, with leaves of the unmodified Desiree plants almost completely destroyed each year. The yield of the GM potato crop was twice as high as the non-GM. Regulations prevented the biologists from tasting the GM Desiree potatoes, but there is no known mechanism for the taste being altered by the presence of the new gene.

Micropropagation of potato varieties at the Department of Biotechnology, University of St Petersburg, Russia

Over 400 R genes conferring blight resistance are known in potatoes, but a similarly large number of genes that overcome resistance have been discovered in *Phytophthora infestans*. If a stack of R genes were transferred to potatoes they should make a potato variety resistant to late blight for many years.

Because the European Union is unlikely to give approval for growing GM crops for human consumption, the biologists granted a license for using the GM technology that they had developed to an American company. Professor Jones who led the research team has been quoted as saying "I think it is unfortunate that American farmers are going to benefit from the fruits of European taxpayers' funded work way before the Europeans".

▲ *Solanum venturii*

9. Write an evaluation of genetic modification of potatoes to make them blight resistant. Consider both arguments for and against, ending with an overall assessment of whether you think they should be banned as in the European Union or approved as in the United States. Try to use scientific language effectively in your evaluation. [15]

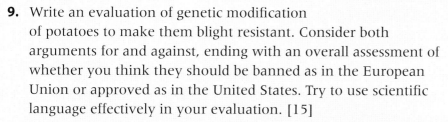

ATL Reflection skills

Consider ethical, cultural and environmental implications

Ethics is the academic discipline that considers the "rightness" or "wrongness" of a particular course of action. Since people differ in their priorities, ethical considerations often can be strongly linked to personal values. It is important to approach these considerations with an open mind.

One strategy for approaching ethical considerations is to employ a systematic approach that relies on a rational framework. First, the motivations of opposing groups can be considered. If it is recognized that both sides have a common goal of maximizing benefit for the community, a compromise position might be discovered. Secondly, the potential consequences of an action should be carefully weighed. The most likely outcome should be most actively considered, but if there is even a remote potential for the consequences to be catastrophic, caution should be practiced. Lastly, we should examine other moral judgments we have made or examine existing practices within our communities that involve related or similar issues and seek the most consistent response with our beliefs about these similar cases.

11 Evidence

Scientific ideas are supported through observation and interpretation of data.

▶ Romans boiled grape juice down to "sapa" in leaden cooking vessels, resulting in a solution of lead acetate, a compound which has a sugary taste. The book *Apicus* contains a collection of Roman recipes; many of those recipes include "sapa" as an ingredient. A minority of modern scholars suggest that lead poisoning was widespread in the ruling class of Rome and contributed to the decline of the empire. In areas where historians disagree, what counts as evidence?

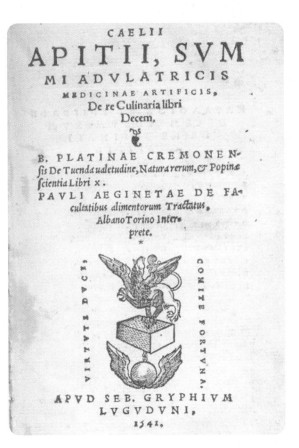

▽ Lead is easily extracted and purified from ore. It is malleable and unsurprisingly was widely used in ancient Rome.

Lead was used for making pottery and eating utensils and in the production of wine. We now know that ingesting lead has a significant adverse effect on our health. Analysis of primary source documents from Roman times suggest that scholars were aware of this, yet other documents indicate dangerous applications for the use of lead.

ength of lead wa
m under a sh
eet. We beli
e **praetoriu**

in pieces during 1899 and 1900. It came
etween Eastgate Street and Northgate
es this part of Chester was the site of
ss commander)

IMP.VESP.VIIII.T.IMP.VII.COS.GN.IVLIO.AGRICOLA.LEG.AVG.PR.PR
"(made) when the Emperor Vespasian was consul for the ninth time and the
Emperor Titus was consul for the seventh time, when Gnaeus Iulius Agricola
was imperial governor (of Britain)"

The number of consulships tell us th
Agricola is the best known of all the
daughter married the great historian Tac
many books have survived from the an
is one. Agricola was governor of Britain i
time he conquered northern England an
be the furthest the Romans ever reached in

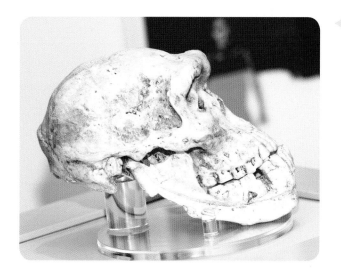

Evidence of the past is often fragmentary. The skull shown here comes from the partial remains of five *Homo erectus* individuals, uncovered in Dmanisi, Georgia. The skulls have features that did not fit existing theories about human evolution and which fueled considerable debate about when human ancestors first invaded European ecosystems and how much variation can exist within a species. Do you know other examples of understanding being hampered by a lack of evidence?

Tollund Man was a well-preserved body of an adult man dated from about 200 BC discovered in a bog in Denmark. Analysis of stomach contents showed that his last meal was a gruel of barley and wild seeds. Under the microscope scientists were able to see that there were no traces of meat, fish or fresh fruit among the contents, only grain and seeds. What is the significance of this fact? How is knowledge of how diets have changed over time useful?

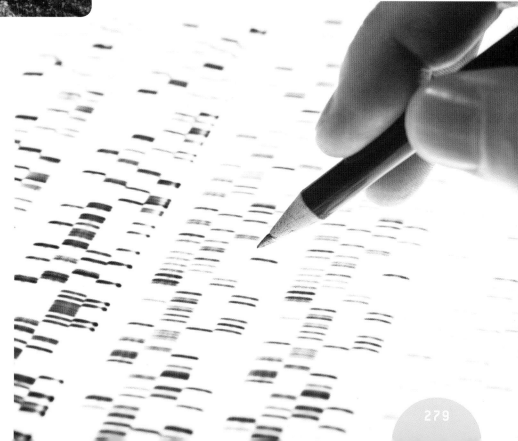

Trials in court involve the presentation of evidence. What types of evidence are admissible? What are the similarities and differences between scientific evidence and the evidence that lawyers use in court?

Introduction

How do scientists gather evidence and use it to expand our understanding of the world? There are many different steps scientists take to achieve this: first of all, they make observations of the natural world and take note of interesting phenomena. This can often lead to hypotheses, which are possible explanations for the observations recorded. Scientists then make some predictions which help them design controlled experiments to test whether the hypotheses are true or not. Carrying out the experiments, they collect data and analyze it; this allows them to draw conclusions, which will ultimately allow the scientists to accept or reject their initial hypotheses, or even formulate new ones. This series of steps is known as the scientific method.

In the scientific method, we distinguish between qualitative evidence obtained through direct observation and quantitative evidence from experiments. Both observation and experimentation can provide evidence for the relationships that exist between variables.

The global context to be explored in this chapter is scientific and technical innovation. Experimental methods, vaccinations, medicine and population study methods are all innovations stemming from human creativity that lead to improved health outcomes.

Key concept: Relationships

Related concept: Evidence

Global context: Scientific and technical innovation

▼ This is John Snow's map of cholera deaths around Broad Street in London, in the year 1854. Snow hypothesized that cholera was transmitted by water, but his contemporaries met this with suspicion and he had no evidence to sustain his claim. That is, not until 1854, when a cholera outburst in Soho allowed him to record cholera deaths on a map of the area. This systematic approach showed the relationship between how close a house was to the water pump in Broad Street and the likelihood of its inhabitants being affected by cholera

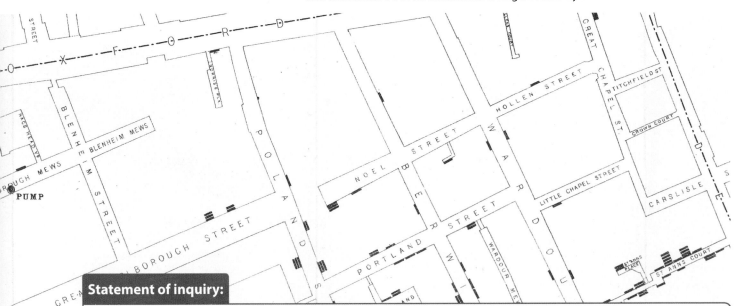

Statement of inquiry:

Healthy lifestyles can be based on evidence of relationships between types of behavior and risks of disease.

In science, relationships can be direct, such as when the rate of cancer incidence increases with number of years smoking, or inverse, for example when increases in vaccination rate lead to decreased incidence of a disease.

When experiments yield interesting results and new relationships between variables are discovered, scientists publish their findings in journals that are edited and reviewed by other scientists. Journal articles outline the significance or implications of a result and indicate areas for further exploration. Published results are often debated within the scientific community and sometimes more widely by the public.

Popular media may often exaggerate the importance of particular studies, making it critically important that readers are scientifically literate and capable of evaluating claims. Reading scientific journal articles allows researchers to keep up to date with the developments in their field and direct their own research, but because published results are organized in tables, graphs and charts and are often subject to complex and specialized analysis, they are not always accessible to non-experts. This is why reputable scientists ensure that there is careful dissemination to the public of research findings, so that they are understood by the public and not misrepresented by journalists.

This engraving shows Roger Bacon, a 12th century Franciscan monk, carrying out an experiment. He was an early proponent of the use of the scientific method and of the use of mathematics to describe the natural world. Why is the scientific method so successful in modern research?

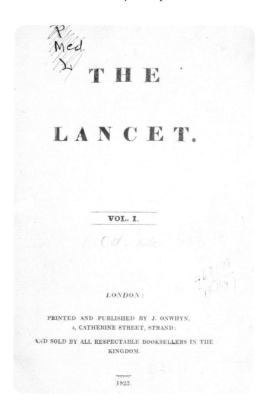

The Lancet, first published in 1823, is a one of the oldest and best known scientific medical journals. Articles within the journal have been reviewed by other researchers to ensure the quality of the research. This is known as peer review

The first mass production and clinical trials of oral poliovirus vaccine (OPV) made from live but altered viruses were conducted in the Soviet Union in the late 1950s. The success of these clinical trials paved the way for the vaccine's key role in the global poliomyelitis eradication campaign. This stamp from Egypt is part of a campaign to promote vaccination

CELLS

What evidence led to the discovery of mitosis?

Cells reproduce by dividing in two. They must do this before they have reached too large a size, because large cells cannot perform functions such as gas exchange as efficiently as smaller ones. Cell division must therefore happen repeatedly as an organism grows. It is also needed to replace lost or damaged cells.

Walther Flemming studied cell division in the 19th century. He made microscope observations in salamander larvae and in the roundworm *Parascaris equorum*. Some of Flemming's drawings of salamander cells are shown here. They provide evidence for division of the nucleus by a process he named mitosis. He made genetic material in the nucleus visible using chemicals called stains.

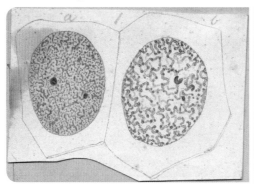
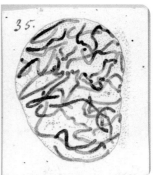

▲ Drawings such as these are a way of presenting qualitative evidence

CELLS

How many times does cell division need to happen to produce enough cells to convert a fertilized egg into an adult human?

Evidence for a scientific prediction can be made by reference to reason.

If all the cells in the body divide at the same time, the total number will repeatedly double. According to this mathematical pattern, the number of cells will follow the sequence 1, 2, 4, 8, 16 and so on until the number of cells in the human body is reached.

To find the number of doublings necessary, we need to know how many cells there are in humans. An estimate obtained by careful research and published in 2013 is that there are 3.72×10^{13} cells in an adult body. This is 37,200,000,000,000 or 37.2 trillion cells.

Try to calculate the number of cell divisions needed to produce 3.72×10^{13} cells. You do not have to work out the complete sequence of numbers—there are easier ways to do the calculation. The answer you should get is that 45 doublings gives 3.52×10^{13} cells, which is nearly enough and 46 doublings gives 7.04×10^{13} cells, which is many more than needed.

Data-based question: *Caenorhabditis elegans* development

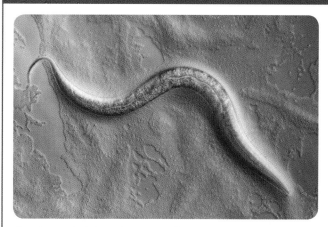

▲ *Caenorhabditis elegans* is a flatworm that is widely used in biological research. It follows a precise pattern of cell divisions during its life and both sexes (male and hermaphrodite) have a fixed total number of cells when they are adults. Here *C. elegans* is surrounded by large numbers of the unicellular bacterium *E. coli*, which is provided as food for it in laboratories

1. *Caenorhabditis elegans* flatworms start life as a single cell. Adult males have a total of exactly 1,031 cells. Calculate how many cell divisions would have to occur to produce an adult male, if all cells divide at exactly the same time (synchronously).

2. The graph shows the number of cells in *C. elegans* in the first 210 minutes of life. Interpret the data in the graph to answer these questions:

    a) Do the cells all divide synchronously?

    b) What is the approximate time interval between one cell division and the next?

3. The total number of cells after 210 minutes is 182. Interpret this data and the data in the graph to answer these questions:

    a) How many cell divisions would be needed to produce 182 cells?

    b) Have all cells completed this number of divisions?

4. The pattern of development in *C. elegans* involves a process called apoptosis (programmed cell death). In hermaphrodites, 131 cells kill themselves by apoptosis. How many cells must be produced by cell division if the final cell total in an adult hermaphrodite is 959?

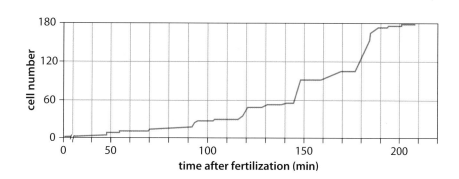

Is there a limit to how many times a human cell can divide?

GENETICS

Leonard Hayflick, an American biologist, discovered that if cells from a human embryo were grown in an artificial cell culture, they would divide up to 60 times but then stop, so 45 or 46 divisions is certainly possible, but apparently not many more. Structures called telomeres may be the limiting factor. Telomeres are the sections of DNA at the ends of chromosomes. Each time a cell divides, the telomere becomes

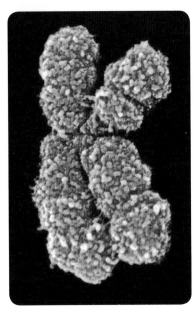

The scanning electron micrograph of chromosome #10 shows the telomeres marked in green

shorter, until it is too short to allow any more divisions. The first cell in a human life (the zygote) has long telomeres, but with each round of cell division they become shorter, setting a limit to the number of divisions that are possible. There is some evidence that the rate of shortening is highly variable between individuals and that a healthy lifestyle leads to a lower rate of telomere shortening (Epel, ES et al. 2004. "Accelerated telomere shortening in response to life stress". *PNAS*. Vol.101 (49). Pp. 17312–17315).

Data-based question: Ageing and telomere shortening

The graph shows the length of telomeres as a function of age. The green line represents the average telomere length for a certain age in a large sample. The blue line represents the telomere length that exists in about 1% of the population.

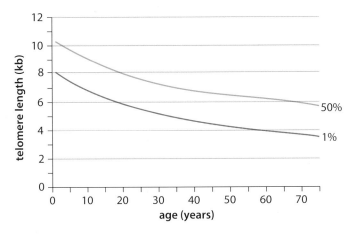

Source of data: Armanios, M. and Blackburn, EH. 2012. "The telomere syndromes". *Nat Rev Gen.* Vol.13. Pp. 693–704

1. Describe the relationship between age and telomere length.

2. Evaluate the claim that telomere length is variable within a population.

3. Suggest some possible causes of shorter telomeres in some individuals.

4. **a)** List three processes which are dependent on mitosis.

   b) If the ability of the body to carry out processes dependent on mitosis decreased with age, what would be some of the consequences?

Are there exceptions to the theory that the number of cell divisions is limited?

Some cells have the capacity to divide endlessly. To do this, they must produce the enzyme telomerase, which lengthens telomeres. Cells that produce telomerase occur in several types of human tissue. In our skin these cells allow the replacement, throughout our lives, of cells that are lost from the skin surface. In males there are cells in the testes with telomerase. They go on dividing throughout adult life, so producing the huge number of cells that develop into sperm. Most cells do not however contain telomerase even though they have the gene for making it. This may be protective as it makes it more difficult for cells to develop into a tumor by dividing endlessly.

A strain of cells called HeLa cells has been cultured in laboratories since 1951. There seems to be no limit to the number of times that these tumor cells can divide. They came from a tumor found in a woman named Henrietta Lack.

The explanation for this is that HeLa cells produce the enzyme telomerase; however many times HeLa cells divide, the telomeres at the ends of their chromosomes do not become too short for further cell divisions.

▲ Human cells will grow and divide in a liquid culture, either in tubes or dishes, but only if conditions are suitable (such as incubation at 37°C)

How is the rate of growth of a tumor determined?

Cancer is due to the growth, and often also the spread, of tumors in the body. Tumors are groups of cells that are dividing repeatedly because the normal controls over cell division have been lost. In some tumors, the cells divide frequently, so the tumor grows quickly and treatment is particularly urgent. In other tumors, the rate of division may be very slow, so the threat posed is minimal.

The rate of growth of a tumor could be measured by scanning it repeatedly and measuring the size on each scan. This would involve periods of waiting between the repeated scans, with the undesirable consequence of delaying treatment. The rate of growth of tumors can be assessed without delay by calculating the mitotic index.

To find the mitotic index of a tissue, a sample is taken by biopsy. The sample is sectioned and stained, so the cells can be examined with a microscope. The number of cells in each of the four phases of mitosis is counted (P, M, A and T) and also the number of cells in interphase (I); N is total number of cells. N = (P + M + A + T + I). The mitotic index is calculated using this formula:

$$\text{Mitotic index} = \frac{(P + M + A + T)}{N} \times 100\%$$

In a fast growing tumor a high proportion of cells are performing mitosis at any one time, so whenever the biopsy is taken, the mitotic index will be high.

The mitotic index of a tumor

The photograph shows a section through a malignant melanoma tumor, that causes life-threatening skin cancer. Nuclei of cells in mitosis are stained purple. Nuclei of cells in interphase are stained brown. Red blood cells in a blood vessel passing through the tumor are orange.

1. How many cells are in mitosis?

2. In what stage of mitosis is each cell?

3. How many cells are in interphase? It is easiest to count the number of nuclei and the red blood cells should be ignored.

4. Calculate the mitotic index of this tumor.

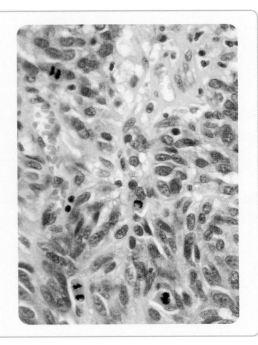

The table shows the survival rates for women with one particular form of breast cancer. The survival rates are shown separately for women with smaller and larger tumors and for three ranges of mitotic index. There were approximately equal numbers of women in each of the three ranges of mitotic index.

Mitotic index	Overall survival after 6 years (%)	
	11–20 mm tumors	> 20 mm tumors
< 0.1	100	100
0.11 – 0.5	100	83
> 0.5	81	79

1. Display the data in whatever graph or chart you consider most appropriate.

2. a) Is there a positive or negative relationship between the mitotic index and the survival rate after six years? (If there is a positive relationship, then the survival rate is higher if the mitotic index is higher.)

   b) What is the explanation for this correlation?

3. Is the size of the tumor or the mitotic index a better indicator of the chance of survival?

4. The women in this trial were all given regular scans of their liver and bones and X-rays of their breasts and liver. What is the reason for these tests?

Finding, interpreting, judging and creating information

- Present information in a variety of formats and platforms.

- Collect and analyze data to identify solutions and make informed decisions.

- Identify primary and secondary sources.

The data in this question is a secondary source because it has been obtained from another primary source. The primary source is a paper in a scientific journal. The correct reference to this primary source is: Medri, L et al. 2003. "Prognostic Relevance of Mitotic Activity in Patients with Node-Negative Breast Cancer." Vol 16, number 11. Pp 1067–1075.

The conventional way of displaying the data is with a bar chart. There are two possible ways of grouping the bars: by mitotic index and by tumor size, giving three groups of two bars or two groups of three bars. You need to decide which allows comparisons to be made most easily.

Looking for correlations in data is a common type of analysis. With large data sets this is usually done with a computer but here the data is clear enough for any correlation to be deduced from a bar chart.

What is the consequence of tumor cells moving?

Broadly speaking, there are two types of tumors: benign and malignant. Benign tumors may grow, but they remain localized and do not damage surrounding tissues, so they do not pose a major threat to health; this is why they are not usually regarded as cancer.

Malignant tumors invade and destroy surrounding tissue. They may also spread to other parts of the body, where they establish secondary tumors, and so are a major threat to health.

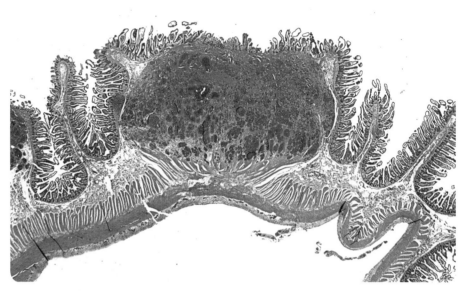

▲ Carcinoid tumor in the wall of the small intestine; to the right and left of the tumor, the normal folded structure of the intestine wall (with villi) is visible. The wall of the intestine is damaged where the tumor is growing, but not elsewhere. This type of tumor can spread to lymph nodes and the liver, but it only happens in about 1 in 30,000 cases. Is this a benign or malignant tumor?

Movement of tumor cells to other parts of the body follows a complex pattern of steps. The tumor cell must break the adhesions that attach it to other cells. It must then move between other cells in surrounding body tissues. Proteins such as collagen, that bind these tissue cells together, must be digested to allow movement between them. The tumor cell must move through body cavities or break through the wall of a lymph vessel or a blood vessel (usually a vein), so it is carried to another part of the body. It must then migrate out of the vessel into the surrounding tissue and establish itself in a position where it will receive oxygen and nutrients. Most tumor cells fail to perform these actions, but if one cell in the primary tumor is able to move and establish secondary tumors, then probably many will do so. The consequence of movement of tumor cells therefore is usually not just one secondary tumor, but many.

Primary tumors can often be treated by surgery. The tumor is removed, together with some of the surrounding tissue. Radiation is sometimes used to kill cells in a primary tumor, either to reduce it in size before surgery or because the location of the tumor makes surgery impossible. This is called radiotherapy. If there are no secondary tumors this may be all that is needed to cure the cancer. It is often impossible to remove secondary tumors surgically, either because of their location or because there are too many. The location of secondary tumors varies depending on the type and location of the primary tumor, but they commonly develop in lymph nodes, liver, brain and bone. The usual approach with a cancer that has spread to form secondary tumors is to treat it with chemicals. This is called chemotherapy. Some of the chemicals that are used kill any dividing cells, including tumor cells. Ironically, these chemicals do not work well with slow growing tumors that have a low mitotic index. In recent years chemical treatments have been developed that target only tumor cells rather than all dividing cells.

Sadly, some cases of cancer cannot be treated successfully. Cancer is the cause of about 15% of all deaths in the world, with a higher percentage in developed countries. Cancer has been a major target of medical research for many decades and there has been immense progress in the understanding of it and the development of treatments, but much more research is needed into how normal body cells change into tumor cells, how they migrate to form secondary tumors and how cancer can be cured.

Cancer treatments have improved in recent years so survival rates with many cancers are much better than they were in the past. However, difficult issues have been raised by some new treatments. Debate these questions with other students:

1 What are the reasons for some new treatments being very expensive?

2 Is there a limit to how much national health services or health insurance schemes should pay for cancer treatments?

3 Should individuals or families be allowed to pay for expensive treatments that only have a small chance of extending life significantly?

What factors in the environment can cause normal body cells to change into tumor cells?

A tumor starts with a single body cell changing into a tumor cell. A group of specific mutations have to take place to the genes in the cell. The chance of any one of these mutations occurring is very small, but the chance of all of them occurring in the same cell is extremely small. The reason why tumors are not infinitesimally rare is that our

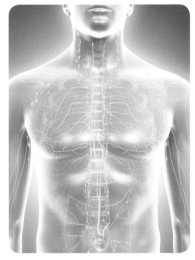

▲ Lymph is fluid that drains from body tissues and is carried by lymph vessels (shown green) to enter the blood system near the heart. The swellings at intervals along the vessels are lymph nodes

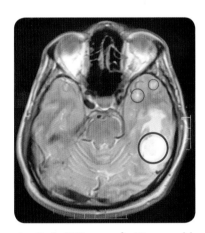

▲ Brain MRI scan of a 39-year-old man with secondary tumors (metastases)

▲ Ionizing radiation released when nuclear bombs are detonated can cause deaths due to cancer decades afterwards. Only two nuclear bombs have so far been used during warfare, at Hiroshima and Nagasaki. The photo shows a later test detonation

bodies contain vast numbers of cells, any one of which could change into a tumor cell, so the collective chance is quite large.

Mutations are chemical changes to the DNA in a cell. DNA is a very stable substance in normal environmental conditions, but various physical and chemical factors can cause mutations, for example:

- high energy (ionizing) radiation: X-rays, gamma rays (Y rays), alpha particles and shortwave ultraviolet (UV) radiation

- chemicals, such as nitrosamines (found in tobacco and smoked foods), benzene, reactive oxygen species (such as hydroxyl radicals) and heterocyclic amines (found in meat cooked at high temperatures).

All of these factors can cause mutations, so we refer to them as mutagens. As mutations cause cancer, they are also carcinogens (a carcinoma is a cancer).

1. Explain how each of the following can cause cancer:

    a) nuclear bombs

    b) artificial sunbeds

    c) smoking

    d) X-rays.

2. Debate whether each of the four causes in question 1 should be made illegal because they increase the risk of cancer.

▲ Some people have suggested that hairdressers have higher rates of cancer than other occupations. This is an example of a hypothesis. Scientists evaluate the validity of hypotheses using data from experiments or other sources. In this case it is important to know if factors in the environment of hairdressers are causing cancer, so that these factors can be identified and removed. What evidence would suggest that hairdressers have an increased risk of cancer?

Data-based question: Global distribution of air pollution

The UN has developed 17 main "Sustainable Development Goals", which are further broken down into 169 targets. These targets are even further subdivided into measurable indicators, allowing evidence of progress to be quantified. Goal number 3 refers to good health and well-being and aims to ensure healthy lives and promote well-being for all at all ages.

Goal number 11 focuses on making cities and human settlements inclusive, safe, resilient and sustainable.

Air pollution is a significant barrier to achieving both of these goals. The specific targets and indicators of success related to air pollution are shown in the following table.

Targets	Indicators
3.9 By 2030, substantially reduce the number of deaths and illnesses from hazardous chemicals and air, water and soil pollution and contamination	3.9.1 Mortality rate attributed to household and ambient air pollution 3.9.2 Mortality rate attributed to "hazardous chemicals, water and soil pollution and contamination"
11.6 By 2030, reduce the adverse per capita environmental impact of cities, including by paying special attention to air quality and municipal and other waste management	11.6.2 Annual mean levels of fine particulate matter (i.e. PM2.5 and PM10) in cities (population weighted)

Source: http://indicators.report/goals/goal-3/

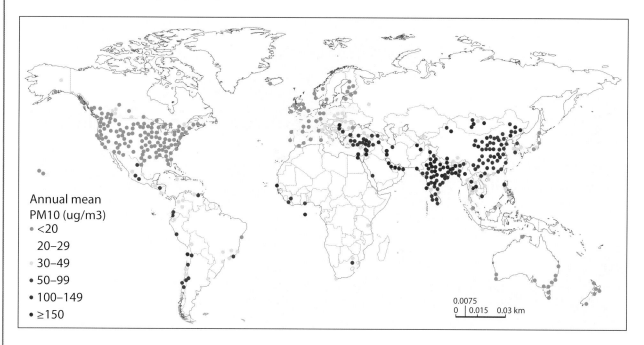

Annual mean PM10 (ug/m3)
- <20
- 20–29
- 30–49
- 50–99
- 100–149
- ≥150

0.0075
0 | 0.015   0.03 km

The map shows the global pattern of particulate matter (PM10). Particulates can be inhaled and damage lung tissue. Further, carcinogenic chemicals might adhere to the surface of the particle and increase the risk of cancer.

1. Outline the distribution of particulate air pollution globally.

2. Predict the pattern of the global distribution of respiratory diseases such as asthma, emphysema and lung cancer.

Lichens are composite organisms that consist of fungi living in close association with algae or photosynthetic bacteria. There are different types of lichen that are sensitive to pollution; generally, the lower the pollution rates, the higher the diversity of lichens.

The biodiversity of lichens was determined at a number of locations in the Veneto region, in north-east Italy. Mortality due to lung cancer in each of these locations was determined from the examination of medical records. The relationship between these two variables is shown in the following graph.

3. Using only the data in the graph, identify the relationship between mortality due to lung cancer and lichen biodiversity in the Veneto region.

4. Explain the relationship between mortality due to lung cancer and lichen biodiversity.

Only men who had lived in one region for their entire life were included in the investigation.

5. Suggest one reason for excluding other men.

6. Suggest two reasons for the points on the graph not all lying on the line of best fit.

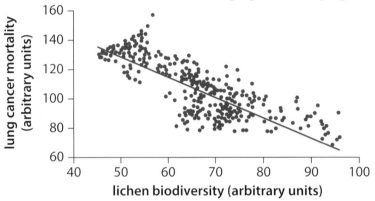

GENETICS

What were the objectives of the Human Genome Project?

All of the genetic information within the DNA of an individual organism is referred to as its genome. In the late 20th century, scientists collaborated in a venture known as the Human Genome Project. This project had a number of objectives including:

- determining and documenting the sequence of the more than 3 billion DNA base pairs in the human genome

- identifying the location of genes

- making the information available to scientists for further investigation.

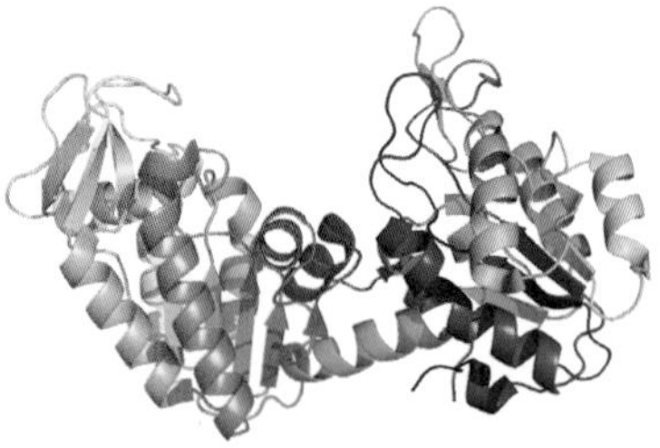

▲ Phosphoglycerate kinase is a protein that is universal in living things

To locate genes, scientists look for specific three-base sequences in the DNA that act as signals to start or stop translation of messenger RNA. A start signal first needs to be located. If a long sequence of bases without any stop signals follows and there is then a stop signal, the long base sequence is likely to be a gene.

The completion of the project was announced in 2003, and the data collected has led to a great range of further research and the development of applications including:

- development of personal genome analysis related to health
- understanding of evolutionary relationships
- comparison of genomes from different species.

How are the patterns detected in the human genome useful in health research?

Medical researchers have used the information from the Human Genome Project to compare the DNA of individuals who have a genetic disease with the genomes of people who are not affected. Differences between their genomes may indicate the possible cause of their condition.

Analysis of an individual's genome is increasingly leading to personalized medicine. This analysis can indicate if a person is at increased risk of suffering from a disease. The individual can then be given advice that may lead to prevention of the condition. The analysis also makes it possible to identify variations in a person's genome that predicts how well that person will respond to certain drugs, meaning that they can be given better treatments with fewer side effects.

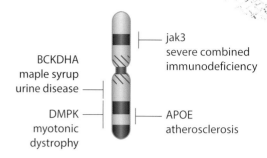

▲ Human chromosome 19 contains over 60 million base pairs, of which more than 85% have been mapped. This process has shown that there are over 1,700 genes on chromosome 19

GENETICS

Determining relatedness between organisms

Comparison of DNA sequences provides evidence of relationships. Nearly all eukaryotic species have a gene for the protein cytochrome C oxidase, an enzyme that is essential for energy metabolism. This gene has common sequences in most species, but over time differences accumulate by mutation. The base sequences for part of the gene in four species of butterfly (*Adoxophyes honmai*, *Diatraea saccharalis*, *Ostrinia furnacalis* and *Ostrinia nubilalis*) are shown in the table.

A. honmai	(5') T	A	C	G	T	A	G	G	G	G	A	G	C	T	A	A	A	T	T	A	G	C	G	C	A	C	G	A	T	C	G	G	G	C	G	T	G	A	T	C	G	T (3')
D. saccharalis	(5') A	T	G	C	A	T	C	C	C	C	T	C	G	A	T	T	T	A	A	T	C	G	C	G	T	G	C	T	A	G	C	C	C	G	C	A	C	T	A	G	C	A (3')
O. furnacalis	(5') T	A	G	G	T	A	G	G	C	G	A	G	C	T	T	A	A	T	T	A	G	G	G	C	A	C	G	A	A	C	G	G	G	C	G	T	G	A	T	C	C	T (3')
O. nubilalis	(5') C	A	A	G	T	A	G	G	G	G	A	G	A	T	C	G	C	T	A	A	G	C	G	C	A	C	G	A	T	A	A	T	A	G	C	T	G	A	T	C	G	T (3')

1. What does the data given here suggest about the relationship between the species in the table?

2. Based on the table, which two species are the most closely related?

A technician is drilling a sample of fossilized Neanderthal (*Homo neanderthalensis*) bone. The sample will have its genetic material extracted and sequenced as part of the Neanderthal genome project. Neanderthals were early humans who lived in Europe and the Middle East from 100,000 to 30,000 years ago

GENETICS

What are model organisms?

Genome mapping has been carried out for a number of species known as model organisms. Species are chosen for this research if they have useful characteristics, such as ease of rearing in laboratories, short generation times, or production of large numbers of offspring.

Model organisms include the fruit fly *Drosophila melanogaster*, yeast *Saccharomyces cerevisiae* and the soil nematode worm *Caenorhabditis elegans*.

The puffer fish *Fugu rubripes* is a model organism because it has a similar set of genes to humans but a much smaller amount of genetic material between genes, making it faster to map. It was the first vertebrate to have its entire genome mapped after the human genome map was completed

Over 60% of human disease genes that have been identified thus far are similar in *D. melanogaster* and *C. elegans*. Scientists have identified about 1,500 gene families that are found in all animals. Some genes, such as those from the human immune system, are less likely to have direct matches in less complex animals. For this reason the mouse *Mus musculis* is also used as a model organism. The mouse genome has a similar layout to the human genome.

The existence of model organisms further illustrates the idea of universality and diversity among living things.

Once a hypothesized gene is identified in one species, similar sequences will be sought in other species. Through a procedure known as "knocking out", a gene can be deactivated in a model organism. The effect of deactivating the gene can give an indication of the function of that gene.

Scientists were able to locate and determine the function of leptin in humans using mice as a model organism.

What evidence established the cause of infectious diseases?

Until the 19th century, it was common to attribute infectious diseases to causes such as exposure to foul odours or evil spirits. Louis Pasteur established that disease-causing organisms exist and could be the specific cause of a disease.

Under carefully controlled conditions, he extracted pus from several sites on a person with a skin infection and cultured the pus in a nutrient solution. Examination of the culture under a microscope showed the presence of a single variety of bacteria.

The process of establishing the specific cause of an infectious disease was formalized by Robert Koch into four postulates.

1. If an organism is suffering from the disease, then the suspected specific cause of the disease should be found in large numbers in the individual with the disease.

2. The suspected specific cause organism can be isolated and cultured.

3. The cultured organism should lead to the disease when introduced into a healthy test individual.

4. The organism that was suspected of causing the disease in the original organism must be found in large numbers in the test individual and should be identical to what was found in the original host.

The gene that codes for the production of the protein leptin has been "knocked out" in the mouse on the left. This allowed scientists to recognize that leptin plays a role in energy metabolism, giving insight into such health concerns as obesity

HEALTH

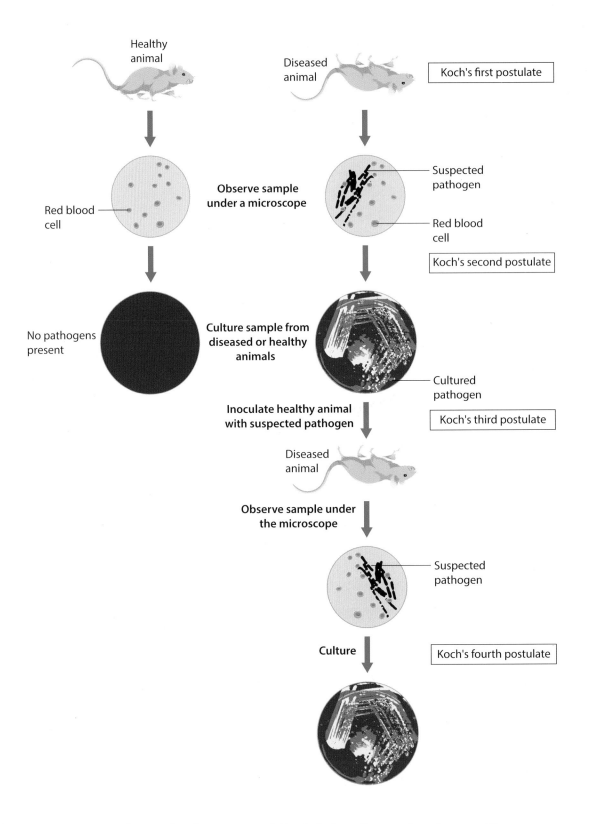

Healthy animal

Diseased animal — Koch's first postulate

Red blood cell

Observe sample under a microscope

Suspected pathogen

Red blood cell

Koch's second postulate

No pathogens present

Culture sample from diseased or healthy animals

Cultured pathogen

Inoculate healthy animal with suspected pathogen

Koch's third postulate

Diseased animal

Observe sample under the microscope

Suspected pathogen

Culture

Koch's fourth postulate

The work of Pasteur and Koch led to discovering the specific cause of infection for several diseases, as well as to the highly successful innovations of vaccinations and pasteurization of milk.

Disease	Specific cause of infection
Malaria	*Trypanosoma sp.* (protozoan)
Measles	measles virus
Tuberculosis	*Mycobacterium tuberculosis* (bacterium)
Amoebic dysentery	*Entamoeba histolytica* (protozoan)
Pertussis (whooping cough)	*Bordetella pertussis* (bacterium)
AIDS	HIV virus

1. Robert Koch hypothesized that anthrax was caused by the presence of rod-shaped bacteria that he observed in the blood of infected cows. Explain how Koch could apply the method above using infected cows, mice, a culture tube and a microscope to confirm his hypothesis.

2. Discuss some possible limitations to Koch's postulates in identifying the cause of a disease.

3. For which types of disease would Koch's postulates not be helpful?

4. What are the limitations of animal models?

5. Discuss the ethical considerations of the third postulate.

How do vaccines work?

Pathogens are disease causing organisms. When a person is infected by a pathogen and develops a disease, recovery depends on their body carrying out an immune response. This results in the production of both memory cells and antibodies against the disease, which will rapidly resist any further infections by the pathogen, so the person has immunity to the disease.

Vaccines work by stimulating the development of immunity. They may consist of a dead or weakened version of the pathogen. Alternatively they may contain a living microorganism that is similar enough to the pathogen to stimulate production of the antibodies needed for immunity to it. Vaccines are usually administered as an injection.

Edward Jenner developed a vaccine for smallpox after noticing that people who had suffered from cowpox survived smallpox. He extracted material from cowpox infections and injected unaffected people with it. The people treated in this way became immune to smallpox.

Unfortunately, despite their obvious success, vaccines are resisted by a vocal minority of people based on questionable evidence. Some of these object to the inclusion of thimerosal as a preservative, whereas others falsely claim links between autism and vaccination.

Thimerosal is added to vials of vaccine containing more than one dose, in order to prevent the growth of bacteria and fungi. When this preservative enters the body, it is broken down to ethylmercury, a mercury compound.

NEW YORK TIMES BESTSELLING AUTHOR

ROBERT F. KENNEDY, JR., EDITOR

THIMEROSAL
LET THE SCIENCE SPEAK
The Evidence Supporting the Immediate Removal of Mercury—a Known Neurotoxin—from Vaccines

Preface by MARK HYMAN, MD
New York Times bestselling author of *The Blood Sugar Solution* and founder and medical director of the UltraWellness Center

Introduction by MARTHA R. HERBERT, PhD, MD
assistant professor of neurology at Harvard Medical School and pediatric neuroscientist at Massachusetts General Hospital

Foreword by U.S. CONGRESSMAN BILL POSEY

INCLUDES THE ORIGINAL OMITTED CHAPTERS ON THE AUTISM LINK

▲ An example of a book that takes issue with the use of thimerosal as a preservative in vaccines

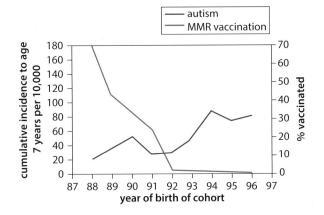

methylmercury
(MeHg)

ethylmercury
(EtHg)

▲ Structural formulas of methylmercury and ethylmercury

There are two types of organic mercury compounds to which people are most commonly exposed—methylmercury and ethylmercury—but they have different properties. Methylmercury is a compound of mercury that can build up in certain kinds of fish and humans are exposed to it when eating this fish. In humans, methylmercury can be absorbed into the blood through the intestine, and at high levels it acts as a toxin, affecting the nervous system. In contrast to methylmercury, ethylmercury is cleared from the human body more quickly and does not tend to accumulate.

Data-based question: MMR and DTP vaccines

A link was postulated between the use of the triple measles, mumps and rubella (MMR) vaccine and the rise of childhood autism. The MMR vaccine was introduced in Britain in 1988 after a measles outbreak killed 17 people. Though very considerable research has shown there to be no connection, some people continue to believe in such a link and propose use of single vaccines instead.

1. Suggest reasons for doctors advocating triple rather than single vaccines. [2]

The MMR vaccination is optional in the UK. The data in the top graph shows the percentage of children vaccinated (MMR uptake) over a 13-year period.

2. Outline the pattern of MMR uptake over the period shown in the graph. [3]

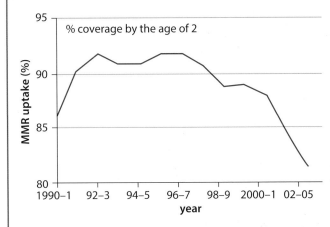

3. Suggest, giving a reason, a year in which the UK media may have carried a story

about research making a link between MMR and autism. [2]

In Japan, the MMR vaccine was introduced in 1989, but the programme was terminated in 1993 and only single vaccines used thereafter.

The data in the second graph shows the incidence of autism in Japan for children grouped by the year that they were born in.

4. Outline the trend in the incidence of autism over the period shown in the graph. [2]

5. Evaluate using the data the claim that autism is linked to the MMR vaccine. [3]

The third graph provides information about the history of the triple DTP vaccine (diptheria, tetanus and pertussis) in England and Wales over a 50-year period. The incidence of pertussis (whooping cough) is shown between 1940 and 1995 (red). A second curve (blue) shows DTP vaccine uptake from the mid-1960s to the mid-1990s. The green bar indicates a period when the British media carried many stories about alleged side effects of DTP vaccination.

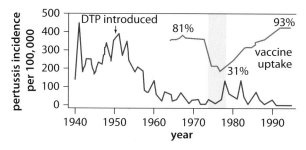

6. Using the data in the graph, explain the changes in rates of whooping cough in the 50 years from 1940 to 1990. [3]

The medical journal *The Lancet* was criticized after it published a paper in 1998 regarding a link between the MMR vaccine and autism. In February 2004, *The Lancet* published a statement by 10 of the paper's 13 co-authors withdrawing their claim that there is the possibility that MMR could cause autism. The journal completely withdrew the research article in 2010, after one of the researchers was found to have acted unethically in conducting the research.

Information literacy skills

Finding, interpreting, judging and creating information

● Use critical-literacy skills to analyze and interpret media communications.

Find an article on the internet about vaccines.

When conducting research using internet sources, it is better to consult sites where the author's name can be located. This shows that the author is prepared to take responsibility for the content of the article and you can evaluate the credentials of the author. What credentials would convince you as a reader that an author is qualified to speak with authority on vaccinations?

Is this website provided by an organization or a corporation? What does this organization or corporation do? You can determine this by clicking on a link that says "About us".

What is the domain of the website? Typically .edu, .gov and .org organizations are more suitable sources than .com, but this will still require some judgment.

Has the author provided links to the sources used to create the content on the website?

Do the citations on the site provide enough information so that they can be partially evaluated without opening them?

What is coronary heart disease?

HEALTH

The wall of the heart is muscle tissue and therefore requires a supply of oxygen and nutrients. Blood pumped to cardiac muscle through the coronary arteries provides this supply. The coronary arteries branch repeatedly to form a dense network of capillaries that serves all parts of the heart wall. Having picked up waste products and become deoxygenated, the blood flows on from the capillaries to the coronary veins which carry it back to the right atrium of the heart.

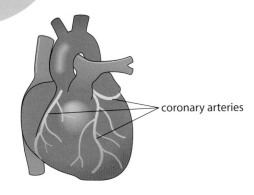

coronary arteries

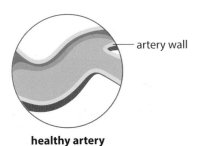

artery wall

healthy artery

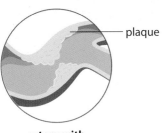

plaque

artery with plaque (blocked)

Coronary heart disease (CHD) starts with fatty deposits known as plaque building up in the wall of one or more of the coronary arteries. The deposits become hardened and make the inside of the artery narrower. These changes increase the risk of blood clots forming within the artery. If a clot is dislodged, it will be carried on to where the artery branches and becomes narrower. The clot may form a blockage, preventing blood from reaching cardiac muscle cells in the part of the heart wall that is supplied by the blocked branch. These cells no longer receive oxygen or glucose, so they stop contracting in a coordinated way – this is commonly known as a heart attack and is a common outcome of coronary heart disease.

What are the factors that contribute to coronary heart disease?

The rates of coronary heart disease vary widely between countries and within populations. There are a number of factors which increase a person's risk of coronary heart disease. New evidence for the relationships between a certain factor and risk leads to modifications in the advice of health officials seeking to reduce the incidence of CHD.

High blood pressure increases the risk. Age reduces the elasticity of arteries. Men are more likely to suffer from high blood pressure than women. Smoking increases blood pressure and deceases oxygen supply to the heart. Inactivity and obesity are contributing factors. Recent evidence suggests that it is the correlation of being overweight with inactivity that is perhaps more significant than being overweight itself. A lack of exercise increases the risk of high blood pressure.

Cholesterol is transported in the blood in two forms: HDL and LDL. High density lipoproteins (HDL) are associated with reduced rates of CHD, while low density lipoproteins (LDL) are associated with increased rates of CHD. LDL in the blood increases plaque formation in arteries. High levels of fat in the blood are associated with increased risk, but this may be because they are correlated to LDLs. Lipoprotein levels are not solely due to diet. Some people are genetically predisposed to have different levels regardless of diet. This may explain why some ethnic groups, such as the Maasai of Kenya, consume large quantities of cholesterol and saturated fat and yet have low CHD rates.

Summative assessment

Statement of inquiry:

Healthy lifestyles can be based on evidence of relationships between types of behavior and risks of disease.

Introduction

In this summative assessment we explore factors causing disease. While completing the assessment think about how choosing healthy lifestyle behaviors can minimize the risk of diseases.

The causes of disease

1. **a)** Outline an example of a disease that has:

    i) an environmental cause [1]

    ii) a pathogen-based cause [1]

    iii) a lifestyle cause. [1]

    b) In each case, outline the evidence that supports that the disease is caused in this way. [3]

2. A human life starts with a single cell that follows a precise controlled pattern of cell divisions leading to the development of an embryo, then a fetus and eventually an adult. The pattern of cell divisions has been studied in simple organisms, such as the flatworm *Caenorhabditis elegans*. In a study, an embryo of *C. elegans* was treated with fluorescent stains, so nuclei appear blue and mitochondria green. Other cell structures are not visible.

    a) What is the overall shape of the embryo at this stage? [1]

    b) Estimate the total number of cells in the embryo. How reliable is your estimate? [2]

    c) If the embryo contained 64 cells, how many rounds of cell division would there have been up to this stage? [2]

    d) What process is used to divide one nucleus into two genetically identical nuclei? [1]

    e) Do the cells of the embryo each contain more nuclei or more mitochondria? [1]

    f) Like whole cells, mitochondria can only be produced by division of pre-existing mitochondria. What would be the consequence if the mitochondria in the embryo divided at a slower rate than the embryo cells? [2]

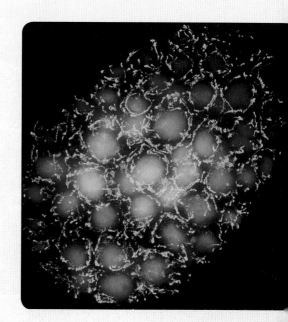

Analyzing data related to coronary heart disease, cancer and childhood mortality

Increasing age, gender and family history are factors which are outside of an individual's control, unlike smoking, high blood pressure and bad dietary choices, all of which are risk factors for declining health.

3. In the late 1960s, Finland had the highest death rate from coronary heart disease in the world, with working-age men in the eastern part of the country carrying the highest risk of CHD. To help decrease deaths from CHD, a community-based project was set up, with the aim of reducing the levels of the three main cardiovascular risk factors: dietary cholesterol, smoking and high blood pressure.

    Between 1972 and 2012, a study was conducted to determine whether the measures taken in the community project were efficient. Over 34,000 men and women, aged 30–59 at the beginning of the study and living in eastern Finland, participated.

    The data in the graphs below shows the reduction in death rates as well as changes in the prevalence of the risk factors, in both men and women (1972 is set as the 100% level for each of the variables observed).

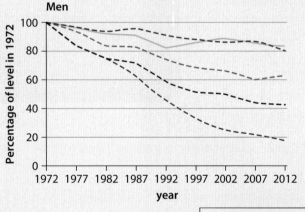

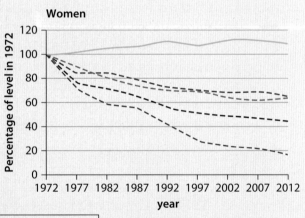

Prevalence of smoking in the population
--- Average blood pressure
--- Predicted CHD mortality based on smoking, blood pressure and cholesterol
--- Average blood cholesterol concentration
--- Actual CHD mortality

a) Estimate the reduction in actual CHD mortality between 1972 and 2012 in men. [1]

b) Identify which risk factor changed most significantly in men. [1]

c) Distinguish between the changes in smoking in men and women over the course of the study. [1]

d) **i)** Distinguish between the actual reductions in deaths due to CHD and the predictions. [2]

ii) Suggest reasons for the difference. [2]

4. The bar chart shows ten cancers with the highest mortality rates globally. The mortality rate is the number of deaths per year in 100,000 people. Lung cancer has been split into deaths in smokers and in people who have never smoked.

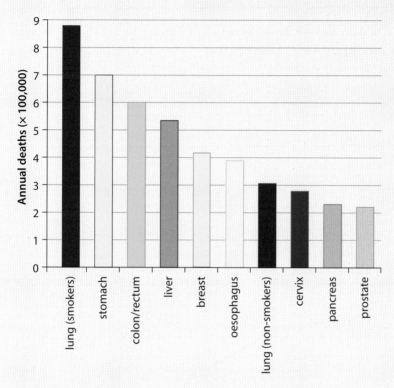

a) Calculate how much greater the chance of lung cancer is in smokers compared to non-smokers. [1]

b) **i)** Deaths due to lung cancer in non-smokers would drop if nobody smoked. Explain this paradox. [3]

ii) Suggest changes to the environment, apart from stopping cigarette smoking, which would reduce deaths due to lung cancer. [2]

c) In research involving 174 patients with lung cancer in Japan, the time taken for a lung tumor to double in size was found to be very variable, ranging from 30 to 1,077 days. Discuss the consequences of the doubling rate of a tumor for the patient. [3]

5. Gapminder (www.gapminder.org) is website that makes a wider variety of data available for exploration, including data related to global health issues.

One of the United Nations' 17 "Sustainable Development Goals" refers to good health and well-being. This goal includes the target of reducing under-5 mortality from such infectious diseases as diarrhea, HIV, malaria, measles, pertussis, pneumonia, as well as reducing deaths due to accidents.

The data shown in the graph represents the trend in under-5 mortality in four countries since 1800, as investigated on Gapminder.

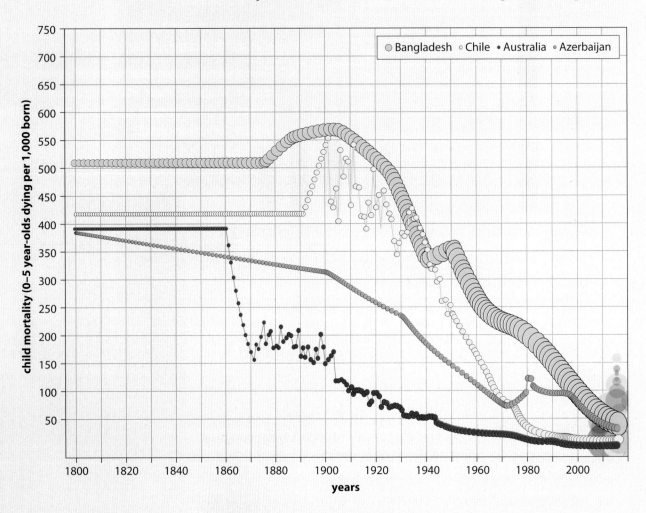

a) State the under-5 mortality rate in Australia in 1800. [1]

b) Compare and contrast the trends in under-5 mortality in the four countries. [2]

c) Suggest reasons for the observed patterns. [2]

d) The Sustainable Development Goal target for 2030 is to reduce under-5 mortality to 25 per 1,000 in all countries. Use the database to find three countries that have reached that target currently and four countries that have yet to reach that target. [2]

6. Explore the other data sets available on Gapminder and develop a question to explore regarding how health indicators have changed with time.

   a) Clearly state your question. [1]

   b) Choose representative countries for your study and provide a justification for this choice. [2]

   c) Produce graphs using the trails functionality on Gapminder. [2]

   d) Analyze your graphs and state your conclusions. [2]

Consequences of smoking during pregnancy

7. The text that follows consists of two extracts from "Molecular Epidemiology: On the Path to Prevention?" by FP Perera in the *Journal of the National Cancer Institute* (2000, Vol 92, pp 602–612).

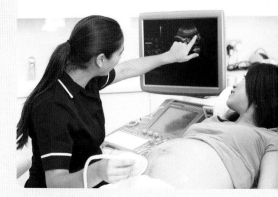

▲ Ultrasound scans are used to check that a fetus is developing normally in utero. Fetal growth is slower in women who smoke during pregnancy

Tobacco smoke was identified in 1949 as a potent human lung carcinogen and still ranks at the very top of the list of environmental carcinogens. It contains 55 known carcinogens, including PAHs (polycyclic aromatic hydrocarbons). PAHs are also found in outdoor air from automobile exhaust and emissions from power plants and other industrial sources; in indoor air from tobacco smoking, cooking, and heating; and in the diet from consumption of smoked or grilled food.

Compared with exposures occurring in adult life, exposures in utero and in the early years can disproportionately increase the risks of many types of cancer later in life. Experimental and epidemiologic data indicate that, because of differential exposure or physiologic immaturity, infants and children experience greater risks than adults from a variety of environmental toxicants, including PAHs, nitrosamines, pesticides, tobacco smoke, air pollution and radiation. The underlying mechanisms may include increased exposure to toxicants, greater absorption or retention of toxicants, reduced detoxification and DNA repair, the higher rate of cell proliferation during early stages of development, or the fact that cancers initiated in the womb and in the early years have the opportunity to develop over many decades.

   a) Explain what is meant by:

   i) carcinogen [1]

   ii) in utero [1]

   iii) cell proliferation. [1]

   b) The text is written in scientific language that non-scientists may find difficult to understand. Write a short and easily comprehensible article to explain to women who have just become pregnant why it would be wrong for them to smoke. [8]

   c) List other pieces of health advice that you would give to pregnant women based on the text extracts. [4]

12 Models

Complex systems can be explored using simplified representations.

> When I was sick and lay a-bed,
> I had two pillows at my head,
> And all my toys beside me lay,
> To keep me happy all the day.
>
> And sometimes for an hour or so
> I watched my leaden soldiers go,
> With different uniforms and drills,
> Among the bed-clothes, through the hills;
>
> And sometimes sent my ships in fleets
> All up and down among the sheets;
> Or brought my trees and houses out,
> And planted cities all about.
>
> I was the giant great and still
> That sits upon the pillow-hill,
> And sees before him, dale and plain,
> The pleasant land of counterpane.
>
> "The Land of Counterpane"
> by Robert Louis Stevenson

This poem describes the author's experiences of models from his childhood. What is so appealing to children about small world play?

Physical models are sometimes constructed for test purposes, for example, full size models of the shape of newly designed cars are placed in wind tunnels to test air resistance. What is the advantage of modelling the shape of a new car before constructing a prototype?

Niels Bohr and Ernest Rutherford proposed a model of atomic structure in which the positively charged nucleus is orbited by negatively charged electrons. According to this model, electrons in orbitals further from the nucleus have more energy, so as electrons move to an orbital closer to the nucleus energy is emitted, usually in the form of light. Electrons do not actually move in fixed orbits like planets. Is the planetary model of atomic structure therefore invalid? Can you use this model to explain the colours of fireworks containing different metals?

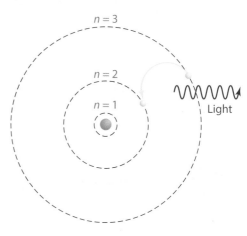

Weather forecasts are based on atmospheric variables such as temperature and air pressure that are monitored at many sites around the world. Complex computer models predict changes in these variables over the following hours and days. How far into the future are weather forecasts accurate in your area?

Introduction

While a system can be composed of just two interacting elements, biological systems typically have many interacting elements, making them very complex and challenging to study. The interactions between the system's elements are often very complicated and can lead to emergent properties. A simple phrase that sums up emergent properties is "the whole is greater than the sum of its parts".

Biologists may not need or be able to comprehend a system in its entirety, so they create simplified models that only contain the features that are important in their research. Despite only being an approximation, these models can still be very helpful, as they are a simplified representation of something in the natural world.

Models can predict how variables change in response to different factors, so they are used to explore cause and effect. They allow us to understand complex relationships and forecast future behavior, hence they are closely linked to the global context of globalization and sustainability.

Key concept: Systems

Related concept: Models

Global context: Globalization and sustainability

▼ Snow geese are migratory birds that breed in the Arctic. They spend the winter in the central region of the United States of America, where they feed on crops such as winter wheat, rice and corn. As more food is available, the overall population of snow geese increases which has a negative impact on the local environment. Modelling this system led to proposals for managing the environment in a sustainable way. Can you think of a different example where a model was used in decision-making?

Statement of inquiry:

Methods of achieving sustainability can be developed using models that explore differences between systems.

Scientists use models to explain phenomena, make predictions and test hypotheses. Models can be used to run simulations of processes that may not be observable with human senses, or might be difficult to observe directly. Simulations can explore changes over timescales that are too short or too long for experiments to run in real time. Analysis of the outcomes of a simulation allows the model to be refined, so that it is closer to reality.

Modelling → Simulation → Analysis →

Models are particularly useful for research into interactions within ecological communities. They can help us to investigate human influences on a local and a global scale. They can be used to predict whether we are overexploiting natural resources and how we can mitigate adverse effects on ecosystems. They can help as answer these general questions:

- how are people connected and how does this impact me?
- how can our way of life, and the systems we have in place, last long term?

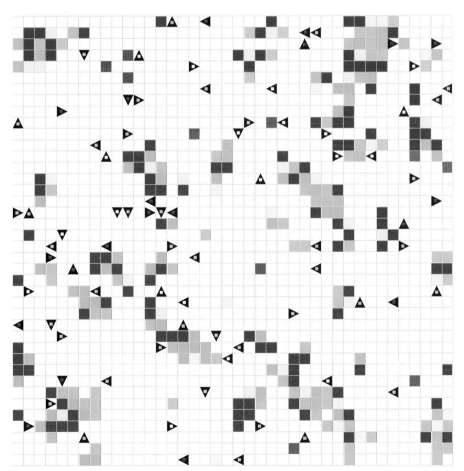

▲ COBWEB is a large-scale ecological simulation program. Here it is being used for modelling interactions between four species of predator (triangles) and four species of prey (squares). Many parameters such as breeding rate can be varied to investigate the effects. The outcome of this particular simulation was that all four prey species became extinct due to overexploitation and as a consequence the populations of all four predator species crashed

How can we construct physical models?

A wide range of methods can be used to construct models. Francis Crick and James Watson used models made from sheets of metal, metal rods and laboratory stands and clamps to investigate the structure of DNA. When their first model was analyzed it did not explain all of the properties of DNA. It was their second model which convinced all biochemists who examined it that they had represented the structure of DNA accurately.

Much more sophisticated methods of constructing molecular models are now available, such as 3D printing. This technology is now widely available and some schools have a 3D printer. The US National Institute of Health has an online database, with the files needed for printing models of tens of thousands of different molecules. Files can be downloaded for free from the NIH 3D Print Exchange (http://3dprint.nih.gov) and used to print models of complex molecules such as proteins and nucleic acids. If you have access to a 3D printer and someone who can teach you how to use it, you could become part of what is now known as "the maker community".

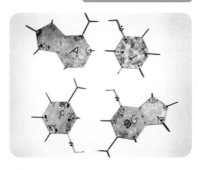

▲ Crick and Watson made sure that bond angles in their model were all correct and bond lengths were in proportion. Why was this important?

▲ Francis Crick (standing) and James Watson (seated) discuss their DNA model, now preserved in the Science Museum in London. Behind them on the wall is a two-dimensional representation of DNA, with the double helix indicated by two ribbons. What other models of DNA structure can be produced?

▲ A model of a ribosome and three different transfer RNA molecules produced by 3D printing

Streamlining in fish

- Make a model barracuda, using any material as long as it is denser than water. You can produce a simplified model without fins.

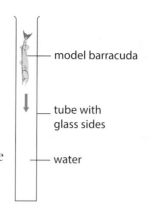

— model barracuda

— tube with glass sides

— water

- Drop the model into a vertical tube of water and time how long it takes to reach the bottom. You could use a large measuring cylinder, but if possible try to contrive a greater vertical drop, to get a more reliable result.

- Make other models with the same volume as your model barracuda, but with modified shapes. Use them to test a hypothesis about the shape of barracuda and its effect on water resistance.

▶ To catch their prey, barracuda can swim at over 40 km/h. Their streamlined shape reduces water resistance, allowing them do this

ATL Critical thinking skills

Is modelling an essential part of all research in biology?

In this chapter, we look at many different types of model and ways of using them.

- Physical models can be an effective learning aid and they can help with visualization.

- Mathematical models can be used to analyze results of experiments and draw conclusions.

- Conceptual models help us think about complex phenomena and make generalizations.

All types of model can be used to make predictions and frame hypotheses and for this reason we might argue that modelling should be the first stage in any scientific investigation.

1. What is the value in starting a scientific investigation by framing a hypothesis?

2. Some biologists argue that before a hypothesis is framed there is an observing stage in most investigations and the resulting observations suggest what the hypothesis should be. Do you agree?

3. Some scientific breakthroughs are the result of serendipity. This is where an observation or discovery is made by a stroke of luck rather than by careful planning. Do you know any examples of serendipitous discoveries and is modelling unnecessary in these cases?

How are models used in 3D printing?

3D printing can be used to construct models, but models are also needed for 3D printing. The starting point in the 3D printing process is computer-aided design (CAD), which involves producing a computer model of the desired structure, known as an STL (stereolithography) file. This model is then used to guide the motion of a printer head to produce the object layer by layer. Plastics were the first material to be used, but other materials including metals are available for model making. Techniques are currently being developed for 3D printing using living cells.

With the increase in human longevity and improvements in transplant science, there is a shortage of organs for transplanting. Recent advances have enabled 3D printing of materials which are compatible with living things, distributing cells using a 3D printer and adding supporting components into complex 3D functional living tissues. An accurate model of the organ is needed that places cells and other structures in the correct relative positions for the organ as a whole to perform its function. 3D bioprinting techniques have already been applied to the generation of multilayered skin, bone, blood vessel grafts, heart tissue and structures made out of cartilage.

▶ Future patient in a 3D skin printer. The patient is having new skin printed onto a leg wound. Organ printing is a proposed organ manufacturing technique where an inkjet-type printer uses cell types instead of ink. The use of a sticky gel provides a supporting framework for the cells. The printer places gel and cells in complex patterns arranged in layers on top of each other. When the gel is washed away, the result is a 3D organ

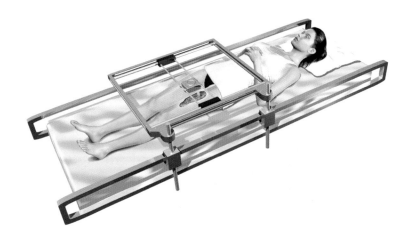

Using computer-assisted design to generate a simple heart-shaped disc

1. Visit the website www.tinkercad.com.

2. Select the **Projects** tab on the left and create a new design.

3. Drag a box shape to the workpane.

4. Scale it down to the height of 2 mm and dimensions 12 mm × 12 mm.

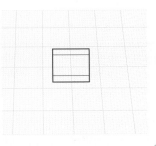

5. Drag a cylinder shape to the workpane.

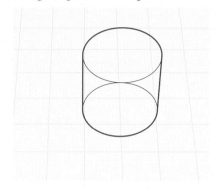

Scale it down to a height of 2 mm and a diameter of 12 mm and copy and paste a second cylinder.

6. Rotate the box shape by 45°.

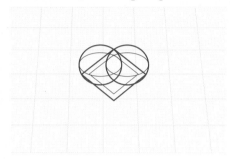

7. Select all items.

8. Group all of the items using the **Group** button on the toolbar menu at the top.

9. Under the **Design** menu, save the item. It can also be downloaded for 3D printing.

10. Pictured here is a model of two kidneys, associated blood vessels and the ureter. Use a CAD application to generate the models of the kidneys shown in this image.

Take effective notes in class and make effective summary notes

Listening is distinct from hearing in that listening is a more active process. Listen to the Ted Talk by Anthony Atala called: "Printing a human kidney".

Before you listen to a video or a lecture, ask "What do I need to learn by listening?" For example,

1. What challenge does Atala mention to explain why there have been so few clinical advances in the field of regenerative medicine?

2. What has been achieved so far and what challenges need to be surmounted?

Choose your mode of note-taking carefully. Verbatim notes record word for word everything that the speaker says. Listeners can often type almost as fast as a speaker talks, but hand-writing is slower, so you would have to type if you want verbatim notes. However, studies have shown that typed verbatim notes are less likely to result in remembering what the speaker said compared to selective handwritten note-taking. This is because making a selection of what to record requires us to think about what we are writing down.

We can think faster than a person can talk. This is why our mind wanders during lectures. These are supplementary activities you can do while recording the ideas of the speaker:

- thinking about questions that the presentation doesn't address

- forming your opinions about what has been said.

If you know that you have guiding questions to answer in relation to the lecture, have the questions in your notes ahead of time, leaving a blank space below the questions and writing down answers as you listen.

Leave spaces between entries in your notes, so that you can add in things later on when you are reviewing your notes.

If you are not understanding the speaker, take notes anyway. You can ask your teacher or do research online to find the answers later on.

Focus more on the big ideas of the speaker than the specific facts given.

How do biologists use graphs to model relationships?

In many experiments, the effect of one variable (the independent variable) on another variable (the dependent variable) is tested. The independent variable is conventionally put on the horizontal x-axis and the dependent variable on the vertical y-axis.

- A bar chart is used if the independent variable is categoric, for example, apples and pears in an investigation of the vitamin C content of fruits.

- A bar chart or histogram is used if the variable is quantitative and discontinuous, for example, the number of eggs laid per clutch by birds in an investigation of clutch size on mortality of nestlings.

- A line graph is used when the independent variable is quantitative and continuously variable, for example, pH in an investigation of the activity of an enzyme at different pH levels.

Line graphs can be used to model a relationship at two stages in a scientific investigation:

1. A graph can be drawn before any experiments are performed to predict the effect of the independent on the dependent variable. The model is then tested experimentally. The graph may be sketched to show the general form of the relationship or it may be plotted using a mathematical equation.

2. When results have been obtained from an experiment and the data points plotted on a graph, a curve is drawn on the graph to model the relationship. This is sometimes done "by eye" but it is better to use a statistical procedure or a mathematical equation to position the curve.

The graphs below show two types of relationship and also the expected type of curve if there is no relationship. Note that the line on a graph is conventionally called a curve even if it is straight!

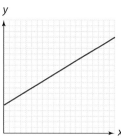

The level of y increases as the level of x is increased.

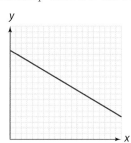

The level of y decreases as the level of x is increased.

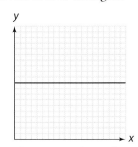

There is no relationship between x and y (when x is increased y doesn't change).

◀ Graphs showing relationships between variables

When we look at graphs in biology, they are often more complicated than the three shown above. Consider the U-shaped line on the graph to the right. The relationship between x and y changes as x is increased. When you describe graphs like this, you should divide the graph up into different ranges of x and say what the relationship is in each range. You should also say at what level of x, the level of y reaches a maximum or a minimum. For example, here, as x increases from 0 to 5 units, y decreases, reaching a minimum when $x = 5$ units. As x increases from 5 to 0 units, y increases.

The relationship where one variable increases when another variable is increased can take various forms. If it takes the form of a straight line, it is called a linear increase. Shown here are three other possibilities:

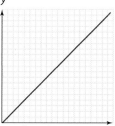

x is directly proportional to y, if there is a linear increase in y as x is increased and when x is zero, y is also zero.

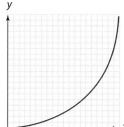

An exponential increase happens if the increase in y is directly proportional to the size of x, so that as x increases, the increases in y become larger and larger.

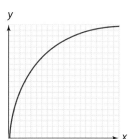

A decelerating increase happens if the increases in y become smaller and smaller as x increases. This is because the level of y is approaching a maximum or saturation level.

a)

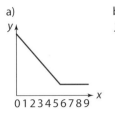

b)

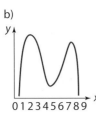

c)

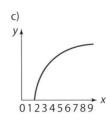

▲ Examples of graphs from biology experiments

1. Describe the relationship between x and y shown in the graphs a), b) and c).

2. Sketch a graph to show the following relationships:

   a) a linear decrease in y as x is increased

   b) an exponential decrease in y as x is increased

   c) an accelerating decrease in y as x is increased.

3. Suggest a biological example of each of the graphs in question 1.

Data-based question: Yoda's law

If plants of a single species grow together in high density, as they grow larger, the smallest plants die due to the effects of competition, so the density, or number of plants per unit area, decreases. The decrease has been observed to fit the mathematical equation $y = x^{-3/2}$ and the process is called self-thinning.

This observation has become known as Yoda's law, following publication of a study by K. Yoda and collaborators, summarizing this relationship as $W = C\rho^{-3/2}$, where W is the mean dry weight of surviving plants, ρ is the density of the surviving plants, and C is a constant reflecting the growth characteristic of the species concerned.

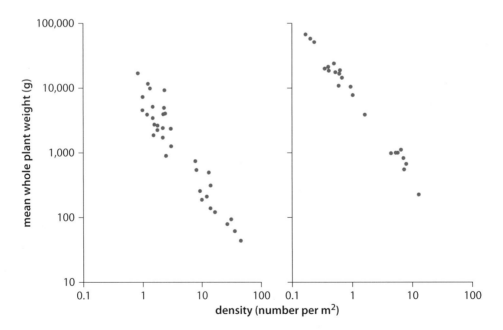

The scatter graphs show density and mean tree mass of pure, dense, even-aged forests of *Prunus pensylvanica* (left) and *Abies balsamea* (right).

1. Compare the mean mass of the two species at:

   a) 1 tree per m²

   b) 10 trees per m²

2. Identify which species was found:

  a) growing at the highest density **b)** with the largest mean mass.

3. Discuss the evidence for a mathematical relationship between density and mean mass.

Note: to approach the next two questions you will need to be familiar with logarithms. If you haven't covered these in maths yet, you can come back and attempt the questions at the end of year 5.

4. Explain how the data could be tested to see whether it fits the mathematical model that is called Yoda's law.

5. A logarithmic scale has been used for both the *x* and *y* axes.

  a) Explain the advantage of this for these graphs.

  b) Predict the shape of the curve if logarithmic scales had not been used.

▲ In commercial forestry, such as this stand of white fir in New Mexico, trees are removed before they die because of self-thinning. What are the advantages of doing this during the growth of a stand of trees? What is the advantage of repeated moderate thinning, rather than infrequent major thinning?

How are statistical samples used to model populations?

Scientists wanting to know about the characteristics of a population face the challenge that it is impractical to study every member of that population. They choose to study a smaller number of individuals called a sample. The sample is used to model the population. An effective model can be achieved if individuals within the sample are chosen at random. To be a random sample, every member of the population has to have an equal chance of being selected. In practice, it can be very difficult to ensure that a sample is truly random.

Stratified sampling is sometimes used to help get a representative sample. To do this the population is divided into different categories (strata) with random sampling in each stratum, and the same proportion of all strata included in the sample.

1. If you ask the first hundred people you meet on a street to answer a questionnaire, what are the reasons for this not being a representative sample of the whole population?

2. Opinion polls before an election are often based on calls to voters using landline telephone numbers chosen randomly. Does this method of sampling give a representative model of a whole voting population?

3. If you needed to carry out stratified random sampling of your school community, what groups would you define as the strata within the school?

Data-based question: Does aspirin lower body temperature in children?

A study was conducted to see how effective aspirin could be in reducing body temperature in children with fever. Twelve 4-year-old girls suffering from flu had their temperatures taken immediately before and 1 hour after administration of aspirin. The results are as follows:

Patient number	Temperature before aspirin (°C)	Temperature after aspirin (°C)
1	39.1	37.6
2	39.5	37.8
3	38.8	37.9
4	39.4	38.8
5	38.4	37.6
6	38.2	37.9
7	39.2	38.3
8	39.5	37.8
9	39.3	38.2
10	39.0	38.4
11	38.8	38.5
12	38.6	37.8

Source of data: Remington and Schork: *Statistics with Applications to the Biology and Health Sciences*, pg 163, Second edition

1. Find the range of temperatures:

    a) before treatment with aspirin   **b)** after treatment with aspirin.

    c) Comment on the variation in both data sets.

2. Find the average temperature:

    a) before treatment with aspirin   **b)** after treatment with aspirin.

3 Evaluate the conclusion that aspirin lowers body temperature in children. To what extent do you think that this sample data is representative of the broader population of children?

How can games be used to model the interaction between organisms?

A mathematical model is a description of a system using mathematical concepts and symbols. Game theory is a branch of mathematics that predicts the optimal strategies in situations where individuals are competing for resources that are open access and are not owned by anyone. In 1833, the English economist William Forster Lloyd published a pamphlet that included a hypothetical example of the overuse of an open-access resource. This was the case with cattle herders sharing a common plot of land on which they were each entitled to let their cows graze.

For each additional animal, a herder could receive additional benefits, but the whole group shared an increased risk of damage to the commons. Game theory uses a pay-off matrix. Quantities can be assigned to pay-offs for certain decisions. Game theory predicts the strategy that gives the maximum benefit to the whole community. What strategy is best for the herder community according to the pay-off matrix below?

		Herder A	
		Cooperate	**Add an additional cow**
Herder B	**Cooperate**	A: second best	A: worst
		B: second best	B: best
	Add an additional cow	A: best	A: third best
		B: worst	B: third best

Game theory can also be used to model interactions between organisms in natural ecosystems. The pay-off for the strategies of an individual depends on the strategies of other organisms. A pay-off matrix is developed to make predictions and offer explanations of why such strategies as cooperation and altruism persist in a population. This can be illustrated using male side-blotched lizards (*Uta stansburiana*), which exist in three different forms or "morphs" in the wild: orange-throated, yellow-throated and blue-throated.

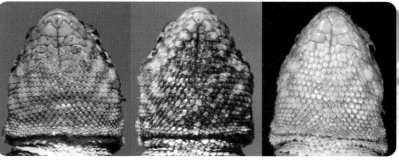

▲ The three morphs of *Uta stansburiana*

Each morph undertakes a different reproductive strategy. The orange-throated morph is very aggressive and defends a large territory, mating with all the females within his territory. The relatively unagressive yellow throat employs a "sneaking" strategy, mimicking both the markings and the behavior of female lizards. They impinge on the orange throat's territory to mate with the females there, ultimately becoming more common as they produce yellow-throated morph offspring. The blue throat chooses one mate and carefully guards her, making it impossible for the sneakers to mate with her, so ensuring production of blue-throated offspring and overtaking the population of yellow-throated sneakers. However, the blue throats cannot defend their mate against the aggressive orange throats. The graphical model here idealizes the changes in frequency of each morph.

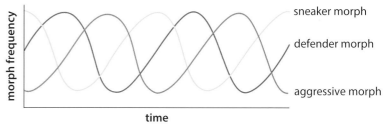

▲ Graph of male morph frequency over time

1. What game does this pattern remind you of: yellow beats orange; blue beats yellow and orange beats blue?

2. What name is given to the type of mathematical pattern shown in the graph?

3. Construct a pay-off matrix for the breeding success of the three colour morphs of lizard.

How can agent-based modelling be used to simulate interactions in ecosystems?

Agent-based models are computer programs that are used to simulate the actions and interactions of autonomous agents. They use game theory, complex systems and other strategies to predict the overall outcome of many individual interactions between autonomous agents. For example, the spread of an epidemic can be simulated, with the agents being the members of the population that interact with each other.

Multi-agent modelling is ideal for simulating interactions between species in an ecosystem. Predator-prey interactions between multiple prey and predator species can be simulated, with variables such as breeding rate and hunting efficiency altered to investigate how stable populations can persist in an ecological community.

Agent-based modelling can also be used to simulate human influences on ecosystems, how adverse effects can be mitigated and how overexploitation of natural resources can be avoided. The collapse in the cod population on the Grand Banks in the north-west Atlantic might have been prevented if models had been created to simulate the catastrophic effects of overfishing.

1. Explain, with examples, what is meant by these phrases:

    a) autonomous agent   **b)** mitigation of adverse effects

2. Suggest examples of:

    a) overexploitation of natural resources, apart from overfishing of cod

    b) adverse effects of humans on ecosystems, apart from overexploitation.

3. Discuss whether it is necessary to re-run simulations in agent-based modelling, to check the outcome.

ECOLOGY

How can the ecological footprint model help our understanding of resource consumption?

The Earth's biologically productive land areas include forests, grassland, cropland and fisheries. These areas provide services that we need:

● supplying renewable resources such as food and oxygen

● absorbing waste we generate, including our carbon emissions.

The ecological footprint is a model that can be used to estimate the amount of productive land area that we each require to provide us with these services. It can be used to find the total areas required for the whole human population on Earth and whether these areas are available. The model results in a quantitative indication that can be used to inform decisions about changes in lifestyle.

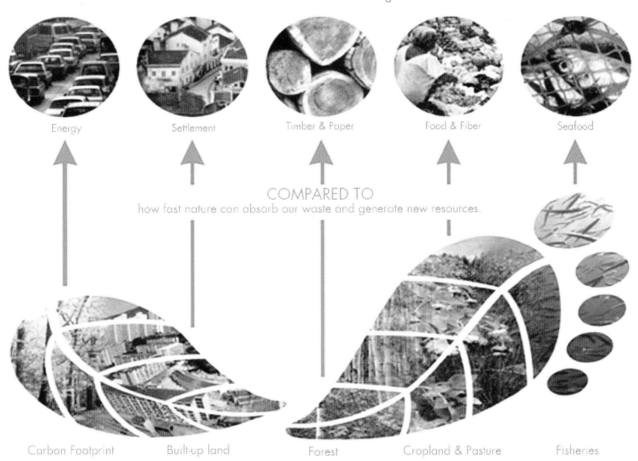

The Ecological Footprint

MEASURES
how fast we consume resources and generate waste

Energy   Settlement   Timber & Paper   Food & Fiber   Seafood

COMPARED TO
how fast nature can absorb our waste and generate new resources.

Carbon Footprint   Built-up land   Forest   Cropland & Pasture   Fisheries

1. Use the graphic model to identify the sources of land as well as the resources and services that we obtain from the land.

2. The organization Global Footprint Network has a web-based tool that allows you to model how much land area it takes to support your lifestyle (www.footprintnetwork.org). Use the tool to discover your biggest areas of resource consumption and identify what you can do to "tread more lightly" on the Earth. Identify which daily activities you pursue that affect your ecological footprint the most.

3. Every year, the organization identifies a calendar day known as "Earth overshoot day". Suggest what this might mean and how this aspect of the model can inform a change in our practice.

4. Compare the ecological footprint of countries across the globe. Explain what patterns emerge.

Summative assessment

Statement of inquiry:

Methods of achieving sustainability can be developed using models that explore differences between systems.

Introduction

In this summative assessment we use a number of different models. Simplified representations can be used to investigate habitat loss and ecosystem changes.

Comparing forest loss in Indonesia and Brazil

The bar charts below show annual forest loss in Indonesia and Brazil, with a correlation curve that indicates the overall trend. Three statistics are given: the mean annual increment for forest loss, a trend line showing the change in forest loss over the years (correlation curve) and the confidence level (p) of the correlation curve.

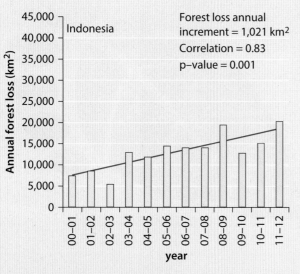

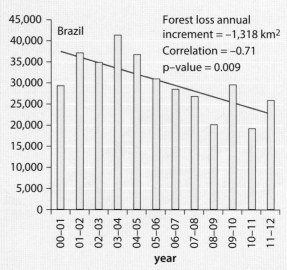

1. **a)** State the annual forest loss in both countries in:

    i) 2003–04 [2]

    ii) 2008–09 [2]

    b) Compare and contrast forest loss in Indonesia and Brazil. [3]

    c) Compare and contrast the correlation curves for Indonesia and Brazil. [3]

    d) Explain what is indicated by the p-values for the two correlation curves. [2]

2. Suggest reasons for forest loss in Indonesia and Brazil. [3]

Designing a FACE experiment

The map here shows the distribution of places on the Earth where forest is being lost and forest is being gained.

3. **a)** Identify two areas where forest is being lost and not gained. [2]

   b) Identify a country where forest is being both lost and gained. Suggest how this is possible. [3]

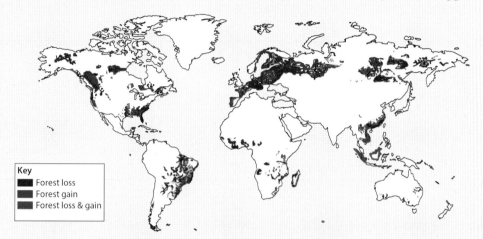

Key
- Forest loss
- Forest gain
- Forest loss & gain

The forecast increase in atmospheric carbon dioxide concentration from 400 to 550 or more parts per million over the next century could have profound effects on forests. A series of six Free-Air Carbon dioxide Enrichment (or FACE) experiments are being set up in representative areas of natural forest around the world to simulate conditions in the forests of the future.

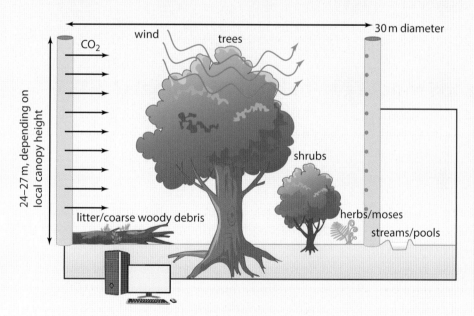

▲ Basic design of a forest FACE experiment

▲ Tower supporting black plastic pipe from which carbon dioxide is released

4. **a)** Explain how you would set up a FACE experiment, including how the forest site should be chosen, how many circular test areas you would establish and what the independent, dependent and controlled variables would be. [7]

   b) Discuss how effectively your model would simulate conditions in forests of the future. [3]

Investigating forest loss using a database

5. Visit the website of the organization Global Forest Watch (www.globalforestwatch.org) or another database that contains information about the status of the world's forests.

   a) Choose a country. [1]

   b) Determine how the country ranks globally in terms of tree cover loss. [1]

   c) Determine the percentage of your chosen country that is covered in trees. [2]

   d) Identify the year on record that had the greatest amount of tree cover loss. [1]

   e) Determine how much of the country is primary forest and what percentage is regenerated forest. [2]

   f) Visit the NASA fires database (https://earthdata.nasa.gov/earth-observation-data/near-real-time/firms/active-fire-data) to determine if there are any active fires in your chosen country. [2]

   g) Using the websites indicated above as well as others, gather further information about the status of forests in your country. [4]

   h) Decide on a method of visually representing your data. [2]

Evaluating zoos as a model habitat

Read the article below from the *National Geographic* magazine and answer the questions that follow.

In what ways do zoos model the habitat of animals?

Habitat is the area or natural environment in which an organism or population normally lives. A habitat is made up of physical factors such as soil, moisture, a range of temperatures, and the availability of light as well as biotic factors such as the availability of food and the presence of predators. A zoo is a place where animals live in captivity and are put on display for people to view. Zoos contain wide varieties of animals that are native to all parts of the Earth and so it is the challenge of the zoo to model a diversity of habitats.

Early zoos like the Menagerie du Jardin des Plantes were more like museums of living animals than natural habitats. Animals were kept in small display areas, with as many species as space would allow.

Today, there is a trend toward giving animals more space and recreating natural habitats. Zoos are usually regulated and inspected by governments.

Urban zoos, located in large cities, still resemble the smaller zoos that were popular 200 years ago. Often, these zoos sit in the middle of cities, making expansion difficult. There is little room for urban zoos to grow, and many of the zoo's buildings are historic landmarks that cannot be destroyed or redesigned.

In many urban zoos, animals are kept in relatively small enclosures. Many modern zoos have developed as sprawling parks in suburbs outside cities. These open-range zoos give animals more territory to roam and provide more natural habitats. This popular technique of building realistic habitats is called landscape immersion.

The San Diego Zoo, in southern California, is the largest zoo in the United States. It is a suburban zoo that houses more than 4,000 animals (800 different species) in its 0.4 square kilometers (100 acres). Landscape immersion divides animals into their natural habitats, such as the tundra (with reindeer and polar bears) or bamboo forest (featuring pandas.) The San Diego Zoo also includes a wild animal park, which is even more expansive (almost 8 square kilometers or 2,000 acres).

Most zoos have specialized enclosures and habitats for specific animals. The Jurong Bird Park in Singapore has more than 8,000 birds of 600 species from around the world. Jurong has more than 1,000 flamingoes in an African wetlands exhibit that features a daily simulated thunderstorm.

Zoos in cold climates, such as Novosibirsk, Russia, must recreate warm ecosystems for animals like lemurs. Lemurs are a type of primate native to the island of Madagascar, off Africa's east coast. The summer temperatures of both Siberia and Madagascar are about the same. However, Madagascar receives about 225 millimeters of rain each summer, making it a humid jungle environment. Novosibirsk gets just 60 millimeters of rain and snow. The difference in winter temperatures is even more drastic: Madagascar is about 15 degrees Celsius. Winter in Novosibirsk is -10 degrees Celsius. The Novosibirsk Zoo has two species of lemur with a specialized heated enclosure with high humidity.

The goal of many captive breeding programs at zoos is the re-introduction of animals into the wild. The California condor, a very large bird native to the west coast of the United States, has been re-introduced to its native habitat after breeding in zoos and wildlife parks. There are several breeding pairs of California condors in the wild today.

Critics of captive breeding programs say that releasing a few animals into the wild does little to help the species population. Animals are extinct in the wild largely due to loss of habitat. The re-introduction of animals, especially large mammals that require vast territory for survival, does nothing to recover lost habitat.

6. Compare and contrast the model lion habitat on the left to the actual lion habitat on the right. [4]

7. Make an actual or virtual visit to your nearest zoo. To what extent is immersive habitat technique practised? [4]

8. Identify an animal that is housed in your local zoo or a zoo of your choice. Conduct research on the features of the natural habitat of that organism.

   a) Compare and contrast the natural habitat of that organism with the one located at the zoo you have chosen. [4]

   b) Evaluate the habitat of the animal at the zoo you have chosen. [3]

Glossary

3D printing	is the printing process that involves making three-dimensional objects by applying repeated thin layers of quick-drying material following digital models.
Abiotic factors	are the non-living factors which influence the environment, including climatic factors and edaphic factors.
Acquired characteristics	are physical characteristics which are acquired by an individual organism during its lifetime.
Active transport	is the movement of substances such as mineral salts through a membrane in living cells against a concentration gradient: i.e. from low to high concentration.
Adaptation	gradually over a period of time, each generation of a particular organism will become better adapted to its environment.
ADH	anti-diuretic hormone, from the pituitary gland, secreted when quantity of water in the blood gets low, allows kidneys to reabsorb water.
Adhesion	is the sticking together of unlike molecules.
Alien species	are species which do not normally occur in an area but have been introduced by accident or intentionally.
Alveoli	(singular alveolus) are the tiny air sacs at the end of each bronchiole through which oxygen diffuses in and carbon dioxide diffuses out.
Amino acids	are the monomer units of all proteins and contain the $-COOH$ and $-NH_2$ groups at either end of the molecule.
Anabolism	is the phase of metabolism that is concerned with the building up of complicated molecules from simpler ones, e.g. formation of glycogen.
Anaphase	is the stage of nuclear division between metaphase and telophase that results in the splitting of chromatids (mitosis) or homologous chromosomes (meiosis).
Angiosperms	(flowering plants) are seed-bearing plants that produce flowers.
Aorta	is the largest artery in the body, carrying oxygenated blood out from the left ventricle of the heart.
Archaea	is a domain of life that includes prokaryotes that live in extreme environments and prokaryotes that are more closely related to eukaryotes than bacteria.
Artery	an artery is a wide muscular-walled blood vessel that carries blood away from the heart towards the body tissue.
Artificial classification	is a system of classifying organisms based on something other than evolutionary relationships.

Asthma	is a disease of the lungs characterized by inflammation and reversible airway narrowing.
ATP	adenine triphosphate is a substance used as a store of chemical energy by living cells.
Baroreceptor	is a sensory receptor in blood vessels that detects blood pressure.
Biceps	is the flexor muscle in the upper arm which bends the forearm.
Biopsy	is a surgical extraction of a sample of cells or tissue.
Biotechnology	is the use of living organisms for the production of useful substances or processes.
Biotic factors	are factors arising from the activities of living organisms (including humans) which influence the environment.
Blood plasma	is the liquid part of blood, which is about 90% water.
Bryophytes	are primitive plants, liverworts and mosses, with simple stems, leaves and roots.
Cancer	is a disease characterized by uncontrolled cell division.
Capillaries	are the narrowest type of blood vessel.
Carbon cycle	the carbon cycle is the constant circulation of carbon between the atmosphere, plants, animals and the soil.
Carbon footprint	a carbon footprint is the amount of carbon dioxide or greenhouse gas equivalents emitted into the atmosphere by the activities of an individual, a community or a company
Carcinogen	a chemical agent that can cause cancer
Catalyst	a catalyst is a substance that increases the rate of a chemical reaction without itself undergoing any permanent chemical change.
Cell membrane	the cell membrane forms the outer boundary of the cell.
Cell wall	the cell wall is a rigid outer wall of plant cells, made of cellulose.
Chemical change	a chemical change occurs in a chemical reaction and produces a new chemical substance. This substance often looks quite different from the starting substances. For example, when hydrogen burns in oxygen, water is formed. This water is a colourless liquid and has none of the properties of its constituent elements, which are both gases.
Chemoreceptor	is a sensory receptor that detects chemical changes.
Chromosome	a chromosome is a long coil of DNA which is made up of genes in a linear sequence which are found in the nucleus of plant and animal cells.
Class	a class is part of the biological classification system. This system classifies living organisms into very large groups called kingdoms, kingdoms are broken down into phylums, each phylum is broken down into classes, which are then subdivided into orders.
Clone	a clone is a genetically identical descendant produced by vegetative reproduction from an original plant seedling.
Closed system	a closed system is one in which no material can escape, though energy can.
Cohesion	is a force of attraction between two identical molecules.

Competition	is a form of interaction between individuals in an ecosystem involving a struggle for access to the same resource.
Condensation	(1; in physics) is the change of state from gas (or vapour) to a liquid; (2; in chemistry) is a reaction in which two molecules are joined together to make a larger molecule, with the loss of water.
Conditioned reflex	a conditioned reflex is reaction that is learned in response to a specific situation or stimulus.
Coronary heart disease	is a heart disease due to blockage of the arteries that supply blood to the heart.
Cytoplasm	is the protoplasm of a living cell which is found outside the nucleus.
Detritivore	is a consumer that ingests dead organic material.
Diabetes-type 1	is a disorder caused by the lack of the hormone insulin.
Dichotomous keys	are the simplest type of key, made up of brief descriptions arranged in numbered pairs.
Dicotyledons	(abbreviation: dicots) are a class of angiosperm with two seed leaves (cotyledons).
Differentiation	involves cells or tissues undergoing a change toward a more specialized function and form.
Diffusion	is the mixing of two liquids without mechanical help.
Diploid	describes a cell which has paired sets of homologous chromosomes in its nucleus.
Diving reflex	is a response to diving in mammals and birds that involves changes in body activities that decrease oxygen consumption.
DNA	(abbreviation for deoxyribonucleic acid) is a nucleic acid which contains the genetic information carried by every cell.
DNA replication	is the production of identical copies of DNA.
DNA transcription	is the copying of the genetic code.
Domain	the largest taxonomic group that includes a group of similar phyla
Dominant	a dominant phenotype masks the presence of the recessive phenotype.
Ecosystem	an ecosystem is a biological community and the physical environment that is associated with it.
El Niño	is an abnormality of ocean currents that results in significant climate and ecological effects.
Electromagnetic radiation	is energy that travels in the form of waves at the speed of light in a vacuum.
Electron micrograph	is a photograph of the image produced by an electron microscope.
Emergent property	is a property of a system that emerges from the interaction of the elements of the system.
Endoplasmic reticulum	is a network of membranes joined to the nuclear membrane. It has a large surface area and is a site of protein and lipid synthesis.
Endothermic reaction	a chemical reaction during which heat energy is taken in from the surroundings.

Energy	is the capacity of a system to do work.
Environment	the environment consists of all the conditions which surround an organism and in which it lives.
Enzymes	are catalysts in biochemical reactions.
Epidemic	is the spread of an infectious disease from person to person in a place where the disease is not normally present at such a high rate of occurrence.
Esophagus	(or gullet) the esophagus is the section of the alimentary canal between the mouth and the stomach.
Eukaryote	is an organism that contain compartmentalized cells with a true nucleus.
Evolution	is the gradual changing of a species of living organism over a long period of time.
Exoskeleton	is a skeleton found on the outside of the animal.
Exothermic reaction	a chemical reaction during which heat energy is transferred to the surroundings.
Exponential growth	occurs when a population size grows at a faster rate as the population size increases
Extinction	is the complete and irreversible disappearance of all living members of a species or group of organisms from the Earth.
F_1 generation	(first filial generation) is the first generation of offspring in a genetic cross (in humans, the children).
F_2 generation	(second filial generation) is the second generation of offspring in a genetic cross (in humans, the grandchildren).
Family	in biological classification, each genus belongs to a family and each family belongs to an order.
Fertilization	(in plants) fertilization is the fusion of the male nucleus (from the pollen) with the female nucleus (in the ovule); (in animals) fertilization is the fusion of the nuclei of the male and female gametes during sexual reproduction to form a single cell called the zygote.
Filtrate	is the clear liquid that passes through the filter during filtration.
Food chain	a food chain is a feeding relationship between organisms in an ecosystem.
Gamete	a gamete is a specialized sex cell formed by meiosis which contains only half the number of chromosomes (haploid).
Gametogenesis	is the formation of sex cells.
Gene	a gene is the unit of hereditary information, composed of a section of DNA which acts as a chemical instruction for protein synthesis.
Genetic code	the genetic code is the code sequence of different bases of a DNA molecule, which controls protein synthesis in cells.
Genetic drift	is the change in the ratio of genotypes within a population due to random events
Genome	the genome is the entire genetic material of an organism
Genome mapping	the process of determining the location and function of genes within a genome

Genotype	is the genetic information about a particular organism as specified by its alleles.
Genotypic ratio	is the proportion of offspring possessing different combinations of alleles
Genus	a genus is a group of closely related species.
Germination	is the initial stages of growth of a seed to form a seedling.
Global warming	is the gradual change in world climate caused by the greenhouse effect.
Glomerulus	a glomerulus is a tangle of blood capillaries located in each Bowman's capsule of the kidney.
Glycogen	is a polysaccharide found in vertebrate animals and is the main energy store in the liver and muscles.
Gonads	are reproductive organs of an animal.
Greenhouse effect	is the trapping of heat energy in the atmosphere because of the effects of greenhouse gases.
Greenhouse gases	are gases in the atmosphere which absorb infra-red radiation, causing an increase in air temperature.
Habitat	is a place in which an organism or a community of organisms live.
Haploid	describes a cell which has a single set of unpaired chromosomes in its nucleus.
Heat energy	is the energy that flows from one place to another as a result of a difference in temperature.
Hepatocyte	is a liver cell.
Herbivores	are organisms which feed on plants.
Heredity	is genetic information passing from parents to offspring.
Heterozygous	describes an organism that possesses two different alleles of a particular gene in a given pair of chromosomes.
Homeostasis	is the maintenance of a constant internal environment of an organism.
Homozygous	describes an organism that possesses identical alleles of a particular gene in a given pair of chromosomes.
Horizontal transfer	is the transfer of genetic information in either direction between two individuals. Genes from a donor are added to the existing genome of a recipient.
Hormones	plant hormones are specific chemicals produced by the cells of plants, which, at very low concentration, can affect growth and development. Animal hormones are special chemical "messengers" secreted in small quantities directly into the bloodstream by an endocrine gland.
Human Genome Project	in 1988 the international Human Genome Project began to identify all the genes in the 46 chromosomes of every human cell. This project was completed in 2003.
Hybrid	a hybrid is the offspring of plants or animals produced from the cross of two closely related species.
Hydrogen bonding	is the strong force of attraction between certain molecules that contain hydrogen, such as water molecules.

Hydrolysis	is the chemical reaction of a compound with water which causes it to break down.
Immunity	is protection of an organism against infection.
Inductive reasoning	is the formation of generalizations based on the observation of patterns
Infrared radiation	is the way in which heat energy is transferred from a hotter to a colder place without a medium such as air or water being present.
Insulin	is a hormone secreted when blood glucose level rises above normal. It stimulates the liver to remove glucose by converting it into glycogen.
Invasive species	are an introduced species that significantly impacts the biological community structure in an area where it is not normally found.
Involuntary actions	are actions which are not controlled by conscious activity of the brain.
Iris	the iris is the coloured part of the eye and controls the amount of light that reaches the retina.
Keystone species	are species whose population fluctuations have a disproportionate effect on the structure of a biological community.
Kilo-	is a metric prefix meaning 1×10^3
Kinesis	is an increase in the rate of movement in response to a stimulus
Kingdom	a kingdom is the highest rank in the classification of living organisms.
Koch's postulates	is a method for establishing the specific cause of an infectious disease
Ligament	a tough, elastic structure of connective tissue that connects bones together at movable joints.
Liver	the liver is a large and important organ which acts as a "chemical factory" and has a wide range of functions.
Mammals	are warm-blooded vertebrates whose skin is covered with hair and has sweat glands.
Mechanoreceptor	is a sensory receptor that detects touch, movement, stretching or pressure.
Meiosis	(or reductive cell division) is division of a cell which results in each daughter cell receiving exactly half the number of chromosomes.
Metabolism	(or metabolic activity) is the sum of all the various biochemical reactions that occur in a living organism.
Metamorphosis	is the transformation that occurs in the life cycle of many arthropods from the egg through the larval and pupal stages to the adult form (imago).
Metaphase	is a phase of nuclear division that occurs between prophase and anaphase and involves genetic material lining up at the equator of the cell.
Micro-	is a metric prefix meaning 1×10^{-6}
Microtubules	are protein based structures that are the components of the cytoskeleton of cells.
Milli-	is a metric prefix meaning 1×10^{-3}
Mitochondria	(singular mitochondrion) the mitochondria are the organelles in the cytoplasm where energy is produced from chemical reactions.

Mitosis	is a division of a cell to form two daughter cells, each with a nucleus containing the same number of chromosomes as the mother cell.
Mitotic index	is the proportion of the number of cells in metaphase to the total number of cells in a sample.
Models	are simplified representations used to explore complex systems.
Model organisms	are species that are chosen for study to represent other species. They are similar enough but they are chosen because they breed in large numbers and have a short generation time, so they can be studied more easily under laboratory conditions.
Mole	is the SI unit of "amount of substance".
Monocotyledons	(abbreviation: monocots) are a class of angiosperm with only one seed leaf (cotyledon) within the seed.
mRNA	is messenger ribonucleic acid. It takes part in the transcription (copying) of the genetic code.
Mutation	is a sudden random change in the genetic material of a cell, which may result in faulty DNA replication or faulty division of chromosomes.
Mutualism	(or symbiosis) is a feeding relationship between two organisms from which both benefit.
Nano-	is a metric prefix meaning 1×10^{-9}
Natural classification	involves grouping organisms based on evolutionary relationships.
Natural selection	the theory of natural selection states that the individual organism which is best adapted to its environment will survive to reproduce.
Negative feedback	is the process by which information about deviation from a norm passes to a controlling organ and produces a correction of the deviation.
Nerve impulse	is an electrical signal which moves along a nerve fibre.
Neurone	(or nerve cell) is an elongated, branched cell that is the basic unit of the nervous system.
Neurotransmitter	is the chemical released by the axon end of one neurone to transmit (or inhibit) the transmission of a nerve impulse across a synapse to an adjacent neurone.
Nucleus	the nucleus in the cell's control centre and is contained within a nuclear membrane.
Nymph	is the immature form of some invertebrates which resembles the adult form.
Oligopeptide	is a short chain of amino acids.
Open system	an open system is one in which materials and energy can escape or enter.
Order	in biological classification, family is part of an order, and an order is part of a class.
Organ	an organ is a collection of different tissues which work together to perform some function in the organism.
Osmosis	is the movement of a solvent (usually water) from a dilute to a more concentrated solution by diffusion across a semipermeable membrane.

Ovum (plural ova) an ovum is the female gamete of animals.

Oval window is a membrane-covered opening between the middle and inner ear.

Ovulation is the periodic release of an ovum (egg cell) from the ovaries to travel down the oviduct (or Fallopian tube) to the uterus, where it is available for fertilization.

Parallel connections occur where flowing material has more than one pathway to follow.

Phenology is the study of the timing of cyclical events such as bud formation or nesting or migration

Phenotype is the observable characteristics of an organism produced by the interaction of its genes.

Phenotypic ratio is the ratio of organisms possessing different patterns of a certain observable feature.

Photon is a unit of light energy.

Photosynthesis is the chemical process of separating hydrogen from water (light stage or photolysis) which then combines with carbon dioxide (dark stage) to synthesize simple foodstuffs such as glucose.

Phylum is a large group of organisms sharing a similar basic structure. A phylum of plants is often called a division.

Physical change a physical change is one which results in no new chemical substance being formed.

Physiology is the study of the functions and activities of a living system.

Pico- is a metric prefix meaning 1×10^{-12}

Pituitary gland found at the base of the brain, it controls the production of hormones by the endocrine glands.

Plasmid is a piece of DNA found outside of the chromosome within a prokaryote.

Population a population is a group of individuals of the same species within a community.

Positive feedback occurs where the end product of a process further amplifies the process that created the product.

Post-synaptic neuron is the neuron that receives neurotransmitter from the pre-synaptic neuron.

Potometer is an apparatus which measures transpiration rates under natural or artificial conditions.

Predators are animals that hunt, kill and eat other animals called their prey.

Presynaptic neuron is the neuron that releases neurotransmitter into a synapse.

Prey is an animal that is a source of food for a predator.

Primary consumers feed on producers (plants).

Producers are animals that can make their own food by autotrophic nutrition and are therefore considered as a source of energy.

Products are the chemical elements or compounds that are produced during the chemical reaction.

Prokaryotes — are organisms whose genetic material is not surrounded by a nuclear membrane, such as bacteria.

Prophase — is the first stage of nuclear division where genetic material condenses and the nuclear membrane breaks down.

Puberty — (or adolescence) is a stage of development when the reproductive organs begin to function.

Pulmonary artery — the pulmonary artery carries deoxygenated blood from the right ventricle to the lungs (the only artery to carry deoxygenated blood).

Pulmonary vein — the pulmonary vein carries oxygenated blood from the lungs to the left atrium (the only vein to carry oxygenated blood).

Pupil — the pupil is the hole at the centre of the iris which appears as a black circle.

R group — is the variable part of a chemical compound, such as an amino acid.

Random sample — is a sample from a population where every member has an equal chance of being selected.

Reactants — are the chemical elements or compounds that a chemical reaction starts with.

Reaction rate — is the rate at which reactants are used up or products are formed in a chemical reaction.

Recessive allele — a recessive allele is a gene that only affects an individual's phenotype if it is part of a homozygous pair.

Reflex actions — are special types of involuntary action of which we are aware, like swallowing, coughing, etc.

Reptiles — are cold-blooded vertebrates which lay soft-shelled eggs on land.

Respiration — is the release of energy in a living organism which occurs when simple products are made from the breaking down of food molecules.

Restriction endonuclease — is an enzyme that cuts DNA at specific sequences.

Retina — the retina is the layer of light-sensitive cells at the back of the eye.

Ribosomes — are tiny particles attached to the endoplasmic reticulum. They are involved in the synthesis of proteins.

Sarcomere — the unit of contraction within a skeletal muscle.

Secondary consumers — feed on primary consumers.

Sexual reproduction — involves the joining of male and female gametes (sex cells).

Skeleton — a skeleton is a structure in an animal that provides support for the body, protection for internal organs and a framework for anchoring muscles and ligaments.

Speciation — is the formation of new species.

Species — is a group containing living organisms of the same kind.

Sperm — is the male gamete of animals.

Starch — is a polysaccharide found in plants, especially in the roots, tubers, seeds and fruit. It is an important carbohydrate energy source.

Statistic	a number which represents a fact about a sample
Stoma	(plural stomata) a stoma is a pore found in the lower epidermis of a leaf, surrounded by a pair of guard cells.
Synapse	is the junction between two adjacent neurones.
System	a collection of interacting elements that has emergent properties.
Taxis	(or tactic movement) is the movement of an organism with respect to a stimulus from a specific direction.
Taxonomy	is the study of the theory, practice and rules of classification of living and extinct organisms.
Telomere	the ends of chromosomes that shortens with repeated cell divisions
Tendon	(or sinew) is tough connective tissue that connects a muscle to a bone. Tendons consist of collagen fibres which are non-elastic, and therefore transmit the contraction or relaxation of the muscle to the bone.
Tertiary consumers	feed on secondary consumers.
Tissue	is a collection of cells which perform a specific function.
Trachea	(windpipe) is a tube through which air is drawn into the lungs.
Transcription	is the copying of the genetic code.
Transformation	is the uptake of donor DNA.
Translation	transfer RNA and ribosomal RNA take part in translation (protein synthesis).
Translocation	is the transport of minerals and products of photosynthesis within a plant.
Transpiration	is the process in which water is lost by evaporation from the leaves through the stomata.
Triceps	is the extensor muscle in the upper arm which straightens the forearm.
tRNA	is transfer ribonucleic acid. It takes part is protein synthesis (translation).
Tropism	a tropism is a growth or movement in plants that occurs due to a specific stimulus.
Tumor	a mass of unspecialized cells formed by uncontrolled cell division.
Unicellular	describes living organisms which are made up of only one single cell, such as bacteria and protozoans.
Ureters	are two tubes which carry urine from the kidneys to the bladder.
Vaccine	a vaccine is a liquid preparation of treated disease-producing microorganisms which can stimulate the immune system to produce antibodies in the blood.
Vector	a vector is an agent (organism) responsible for carrying pathogens from one organism to another.
Ventilation	is the movement of air in and out of the lungs.
Vertical transfer	is the transfer of genetic information from parent to offspring.
Voluntary actions	are actions which are controlled by conscious activity of the brain.
Zygote	is a fertilized egg produced by the fusion of the nucleus of the male and female sex cells.

Index

Although we have made every effort to trace and contact all copyright holders before publication this has not been possible in all cases. If notified, the publisher will rectify any errors or omissions at the earliest opportunity.

Links to third party websites are provided by Oxford in good faith and for information only. Oxford disclaims any responsibility for the materials contained in any third party website referenced in this work.

The authors offer heartfelt thanks to Alexandra Tomescu for all the work that she has done on this book. It has been a long and at times difficult gestation, but Alexandra's comprehensive understanding of science, her resolute desire to make the text comprehensible and appealing to students, as well as her accuracy and attention to detail have all been invaluable.